P9-BIX-005

THE

NEPPI MODONA

DIARIES

The

NEPPI MODONA

Diaries

Reading Jewish Survival

through

My Italian Family

KATE COHEN

DARTMOUTH COLLEGE

Published by University Press of New England

Hanover and London

Dartmouth College

Published by University Press of New England, Hanover, NH 03755

© 1997 by the Trustees of Dartmouth College

All rights reserved

Printed in the United States of America

5 4 3 2 1

CIP data appear at the end of the book

Frontispiece: Aldo's Notebooks.

UNIVERSITY LIBRARY
UNIVERSITY OF ALBERTA

TO MY FAMILY,

FOR LOVE OF LIFE AND WORDS AND FAMILY,

AND FOR THOSE LONG, LINGERING,

SHABBAS DINNERS

CONTENTS

ACKNOWLEDGMENTS

Rachel Neppi Modona made this book possible, by preserving the writings of her husband and son with care and love, and sharing them unhesitatingly with me. She opened her home and her past to me, and for months she answered all my questions, no matter how ignorant, with remarkable patience. Her generosity was immeasurable, as is my gratitude.

Lionella Viterbo's wit and insight refreshed my perspective on her family's story and on the Holocaust in general. Each conversation we had and letter she sent about her experience was a revelation of passion, humor, critical thought, and honest—even painful—introspection. I thank her for her willing help and for the example she set of analyzing the past with rigor and compassion.

Marianne Hirsch has supported this work from the very beginning, from getting the grant to getting published. I thank her for all she did behind the scenes to bring this book into being; I can only guess at the extent to which she used her tremendous energy on my behalf. I am, however, quite certain of how much she both encouraged and challenged me—in large part by affirming that my point of view had a place in the literature of the Holocaust.

I could not have written this book without the James B. Reynolds Scholarship for Foreign Study awarded me by the Dartmouth College Committee on Graduate Fellowships. That money allowed me not only to travel to Italy to do my research, but also to shirk paid employment for a year after my return, in order to write. I am aware of my great fortune; it is a luxury afforded to few writers. I would like to thank in particular Susan Wright, the committee's executive secretary, who attached personal notes of support to the committee's official letters.

Lyon and Marcia Greenberg also eased my financial burdens after my return home, with unflagging good will and faith in my abilities. Their patronage of the arts takes many forms; this one, the least public, has perhaps made the greatest difference.

Silvia Baldi and Manuela Sadun Paggi both offered their thought and knowledge—Silvia's in the form of her dissertation and Manuela's in the form of copious letters—to my research. Nancy Canepa generously contributed time, expertise, and good humor to the cause of accurate translation: she managed to give me long lists of corrections to my manuscript without making me feel like an idiot.

I thank Nancy Kirk, Margo McClung, and Noel Perrin for their encouragement and advice about publishing. Nancy went so far as to read the entire manuscript in a fairly rough state (for which I apologize) and helped give me the confidence to edit Leo's and Aldo's writings more aggressively.

Thanks to the University Press of New England and Dartmouth College for taking a chance on a not-exactly-academic book and an untried author. I hope, with all my heart, that the risk pays off.

Affection and gratitude to Peter Bien, Catherine Turrill, and Terry Osborne, who have for years inspired and encouraged my writing life, first as professors and academic advisors, and then as friends. Thanks also to Peter Demchuk and Mary Crittendon, who offered unexpected praise just when I needed it.

I had many readers to whom I am grateful. Thanks to Amy Cohen for her enthusiastic marginalia and her help with the glossary, to Mary Hill Cole for an historian's perspective, and to Melissa Hale-Spencer for her unmatchable passion and interest. Melissa was also one of four proofreaders who saved me from error and embarrassment; I thank her, my mother, Judy, and my friends Kathryn Rathouse and Andy Schotz.

As usual I called on my parents for all manner of help, especially the last-minute kind. My father, Ralph, helped me through some sticky bits of prose, tinkered with my subtitle, and wrestled with my arguments as no one else did. My mother picked countless nits from my manuscript, and cushioned my way through this whole process with her optimism and confidence in me. They both taught me to think and write about the world and to believe that someone might want to read the result.

For his belief in me, for his love, and for my utter security in both, I thank Adam Greenberg. The next one will be a best-selling novel, I promise.

May 1996   K.C.

PART ONE

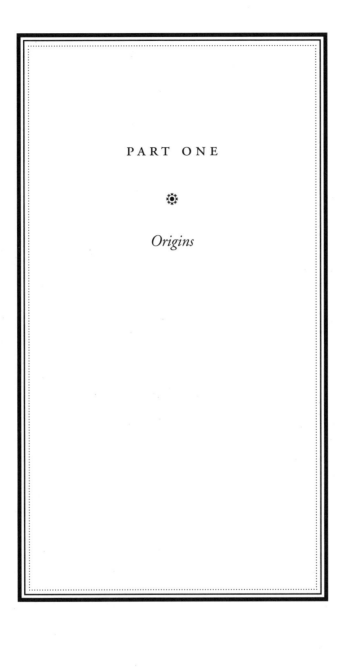

Origins

Via dei Banchi, 5

❋

THE APARTMENT in the center of Florence was dark and old, full of heavy furniture and muted colors. I was restless. I was meeting the Neppi Modonas for the first time—relatives of my father's, they were an obligatory stop on our family trip through Europe. My parents did most of the speaking, but I was still called upon every once in a while to refocus my eyes in the dim light and smile attentively. It was an afternoon visit, and the apartment must have had all its shutters drawn against the sun. But I didn't think about why it was dark, I just wanted to get back outside where I could speak or not speak as I pleased, where I could focus on myself and my effect on passersby, a newfound and fascinating subject. I was twelve. Rachel was seventy-five, I now calculate, but I don't remember her as she was. That must be partly because my later images of her have obscured the first, partly because she probably deferred to her husband. That's hard for me to imagine now—she seems so tough and commanding. But he was the English-speaker in the family and, as I learned later, she was devoted to him. Aldo was eighty-seven, gentle, frail, kind-looking, spoke slowly, smiled often.

But the one I remember best, the one who probably didn't say a word, was the son, Leo, fifty years old at the time. His presence made urgent my need to escape. He was stooped, his skin sagged, and the area around his eyes was dark—or perhaps I'm just inventing qualities that would make a sickly fifty-year-old frightening when I can't quite remember why he was. Most likely, he simply carried an air of sorrow, which is frightening enough for a happy twelve-year-old girl. Of the three, he seemed the closest to death.

When I returned to that apartment on Via dei Banchi in 1987, both Aldo and Leo had died, Aldo in 1985, Leo in 1986. (I still do not know what caused either

3

death—I cannot seem to ask directly in Italian what would long ago have become clear indirectly in English. I do know that Aldo was ninety when he died and a victim of stomach ailments, and Leo a diabetic.) I was on vacation in Chianti with a friend and came to Florence on a day trip, partly to see Rachel. My friend came with me to the dark apartment; she spoke Italian, and I offered my high school French. Rachel was a teary mess. I didn't know if I should hug this woman I barely knew, or how to comfort her. She spoke of Aldo and Leo incessantly and started to cry as soon as she had composed herself from her last bout of tears. She showed us several testimonials that had been written about them, books dedicated to them, honors they had received—they were both academics, both apparently esteemed in their fields. My friend translated as best she could, and I nodded and appreciated as best I could, and we left as quickly as decency allowed.

In 1991 I came to Italy on an academic program. I called on Rachel soon after I got to Florence because I knew the longer I waited the greater the guilt. We took a taxi to her daughter's for dinner; it was the first time I met Lionella. She was warm and lively and made me feel comfortable, or at least more comfortable than I had expected. My Italian was awful and I made a poorly calculated criticism of Desert Storm (Lionella and her husband, Giuseppe, had just returned from their daughter's wedding in Israel, where Patriot missiles were greatly appreciated), but I felt the elation of having to speak another language and getting along well enough.

After my program, I spent about two weeks with Rachel, on and off between trips, living in the dark apartment, sleeping in what I thought of as Boo Radley's old room in *To Kill a Mockingbird*. There were mothball-filled drawers and things you didn't think you should touch and rules, rules, rules. Especially in the kitchen. There were five towels hanging by the sink, one for drying hands, one for drying dishes, one for drying the table after it had been wiped down, one for drying pots. I don't know what the fifth was for, and for this I'm sure I was reprimanded. I didn't dare cook anything or even bring anything into the kitchen except for the odd package of cookies. I hadn't had much experience with a kosher household, and I didn't want to make mistakes. It was like living with your grandmother, except without getting spoiled. I had never before thought of myself as riddled with vice, but I slept too late, I read in too little light, and I perpetually used the wrong towel. For these sins I was scolded in a teasing naughty-little-girl sort of way.

One weekend when we were at Lionella and Giuseppe's farm, Sensano, I realized too late that I was forbidden to write on a Saturday, the Sabbath. In my family Friday night was a sort of family night with a couple of prayers and a nice dinner, and Saturday was ignored. Here I was, a compulsive letter-writer with a journal as my only English-speaking companion, being admonished not to touch my pen. The injustice! I felt as if I were being punished for being Jewish—after all, a Christian guest would have been forbidden nothing. But it was worse, because I felt as if I were being punished for not being Jewish enough, not knowing the rules. If I had, of course, I would simply have cheated.

I felt terrible. And I wrote anyway, and defensively confessed, and was chuckled at, the naughty girl. I was twenty-one, tired of traveling, and missing my sense of humor as well as my boyfriend.

Back in Florence, Rachel still cried frequently at the mention of her husband and son, still kissed their pictures before going to bed every night, still pulled me by the wrist, in an old lady pinch, from bookshelf to bookshelf to show me the same dedications over again.

Her work at that time consisted of typing out Aldo's diaries so that a typist could copy them properly and a printer could bind them. She showed me a finished work, with a red cloth cover. It was called, "Tale of Life Lived" ("Romanzo di Vita Vissuta") and it was about World War II. Rachel had told me something of this period, a complaint about some nuns, and a story about silverware, I think, but since Italian was still an effort for me, and I knew so little of the history, I was instantly lost. Still, I was interested. Here it seemed I had a chance to get the story straight. But I read too slowly and was not allowed to take the red book, as we called it, to my room, so I didn't get very far before I left for home.

The fall after graduation I found myself covering the distinctly unhistorical politics of village school board meetings for a local weekly and thinking about the Red Book, which had acquired capitals in the intervening year. I was sure it contained some heroic stories and that I should be its translator and liberator. So I asked Rachel to send me a copy and when it arrrived I scratched and scrabbled at its cover of brown mailing paper and twine. It was a treasure and now I owned it.

For a long time I just sort of glanced through it, perhaps sensing that what it possibly contained was more romantic than what it actually did. I did not want to break this magic spell, this triple spell, of an unread, unpublished book in a foreign language. If it had been in English, it would not have been so easy not to read it, simply to glory in it as a possession—a possession whose worth might be greater unexamined.

Indeed, when I finally read it, dictionary at my side, I found no heroics but rather a pompous and stiff sort of writing. Aldo referred to himself as "Prof. N. M.," praised his own diligence and religious faith, and when the journal at last took on warmth and familiarity it degenerated into a kind of ship's log: "In the

Rachel Neppi Modona with one of Aldo's notebooks (1993).

afternoon, a new aerial bombardment of the Village. Weather sultry, cloudy, and foggy."

But the greatest shock to me was that this man, this victim of Mussolini's racial laws, this paragon of gentility and intelligence, was a member of the Fascist Party.

Meanwhile, I wrote to Rachel to thank her for sending me the book and to ask her about her memories of the time—I had decided I wanted to write about it—and she wrote me back to say there was another diary, Leo's. I didn't take much notice of this information, perhaps because it came in Italian and passed only half understood, and therefore unmarked, into my brain. Leo was born in 1932 and was not quite seven years old when his diary began, but I did not know this at the time, nor did I know that he was a veritable prodigy, having (according to both his mother and sister—whose rare agreement signaled that the story might well be true) learned to read and write one week when he was sick in bed at the age of five. He had intended to become a writer, which is clear not only from his own statements but from his joy in making up fictional names for the people in his diary, titling his book, and numbering his chapters. He is playing at writing a novel, though he wisely chooses to write about his own life, far more interesting than most fiction.

I knew none of this, and when I next arrived at Rachel's apartment and she offered to show me her son's journal, I had almost forgotten it existed. I took it home to read (assuring Rachel that I would be extremely careful) and came back the next day demanding to know the year in which Leo was born. Nineteen thirty-two? Not quite seven when he started this? Seven? Nineteen thirty-two? Seven years old?

Rachel still insists that he started the journal when he was seven—his age at the beginning of the story he tells. However, it's not a daily log of events, but a seamless narrative, suggesting someone looking back. Lionella thinks he started it in 1941, at age nine.

He was, in any case, a child. And he had written a beautiful book. And so I became fascinated with the one Neppi Modona I had shied away from, the one with the pale, gloomy, tired figure I had met when I was twelve. Was this charming, funny, self-possessed, observant boy the same person? Pictures of both Aldo and Leo dot the apartment, all black and white, all framed, many of them duplicates so that their presence would be felt in all the rooms. Rachel's bedroom contains at least five of each, a small one of each on the pillow next to hers. And in the hallway leading through the house from the doorway to the kitchen there are particularly large ones in silver frames on a bookcase. Rachel kisses these every

One of the many pictures of Leo in Via dei Banchi, 5.

night before bed. In all of his, Leo is a man, not a boy, and though not frightening as I had remembered, his face is gently sad. The gaiety in his youthful writing was utterly absent in his adult face; something had happened to him, a change that does not, I think, happen to everyone simply on account of growing up.

So when I began to visit Rachel at Via dei Banchi, 5, daily, it was partly to find out about the war years, and partly to discover what had happened to Leo. Why did he become a teacher (French literature) and not a writer; why was he so sad? What happened to that most unusual creature—the merry, thoughtful boy?

Via dei Banchi connects the Piazza di Santa Maria Novella with the Piazza del Duomo. Behind Santa Maria Novella is the train station, where fresh Birkenstocks and backpacks arrive daily, and worn ones are carried away. Buses and taxis swerve the new arrivals past the church, around the sharp left onto Via dei Banchi, merge with the Via dei Cerretani traffic, and deposit them in the vicinity of the Duomo and its piazza, both oddly spacious for the packed little city. Sometimes the tourists walk from the station to the center, and frequently I found myself in the stream of them, among umbrellas, belly packs, sunglasses, maps, and cameras. Usually it was my language they were speaking, but I didn't want them to know that, didn't want to speak. I felt like a spy whose fellow Americans would blow my cover if I weren't careful. In an effort to look like an Italian woman, I did not smile—Americans smile incessantly.

I'd walk past the embroidery store, the liquor store, and slow down at the Banca del Vecchio to nod to the bank's security guard. "Buon giorno," I'd say, and if it was the round, balding brunet with the easy smile, he would say, "Buon giorno" back. The stern, grey-faced one with the Germanic mustache would only nod. I'd turn onto the threshold at number 5, grasp a handhold set in the stone doorframe, and ring the bell for Neppi Modona. The doors are wooden, enormous, fitted with iron. Only the locks look modern. After waiting for what seemed each time like a very long time, I'd hear a buzz and a click and push the door open. There is a small vestibule, dim, with four mailboxes and marble floors and another set of doors. Beyond them are an entrance to the bank, an entrance to the garden, and a little room where one of the guards would be sitting drinking coffee when I came back down.

The building belongs to Rachel. The bank pays rent to her, as does the office that shares her floor, and the elderly lady in the little apartment above. This struck me as very odd. In America banks don't tend to have little old landladies, and for that matter, they tend not to share buildings with private residences. Perhaps even odder was that someone lived in this building at all, this imposing stone building with great wooden doors, this piece of *architecture* looking perfectly at home between Santa Maria Novella and the Duomo.

Rachel was usually waiting for me when I got to the door of her vestibule, which has two bells, one for Professor Neppi Modona and one for Studio Festini, the office next door. Sometimes she simply left the door open and hurried back to the kitchen, where she had left something bubbling. I established the wise habit of arriving in time for lunch. I'd put down my things in her hallway and walk quickly to the kitchen at the end to do my chores. I put the glasses on the dining room table, and the bottled water, and the wine. I sliced bread—Rachel said I did that very well—and put that on a little plate, and placed it on the table. The placemats and napkins were in the buffet in the dining room; hers I placed on the side of the table facing the television, mine facing her. Then came the food, starting with pasta, rice, or soup, and followed by meat or chicken with vegetables. The *minestra* went on the plates, and the *secondo* was brought in its dishes, covered, to wait. Sometimes she made a dish of rice and peas, pink with tomato and shiny with olive oil. Sometimes, angel hair pasta, browned in oil and then boiled in water and tomato juice. Sometimes spaghetti with a little meat sauce. Rare treats were fresh cheese ravioli or pizza made with matzoh. To keep kosher, we would eat fish after these cheese-filled treats, or else eat them in the kitchen first, or else get new plates and forks in between. The second course was often chicken loaf or chicken meatballs, or beef rolled around sausage, or fried fish with avgolemono sauce. Plus garlicky spinach, or beans cooked in tomato, or sweet frozen peas, or an endive salad. And then, eater's choice from the fruit bowl.

The one o'clock news was on as we ate. Headlines were written on the top of the screen, which helped me some, but really it was only international news I understood. Italian politics remained impenetrable to me. I struggled with newspapers as well, but writers there don't have the American habit of recapping the issue in every new article—they seem to assume that one has been paying attention for quite some time. And I was embarrassed to ask questions like, "O.K., let me get this straight—who's the Prime Minister?" In Italy, which has seen more governments than years go by since the end of the war, this is not as stupid a question as it might be. Still, it was too stupid for me. So sometimes I would daydream through the news, or focus on my food. Rachel, on the other hand, paid attention and often commented on news items with the Italian equivalents of "My goodness," "Can you believe it?" and, her favorite, "Cretin!"

Then we cleared the table and washed and dried the dishes, a complex ritual in which I had my chores and she had hers, and one was not to confuse which towel was to be used for which task. I found that, since my stay with her two years before, the endless rules and rigid routine had become a pleasant game and not a burden. Certainly, like most people, she was easier to visit than to live with. And I was grateful to her for her stories, her confidences, and her elaborate meals—for she would not have indulged thus on her own: I was company, and treasured company at that.

After the kitchen was cleaned (and increasingly before, as she began to trust me with her dishes), she returned to the dining room to watch *Beautiful*, which is what the American soap opera *The Bold and the Beautiful* is called on Italian television. I made the coffee and then joined her for *Santa Barbara*.

I had watched the soap some in America and had no trouble with all the family connections and plot twists, though these episodes seemed to be several years previous to the ones I had watched. But of course bad writing in another language is much easier to understand than good, since clichés are, by definition, expressions, ideas, and situations one has encountered before. So we had a fine time, she crying "Cretin!" and "Stupid!" and "Idiot!" and, much more rarely, "Poor thing, you're too good!" to the few characters with whom she sympathized. I generally held my tongue, since, except in the case of irredeemable villains, she always sympathized with the men at the expense of the women, and with the parents at the expense of their children.

Around 3 P.M., the television finally dark, she would say, "Let's get to work" or "Have you brought your work?" I did not need to coax her to talk, but I had little control over what she said. If I asked about a man Aldo had mentioned in the context of the war, she might tell me what he had done in 1963, or what he was doing now, or even more likely, what his son-in-law was doing now. People came in families, and could not be described independently of them, and all information available about subsequent generations had to be removed from the chests of her memory, displayed, smoothed out, folded, and replaced. The effect was hypnotizing. It seemed to me that Italy was populated by cousins of her mother-in-law, who figured in almost all the stories, and that these cousins, who had died just a few months before at an impressive age like 102, were invariably the owners of some lovely villa whose location had to be described precisely (though street names were the only names Rachel had trouble remembering).

Throughout, the narrative was accompanied by the Italian ritual of "Understand?"/ "Understood"—so automatic as to cease to be question and answer— so that I found myself prompting her to go on even when I had no idea what she was talking about. Sometimes I would ask a question she had answered the day before, but, befuddled, I had not connected the stories with the names, or the names with the roles. "But didn't I tell you that?" she would ask and then

immediately tell the story over again from beginning to end, despite my at-
tempts ("Yes, of course, I had forgotten") to cut her off. She persisted, too, in
declaring that "the names escape me," when in fact she remembered all four of
Luisa Gallichi's sisters' names, the names of children she had never met, the
names of Allied soldiers met in passing during the liberation.

Her memories of the war were not walled off from her memories of the rest of
her life, as my interest was. She saw it as a specific time period in the life of her
family, but not more significant, it seemed, than if one were to distinguish one's
College Years from the rest, and perhaps less vivid than an athlete's Glory Years.
She did not feel some cosmic leap from the logic of peace and equal rights to the
insanity of Jewish persecution and war back to logic again, perhaps because fifteen years of Fascism had prepared her for insanity, and life only slowly returned
to logical—what with strangers in her house for two years after the war, and the
Allies in Italy long after that. When trouble began and when it ended aren't that
easy to tell—several times in Aldo's diary he says, more or less, "And this is when
things really started to get bad." Also, I think, Rachel herself did not change during the war, did not learn anything new about herself and the world; she is not a
discoverer, but rather a person who is always confirming what she long suspected
was true. So the war takes on no special importance in her picture of herself, and
therefore takes on no special importance in her recollections. She was aware that
they were good stories, perhaps, and aware that that's what I wanted to hear
about, but she had other good stories too, which surely I would want to hear.

"Fascism. It Was Like That."

.... ❂ ....

"ES," ANSWERED RACHEL on one of my first visits, "Aldo was a member of the Fascist Party, but of course he had to be." He had to be to keep his job—it was a little like loyalty oaths during the McCarthy era, only it was in a country where finding another job, a job other than the one you had been trained for all your life, was almost impossible. University professors had to swear allegiance to the party in 1931 and 1932; of approximately twelve thousand, eleven refused, three of whom were Jewish. Aldo did not refuse. He was focused on his career, his family, and his faith rather than on politics, but he was certainly not a natural enemy of Fascism—nor was Fascism his natural enemy, until six years after he joined.

Aldo Neppi Modona was born in Florence in 1895, forty-seven years after the Jews in its ghetto were freed. His family, solidly middle class, instilled in Aldo, in addition to a strong religious faith, a reverence for the monarchy and the nation. Jews had been liberated from the ghettos and given full rights as citizens when Italy was unified into a nation, beginning in 1848. King Carlo Alberto had presided over the unification, so Italian Jews tended to be devoted to their king and country. Renzo De Felice wrote in his *History of the Italian Jews Under Fascism*, "They were in a sense doubly Italian, because Italy for them, more than for other Italians, represented emancipation, civil equality . . ."[1] Other writers have suggested that Italian Jews became super-patriotic to prove they were worthy of the gift of citizenship. To be fair, though, the newly born Italy *was* good to Jews. When Aldo was growing up, the Jews in Italy had been free for less than a lifetime, and already they were fully enmeshed in Italian political, commercial, academic, and social life—some to the point of barely distinguishing themselves

13

from their Catholic neighbors. Aldo practiced his Judaism fervently, and the fact that he was Jewish was probably a strong part of his love for his country. His father wrote him once, "Let us hope the Supreme Lord helps everyone for the fortune of Italy, for the tranquility of the family, for prosperity and a better future for the Nation."[2] God and country were united, perhaps even more for Italian Jews than for Italian Catholics. Rabbis at the time blessed the royal family from the pulpit, and given the situation of Jews in many other European countries at the time, they had some cause to do so.

In 1915, Aldo volunteered for the army and fought as an infantry officer throughout the war, leaving as a captain (he was promoted to major in peacetime). The war ended both well and poorly: The Italians were on the winning side, but they felt slighted when the winners divided the spoils, and they were ambivalent about the price they had paid in lives. The Socialist Party, which had opposed intervention from the start, was able to inspire a certain anti-war sentiment in the victorious country. The party urged rebellious workers and peasants to blame their economic woes on the middle- and upper-class officers who forced the country to intervene in a war that benefited only the rich. Officers who expected to come home to cheers and gratitude were thus shocked to be greeted with bitterness and suspicion. They were spat on in the street and eventually advised by the army not to wear their uniforms in public.

A letter from Aldo's mother Ada expressed the indignation and disbelief the officers felt.

> I don't see the flags! But doesn't everyone understand that it's the most beautiful moment in five years? Our troops destroy, undo and disband that Austrian Army and there's no outburst of jubilation, no demonstrations of gratitude to our soldiers! Do they think perhaps that it's just a simple evening stroll? Ah! I'd like to have them sent to help at the passage of the Piave, my calm citizens.[3]

Aldo was devoted to his country, proud of his war service, and anguished to see his devotion and his service devalued. The antidote to this anguish, for many veterans, was the Fascist Party, which sought to restore that sense of loyalty and nationalism that makes war such a pleasure—the sense (experienced to a small degree by anyone who has marched in a parade, sung in a choir, or cheered at a ballgame) of shared belief and action. That sense of concert is so powerful it can turn ordinary humans into a glorious abstraction—Italians into Italy, for instance. In fact, what Mussolini and his *fasci di combattimento* seemed to offer was a sort of military without war, where one could have superiors and be superior, wear uniforms, and enjoy the freedom from thought that comes from being a small part of a whole. Mussolini's "platform" was shaky at best, but the general idea was to guard against Bolshevism and to make Italy strong economically and important in the eyes of the world. Order was to prevail, and indeed, with the suppression of strikes and peasant revolts and with the destruction of Fascism's political opponents, it did.

In his *Story of a Fortunate Jew*, Vittorio Segre describes his father's feelings after World War I:

> He was convinced, like many landowners of the time, that nothing could stop the "Bolshevic Hydra" if not a new patriotic regime capable of forcing the shirkers to recognize the contribution of the fighters to the country. He couldn't accept the social transformations that the war had imposed. He had gone to Turin to join, out of anger more than conviction, the Fascist party that was being formed with the support of the police and the army.[4]

Aldo did not join right after the war, but not because he was Jewish. Segre, after all, was Jewish. Jews joined the party in the same proportions as their Gentile neighbors: that is, a little over ten percent of the population.[5] "The philo-Fascism among Italian Jewry was only natural," writes historian H. S. Hughes; "Mussolini's movement was both patriotic and predominantly middle class; so were the Jews."[6] Patriotic, as I said before, because they believed their country to be free from the anti-Semitism that plagued their European neighbors, and because they were enjoying full rights and generally flourishing. And middle class in disproportionate numbers—eight percent of all university professors, like Aldo, were Jewish, though Jews constituted only one tenth of one percent of the general population.[7]

Moreover, unlike the party that was to rule Germany ten years later, Mussolini's new party did not espouse anti-Semitism or any sort of racism when it came to power. On the contrary, Mussolini frequently stated that Italian Jews were valued equals.

Memo Bemporad declares in his memoirs:

> Infinite were the Italian assertions, in this period, from Mussolini himself on down, not only of the non-existence in Italy, but also of the absolute impossibility that in our country one could develop or in any way arrive at a racial campaign.
>
> . . . Mussolini, in "The People of Italy" [wrote]: "Italy does not know anti-Semitism and we believe that she will never know it . . . [I]n Italy absolutely no distinction is made between Jews and non-Jews, in all fields, from religion, to politics, to the armies, to economics . . . Italian Jews have here in this our beloved land a new Zion, which after all many of them have defended, heroically, with their blood . . ."[8]

So Aldo probably did not oppose the regime. If he had been more political, he might even have supported it earlier, as a patriot and as a professional dedicated to order. He even jumped just a little before he was pushed, joining the National Association of Fascist University Professors at its inception in 1929. His leather-bound membership card, with a profile of a Roman soldier embossed on the back, lies among his military badges and medals today. In 1932, or rather, Year XI of the Fascist regime, he formally joined the Roman chapter of the Fascist Party.

But he was not a political man. His life revolved around religion and family and his career, which was flourishing: publications accepted, organizations founded, and so on. Rachel tells the story of a professor who successfully prevented Aldo from getting a coveted seat at the University of Florence in the mid-thirties; the man was a Fascist and an early anti-Semite, a prejudice she says he acquired in Germany where he studied. But Aldo found work at a high school, which is not the step down it is in America—and not unusual given the very limited number of seats in universities, every one of which is filled by a formal contest. In the summer, Aldo taught at the University of Perugia. Since their lives were not terribly shaken by the turn in Aldo's professional fortunes, Rachel is more amused than angry when she tells the story of the meddling Fascist, and she explains, without a hint of irony, that things were basically good under Fascism, that the trains were never late.

Around the time that Aldo had to swear allegiance to the Fascist Party in order to keep his job, Leo was born. They wanted to name him Leone, for his grandfather. *Leone* means lion.

When Leo was born, we wanted to call him Leone. But when we went to declare that Leone Neppi Modona had been born, they said, "We're sorry. Leone is not allowed. It's the name of an animal." And Aldo said, "What? There've been popes named Leone!" And they said, "Well now you can't." One couldn't use names of flowers. For example, here, Rosa, at that time one couldn't use it, Rosetta, yes, Rosina, yes, Rosa no . . . So Aldo remembered that lion, in Latin, is Leo. So he said, "Can I call him Leo?" He says, "Yes, yes." And so, Leo came.

But why couldn't one?

Fascism. It was like that. (Laughs)

One didn't know why? A reason . . .

No, no reason, we didn't know. No, no.

A philosophical reason?

No, no, no, no, no, nothing.

Nothing.

It became prohibited *in the sense that Mussolini didn't want these names.*

The loyalty oath was probably accepted in much the same spirit—"Fascism. It was like that"—simply another hoop to jump through. Slightly ridiculous, but at least the joke was shared among all Italians. Even today, Italians maintain a bemused irritation in the face of all their bureaucracy, the complexity of which would frighten the most officious member of the IRS. Somehow it is all deadly serious and all a joke at the same time, even for the bureaucrats themselves—you argue for forty-five minutes about why you are being asked to fill out a form you had been told not to fill out, when suddenly your request will be granted, paper-free.

Then, as now, the bureaucratic tangle was partly irritating, partly laughable. Most serious opponents to Fascist ideology were dead or in exile, and for the time being, Fascist economic measures were actually working. Memo Bemporad remembers when Fascism seemed to be a good thing.

> We are almost to 1930. Yesterday. I was, as they say, in the flower of my years; Italy marched strong: the lira was stronger than almost all foreign currency; a certain order reigned, everyone worked flat out: industries and businesses flourished. They weren't all roses, true, but that's how it was. Fascism had already made its garbage, but not only garbage.
>
> Maybe one could have predicted then that all would go to pot and the infirmities and troubles would come, because the error, as we know, in authoritarian and totalitarian regimes is "in" the system. But then things were "good!"[9]

Things were good for Aldo Neppi Modona. In 1928, when Aldo was thirty-two and on a grant to study in the Aegean, he met Rachel Fintz (aged twenty-one) on Rhodes, an island recently taken from the Turks by the Italians. Her community must have felt both alien and familiar to Aldo. There were no imposing *palazzi* and no paved streets in the Jewish quarter where she lived, and the quarter was just that—Jewish. Utterly. Nearby there was a Turkish quarter and a Christian quarter, but there was not much interaction; the communities were for the most part closed within themselves. Rachel said that intermarriage was unthinkable on the island; "we were like a family." Sabbaths and other holidays were celebrated in separate houses, but children up and down the streets were all called inside at once and every household in the quarter lit its candles at the same moment.

That intoxicating unison was lost in the largely assimilated and cosmopolitan Florence. Aldo was a deeply religious and strictly observant Jew, but his neighbors most likely weren't, not even his Jewish neighbors. Some part of him must have thrilled at this sense of community. That quarter of that tiny island probably did not have the insular quality that one might expect either; rather, since Rhodes belonged first to this nation and then to that, and since the Jews themselves felt connected to nations far and wide, it had an international awareness. Rachel, like all Jews on Rhodes, spoke French, having attended the Ecole Alliance Israelite. She also spoke Greek (her parents were from Patmos), Ladino (a Spanish-Hebrew hybrid analogous to Yiddish), and, more recently, Italian.

When Aldo proposed, she was, she says, surprised. She protested that she was not beautiful, not rich, and did not have a degree. And that she just met him. And he answered that she was beautiful to him, that money was not important, and that a degree was not necessarily a sign of intelligence. And that she was right, they should get to know each other. Two weeks later they were officially engaged. As he traveled among the other islands for his studies he wrote to her daily at least, letters addressed simply to "Gentilissima Signorina Rachel Fintz, Rodi."

They got permission from his reluctant mother, who was able to check out Rachel's credentials through various connections, and returned to Florence, where, on February 11, 1929, they were married. Two years later, Lionella was born, and a little over a year after that, Leo followed. Aldo was teaching at the University of Pisa, filling in for someone else. They lived with his mother, Mamma Ada, who encouraged and supported her daughter-in-law and generally arranged the household; Rachel revered her and honored her authority—she sounds grateful for it when she speaks of it today. The children had nannies, the household had a cook and a maid. Kosher was kept scrupulously, and there were plenty of beautiful dishes to keep it on.

As an army officer and a member of the academy, Aldo was certainly accustomed to following rules, to being passed over for less deserving men, to being part of a system. And he was a patriot. "La Patria, l'unica Patria," he writes in his diary, "the Fatherland, the only Fatherland." He even told his bride-to-be "that before everyone, before my mother, before my wife, comes the Fatherland." On Fascist holidays and veterans days, he proudly wore his uniform, medals and all. So signing up with the party could not have disturbed him too much.

Lionella says that, as children, she and Leo "had to say 'Long live the King,'

The Neppi Modonas dressed up for a Fascist holiday (1936).

etc.; they had raised us as monarchists, according to the ideals Papa had. He fought in the war . . . And—I don't know—he also respected Mussolini, maybe even Mamma did. Papa joined the Fascists to survive because he had to work; however, I saw the photograph of Papa with the children, with Papa in his uniform. There he is a Fascist standing next to Mamma all smiles, all accepting, it's not faked, their expressions. It means that in short, they had accepted [Fascism] without suspicion."

"Never, but Never"

.... ✸ ....

THE MID-1930s brought Italy closer and closer to alliance with Germany. On October 2, 1935, under a trumped-up pretext of retaliation, Italy invaded Ethiopia. The Fascists needed an empire; they had grand visions of returning to the glory of ancient Rome. The invasion brought the condemnation of Britain and France (as imperial powers in Africa, needless to say, their motives were not entirely pure) as well as economic sanctions. When those two former allies of Italy became the enemy, Germany became the natural ally. With Germany, Italy entered the Spanish Civil War on the side of the Fascist Franco in 1936. In an effort to solidify this new Fascist alliance, Mussolini allowed anti-Semitic elements of the Fascist Party to emerge.

In September of 1936, Roberto Farinacci, leader of a Fascist squad, warned Jews who proclaimed their Fascist allegiance, "It's not enough: it will be necessary to give mathematical proof of being a Fascist first, then a Jew." In April of 1937, a book by Paolo Orano called *Jews in Italy (Gli Ebrei in Italia)* was published. It came to be known as "Orano's bomb." Journalist Fausto Coen said that "taking his cue from the support of a very small number of Italian Jews for the Zionist cause, Orano in substance put all Italian Jews, Zionists or not, before this dilemma: either you consider yourselves temporary guests in our country and therefore cannot claim to be considered Italian like the rest; or, if you want to be Italian like everyone, forget being Jewish."[10]

According to his journal, Aldo was not unaware of the forces that were gathering against him (remember, though, that he took notes throughout these years and expanded them later into memoir—he has had the benefit of hindsight). Anti-Semitism in the press, which the Fascist regime had let simmer for about a year following "Orano's bomb," was carefully brought to a boil, as Mussolini sought Hitler's favor, and prepared Italy to accept a racist ideology. The Red Book opens with a scene from Aldo's summer job at the University of Perugia in 1938.

Prof. N. M. . . . went on preparing, bit by bit, the numerous lantern slides for the projections, and in the few, very few half hours of repose, every once in a while he read newspapers and monthly magazines. So it was that, strolling through the Corso Vannucci, the principal artery much beloved every late afternoon, with café tables full of students and some professors, as well as Perugians, he saw in a bookstore window the latest issue of *Vita Italiana [Italian Life]*, the monthly magazine published by Giovanni Preziosi; and it hit him that a good part of the articles attacked the Jews furiously. For the most part they did so with a generic ethical philosophical background, but there were plenty of clear hints and facts and aspects of real life, of relationships between Jews and non-Jews in Italy: what was all this? Very surprised, Prof. N. M. bought the issue and quickly glanced over its contents, strangely alarmed at the freedom of speech allowed to various authors and to the editorial staff. But what does this mean? Under a totalitarian regime, nothing can slip through or happen unbeknownst to the superior organs; so there must be a motive in all this. But how does this fit with the recent official declaration of the government that Jews in Italy don't constitute a racial problem and that no difference should be made between them and others?

Certainly that kind of language isn't common among us, where no one is concerned about one's religious faith and where furthermore there has been ample welcome for students and refugees and those coming from states where the wind of anti-Semitism blows. "Enough, let's hope it's an isolated case," our professor thought, though he was hardly persuaded, and having put the issue in an envelope, he sent it to his family, not hiding his own concern. Indeed, it wasn't unfounded! After a few days came the famous declaration of the ten professors on racial criteria, including a clear point hinting at the separation—for now theoretical—of the Jews from all the other Italians; then came the commentaries, inspired from on high in the press . . . "Point of arrival or of departure?" the papers asked themselves, with a hypocritical question mark, when by now all the machination under German pressure was evident: if you weren't blind or deaf to all that was happening in the rest of Europe, you understood what was being prepared. All the same, given that in Italy there has never, but never been the slightest hint at distinctions of that kind; given that Italians of the Jewish religion were perfectly incorporated into national life, had participated in the Great War, in the Ethiopian War, was it possible that they wanted to proceed with a separation so alien to the Italian way of thinking, so contrary to that spirit of religious tolerance that has always existed here?

Let's not talk about subsequent issues of *Italian Life*; let's not talk about the first issues of *Race*, full of false and tendentious declarations, of statistics constructed on manufactured data, of the denial of every form of heroism and sacrifice performed by Jews, going so far as to say that their acts of valor in the last war were fictitious, not to mention so many unfounded accusations of shameful immorality, in the ethical-social area, which is so alien to that purity and elevation of life which, innate in the Jewish religion, is a constant guide for the Jew—rare exceptions being nothing in comparison—and above all pointing out the hatred of *gentiles* commanded (!) by the *Talmud*, the code of Jewish life elaborated through the centuries, while love for one's neighbor and respect for every commandment and form of life of the country where a Jew lives is actually commanded, and has always been scrupulously observed by Italian Jews, with sincere loyalty and profound attachment full of recognition of the perfect equality of treatment.

So far had Aldo come to believe in the good nature of his nation and of the perfect acceptance enjoyed by Jews that he's willing to claim that "never, but never" has Italy experienced anti-Semitism. In this, he allows his historical perspective to be skewed. The history of Jews in Italy is a long and complicated one, but since the 1500s, with a brief respite during the Napoleonic age, Jews in all cities (except Livorno) were forced to live in ghettos, their rights often dreadfully restricted. The anti-Semitism had been religious in origin, and, in fact, decreed officially by the Pope in 1555. It was not racial—in that sense, Aldo was technically right when he said that "these distinctions" were not made before. And certainly Italy had been kinder to the Jews than other European nations—many Jews came to Italy from Spain in their escape from the Inquisition, for example. But Jews had been legally equal to their Catholic neighbors only since the unification of Italy, 1848 at the earliest, 1870 at the latest—a single lifetime. And yet, a single lifetime, the lifetime also of the nation and its constitution, was enough to convince this educated man, this historian, to believe in his country.

That lifetime was not by any means free from anti-Semitism, either, though it was free from government-sponsored anti-Semitism. Rachel tells the story of a cousin who encountered it before the racial laws, when the "spirit of religious tolerance" Aldo describes was supposed to be reigning:

Marianna was a school inspector. And once she went to inspect a nun's school, in a convent. She did the inspection, etcetera, and when the Mother Superior accompanied her to the door she said to her, "Ah, we are very pleased, because in this school, a Jew has never set foot!" And she, who was Jewish, she says, "I'm sorry to say that on the contrary, I'm Jewish." (Laughs) Understand? Oh, she was very upset, this Marianna. This was before the racial laws.

This event must have been out of the ordinary (since Rachel remembers it sixty years later) and it does take place in a convent, where they were still saying that Jews killed Christ. But they were saying the same thing throughout the overwhelmingly Catholic country; it was a popular belief. Perhaps it lay dormant in the common consciousness, one of many inherited opinions, but there it was, making anti-Semitism just a little less "alien to the Italian way of thinking."

In mid-July, 1938, as Aldo recalls, a group of "racial scientists" published a manifesto asserting that there was a pure Italian race that had to be preserved and that, moreover, "Jews do not belong to the Italian race." Aldo withdrew to a retreat in Gressoney for a few days. He later recorded his thoughts.

And notwithstanding his innate optimism and his effort to calm his thoughts, the news that little by little appeared in the newspapers showed that they were clearly starting to apply racist principles.

Who took all this seriously? Certainly not right-minded people, while the first articles were skillfully twisted in order to present the new political-racial ideal as something . . . transcendental, human, hygienic, and I don't know what. What a surprise for the public! At Prof. N. M.'s *pensione* one could catch conversations in low voices: "Such and such is Jewish, he is the manager of X factory, he has a position of great responsibility, how could he be replaced?" "On such and such, a Jew, depend all the workers of the X military shipyard, he has always been supported by Fascism, how will they find a technician of such value?" and so on. And the professor, instead of joining in, as he had always done, with the other lodgers, without any intention of keeping himself at a distance or hiding his own religious faith, stayed all alone, skimming books without interest, taking solitary walks, and above all thinking, thinking . . . He thought back over his entire past, he saw himself again exultant in his uniform as a sub-lieutenant, lieutenant, captain, first captain, major of an infantry complement, proud of serving *his* Fatherland and *his* King, by whom he had been received some years earlier in a private audience, at San Rossore, to explain to him, as an appointee at the University of Pisa, his scientific activity, to show him the completed research for the Pisan volume of *Inscriptiones Italiae* and of *Forma Italiae*.

But then he concluded that for himself, as ex-combatant enlisted in the P.N.F. [National Fascist Party] since 1932, there could be no doubt that he would be left to his career in the public schools, as a teacher of classical letters in Umberto I School of Rome. And such optimism he tried to instill in others, when he visited campground friends, where there was no dearth of cultured and thoughtful people who had become literally disoriented and perplexed.

So that, when they read in the paper that the enrollment of Jewish children in school was prohibited [in September, 1938], the professor wanted to believe it was a provision limited to real and true enrollment in the first class of every level of school and not to the passage through successive classes of those who already went to school. He even immediately wrote an express letter to an important person so that he would endorse such an interpretation and he gave a little hope to lots of parents and a little comfort to lots of children who were attached to their professors and their classmates. Vain hopes, illusions of a soul too good and trusting in the understanding of our government!

The first official measure against the Jews was a direct hit on Aldo and his children. In September 1938, the headlines read: JEWISH PROFESSORS AND STUDENTS EXCLUDED FROM STATE, STATE-CONTROLLED, AND OFFICIALLY RECOGNIZED SCHOOLS. The article explained:

To trust the didactic function to Jewish teachers would mean to subject young people, in the formative period of their character and their mentality, to the direct influence of Judaism . . . The decree frees therefore not only teaching, but also high culture, from every Jewish influence and finally takes steps to remove from the young every contact that is injurious to the spiritual integrity of the race, denying Jews entrance to the schools.[11]

Finally, in October 1938, the Grand Council of Fascism publicly agreed: there could be no Jewish patriots. The published records of the meeting on the Defense of the Race state:

The Grand Council of Fascism remembers that world Judaism—especially after the abolition of Freemasonry—has been the animator of anti-Fascism in all corners and that foreign Judaism and exiled Italian Judaism has been—in all periods, culminating in 1924–25 and during the Ethiopian War—unanimously hostile to Fascism.

The immigration of foreign elements—which has become strongly marked since 1933—has worsened the Italian Jews' state of mind towards the Regime, which they do not sincerely accept since it is antithetical to that which is the psychology, the politics, the internationalism of Israel.[12]

On November 11, 1938, the headlines read: LAWS FOR THE DEFENSE OF THE RACE APPROVED BY THE COUNCIL OF MINISTERS. First on the list of what members "of the Jewish race" could not do was serve in the army, in peacetime or in war. They could not own land or businesses worth more than a certain amount, care for non-Jewish children, work in local or national bureaucracy, or insurance companies, or banks with national interests. They could not belong to the Fascist Party, have parental rights to their own children if the children were not Jewish, or employ "Aryan" domestics.

Technically, according to a long list of exclusions, Aldo and his family could apply to be "discriminated" from the rest of the Jews on the basis of his service in the Great War. In 1937, he had even been promoted to the rank of major. And yet the damage was done—Aldo's patriotism, his "Italianness" were questioned.

> Am I not Italian like all the rest? . . . It's true that some Jewish elements in Italy have felt the need to stress such a division in the face of others; for them, tracing back into very distant Palestinian origins, Italy would be an adopted fatherland. But it was a very limited movement and anyway a movement to condemn, because beyond some useless theoretical articles and some polemic in poor taste there was the uncontestable reality of all the dead, of all those wounded or damaged by the Great War of 1915–1918. By their own sacrifice they had demonstrated how the Jews respond when their Fatherland calls them as Italian citizens to fulfill their duty.

That he fulfilled his duty was one of Aldo's greatest sources of pride. He had saved drawers full of memorabilia from his service in World War I. Heavy medals in blue velvet boxes, commissions on parchment, military identification cards, pictures of himself in uniform. Everything in little unmarked boxes or envelopes labeled so lightly in pencil that they must be opened anyway to identify their contents.

His service, his recognition by the King himself, was proof for him that Jews should be treated as equal citizens, that they had equal claim. He sees the other side; he sees that Zionists might at least appear not to be totally loyal to Italy and that recent refugees might have less claim to be treated as Italians. But his family had been in Italy for centuries, he served in the Great War, he even joined the Fascist Party. The government was making a mistake. And, through the press, it was misleading the Italian people, Aldo's comrades.

Jews Don't Have a Warrior Spirit:
An Article from the "Defense of the Race"

In an article entitled, "Jews and War," today's issue of "Defense of the Race" points out as one of the characteristics of the Jews most evident and most generally observed in the course of the centuries is the irreconcilable difference between their concept and the Aryan concept of heroic virtues. Not only does the Jew not have a warlike spirit and military sentiments, but even more, the Aryan idea of courage and the eminently Nordic Aryan sentiment of honor do not in the least conform to his spirit . . . Jews as a whole are distinguished by a very high percentage of shirkers, for which, in short, the percentage of their dead has been for certain nations noticeably lesser than the percentage of Aryan dead . . . The "Defense of the Race" observes: "it's evident that for all the Jews who desired it, they were assigned to more profitable and at the same time less dangerous posts."[13]

One day I was helping Rachel clear out a bookshelf in Aldo's study. It was piled with offprints from academic journals, articles clipped from thirty-year-old newspapers, mimeographs of a curriculum vitae, rough copies of official letters. Everything had to be pulled from its manila envelope, unfolded, read, sorted. Nothing was to be thrown out. I came across what looked like a short story by Aldo, who wrote, as far as I knew, only memoirs and academic treatises. I handed it over to Rachel and she immediately read it aloud, in a kind of affectionate, admiring tone. She had never seen it before.

A Meeting of Two Trench-Mates

By Aldo Neppi Modona

(Rome, October 1938)

In the uncertain light of dusk under the trees along the Tiber he thought he could make out the figure of an old comrade-in-arms; he quickened his step and reached him:

"Carlo! Yes, it is you! How happy I am to see you! Don't you recognize me?"

"Ah, yes. Isaac."

"Of course! Ah, how the old dear memories return when I look at you again! Do you remember? Those months spent together in an intimate communion of spirit in the trenches of the Sleme with the 42nd! It's an image that will never leave my mind! A memory that has never faded, you know!"

"Not even now, after your separation from us Aryans?"

"What are you dreaming about? Do you think that maybe I feel Italian like that, when it suits me? I was born Italian, as were my parents, and on back until at least 1500 and maybe even farther back than that, my ancestors were all Italians by birth and sentiment, and such are my children and such will they remain. And so my affection remains exactly the same for my comrades and for all Italians, with whom I have shared all my fears and all my joys. Perhaps you have forgotten the enthusiasm we had as soldiers?"

"Oh, no, I remember it; then one didn't think about this difference, but now that it's been made clear, it surprises me that you can stay so enthusiastic."

"You must not be aware of all the upbringing I've had, and which my fellow Israelites have had, of pure Italianness, of vibrations in my, in our heart perfectly in unison with yours, with all of yours: who delved into ancient origins? My perceptible world, my affective world was Italy. For her I voluntarily ran to fight, all the rest of the world was far away for me. And yet all this was implicit, evident, when we shared the most intimate confidences in the long hours of exhausting waiting and when we had learned to be indifferent to the ta-poom of the light cannon pointed right on our dens! Remember the time when, still a novice, having just arrived in the trenches after basic duty of only one month, as sub-lieutenant of the ground militia, at the first hit of an Austrian gun, I rushed outside all happy to be able to 'fight for real.' I put the whole platoon in action and then I see the Captain rushing out enraged, yelling 'Stop, silence, everyone into the shelters. We don't respond. They are the usual daily provocations for which there is an order not to respond.' And in fact, after a little, all was quiet. But meanwhile I was so upset to see that my first enthusiasm had to be checked and that I had to wait longer to feel the emotion of the attack and the counterattack . . . What lovely times, even with all the war, how we felt united with all our comrades, respected and obeyed by our subordinates, loved by superiors . . . and how deeply we became attached, with all our hearts, to our commanders.

"You can't imagine how much I suffer now to think that for them—for my Major, for example, for the man I would have done I don't know what for, who always told me that he placed all his faith in me . . . I could no longer be considered the same as before . . . [D]idn't I feel that I was doing all this as a duty, as an honor, ready to sacrifice myself for my Fatherland, for Italy, for the King, our Supreme Leader in War?"

"But not everyone thinks and feels as you do."

"No, no, Carlo, you're wrong, a tremendous number of us think and feel this way . . . ask all the veterans, so many of whom are decorated and wounded, and you will see how much they suffer to feel themselves misunderstood . . . And you know what hurts me so much now? Your coldness, your incomprehension . . . When with our efforts we succeeded in saving the Company that had been left isolated at Tagliamento, when we felt so proud at having kept our unit together, at having led it methodically to the established destination. And we had the Major's praise for the cold blood and anti-defeatist enthusiasm with which we encouraged the infantrymen, and we embraced each other crying, swearing to die rather than see the enemy advance beyond the fixed limit of the Piave. Did you suspect that my heart beat in a different way than yours, that it was less sincere than yours, that I wouldn't have known how to be faithful with all the passion of my soul to the oath given to His Majesty the King? Didn't this perhaps mean, for me as well as for you, death rather than dishonor?"

"Yes, of course, then I didn't make any distinction between us, but because they hadn't ever made us understand the difference of race."

"But didn't I know I was Jewish, and didn't you know and didn't everyone know? And if I have had the honor of fighting at your side, wasn't I also subject to the same duties, with the obligation to fulfill them scrupulously just like you? Oh, what pain to feel ourselves so Italian, so sincerely attached to the Dynasty and to the Regime that has saved Italy from Bolshevism . . . [B]y the way, we met once after the demobilization, in Florence, in October of 1919, remember?"

"Yes, when you had just recovered from a serious illness."

"Exactly, I'd had typhus just as I returned home and we opened our hearts to each other about the pain of having reentered our cities almost on tiptoe . . . Remember our dreams of the reception that would be made at our return, after victory? We said: What joy to be able to parade under the windows of our houses, at the head of our units, content to have done our duty to the last . . . and instead returning one by one, like so much small change, in the dark, we were almost supposed to be ashamed of the years we spent at the front . . . [I]t was atrocious, you know, how much I suffered for it, and you too, you told me you couldn't believe your eyes . . . So think whether my enthusiasm for the Fascist movement was sincere, the movement that gave us liberty again, that made our hearts beat anew with passion and pride, that made spiritual values honorable!"

"But you shouldn't lose heart, you should resign yourself to the new situation and submit yourself to it."

"Of course, without arguing and without complaining. But I thought that to old comrades we could open our hearts to make it clear how much we were suffering to find no more affectionate greetings, even in those we were closest to, in those who have risked death with us for more than three years, minute by minute . . . Those bombs that exploded two steps away from us were thrown against me as well as against you, because we were and we are both Italians. And during the long months of comradeship at the front, scrutinizing as we did to the depths of our inner beings our hopes, our affections, never for a single minute on anyone's part was the smallest difference in feeling found, the object of our affections being identical, identical being our spiritual aims, identical our fundamental faith in the goodness of the Creator and of the Ruler of the Universe: our religions have much in common in the original substance. How it hurts me to see that you don't want to understand any of this . . ."

"No, it's not that I don't want to, but, I repeat, I'm surprised, I thought that your love for Italy had gone cold, that it was, let's say, transitory, changeable according to the time and the situation. And so I was a little disconcerted to find you like this, just as before . . . and I ask myself if he can really be sincere . . ."

"Oh Carlo! I understand and I suffer terribly from this doubt of yours. I realize that one can't assume an emotional national identity in someone who recently came from outside, maybe, in someone who had, before ours, other fatherlands; but he who never had another fatherland other than maybe going back centuries and centuries, maybe millennia, for what could he feel more affection if not for that which was the fatherland for all the preceding generations who had their upbringing, affections, memories here? Try to understand me, think about what I said to you and if we meet each other again, maybe even another time as soldiers, try to show me that you have understood. In any case, for me you will always be my friend Carlo, as every Italian will always be my closest life companion . . ."

Isaac departed, alone with his troubles.

Carlo followed him with a look.

It is a measure of Aldo's isolation that he wrote this story, a record of what he would say if he could, if there were someone to say it to. Surely Aldo's dignity would not allow him to issue this plea out loud. After fighting for his country, to stoop to begging for recognition—"please, don't listen to them, I'm still just like you . . ." Who could say such a thing, who could meet with a snub and press the point? Only a man who didn't care what people thought, only a man who wasn't pained by that snub. A man as hurt as "Isaac" is could not have done it. And that is why, as a short story, "A Meeting of Two Trench-Mates" doesn't work; it pictures a scene that couldn't really happen. The anguish is real, but the scene is simply not possible. Aldo would not have had to write it if it were.

He couldn't say how he felt to anyone; with Rachel, perhaps it was understood. But he needed another kind of comfort, precisely the kind he could not get, the comfort of his comrades. He couldn't tell them how he felt, so he wrote it here. Aldo felt not anger at the injustice of the racial laws, but anxiety, lest his old comrades think him less devoted, less patriotic than he was. Lest his Major should believe that he were less worthy and reliable. He loved the system, believed in it. He loved his Major, His Majesty, and the Fascist Regime. And he loved order. So he is willing to despair rather than to fight, to suffer rather than to challenge. Not to submit, not to resign himself to these laws would disrupt the order—just as Jews are accused of doing by having two Fatherlands, two loyalties. If he refuses to submit to his own oppression, he justifies that oppression: he is the disloyal Jew. All he can do is obey the rules and remain a model citizen. Maybe then Mussolini will realize that Jews can be good Italians, maybe he will realize his mistake.

But Aldo, in arguing his case as an impeccable Italian citizen, implies that those Jews who didn't fight, those who didn't swear allegiance to the King, those whose families don't reach back into the 1500s, those who don't embrace Fascism are somehow less worthy of being Italians. Recent refugees, Zionists, pacifists—they are all left undefended by his argument. The Fascists—and indeed the Nazis—were brilliant at dividing their enemy, encouraging them to abandon one another as they sought to appease the government.

In fact, in defending only the Jews who are like him, Aldo merely succumbs to an understandable but selfish urge to plead his case, to vent his own, deserved sorrow. Others actually struck out against their fellow Jews. Mainstream Italian Jews (active Zionists and anti-Fascists were a small minority[14]) often felt that they were being blamed for the beliefs of their Zionist brothers; they often blamed their oppression on the Zionists and Jewish anti-Fascists instead of on the government. "At that time," writes Vittorio Segre, "there were still nonetheless people who convinced themselves they could win the favor of the regime with public demonstrations of loyalty to Fascism and of distance from those Jews considered to be enemies of the regime."[15] Segre's father, a decorated veteran and Fascist, was in fact approached by his cousin Ettore Ovazza, Jewish publisher of the pro-Fascist magazine *La Nostra Bandiera (Our Flag)*, to join in a plot to attack another Jewish magazine, *Israele*, which "defended with courage and dignity the position of Italian Jews supporting their right to be Zionists." Ovazza said that "a 'punitive action' by Jews against that periodical would demonstrate to the government the patriotism of Jewish Fascists and at the same time would do something the party would appreciate."[16]

Segre's father declined. He said, "To attack our coreligionists in miserable times such as those that we are going through, in order to ingratiate ourselves with a regime that has betrayed us, is an act of servants, not of men."[17] Ovazza and his men destroyed *Israele*'s press shortly thereafter.

Segre's father was unusually clear-sighted. Aldo, though an intelligent man, tries so hard *not* to be betrayed by the regime he had believed in and served that he misses the point. It's not that the most patriotic, war-honored, Fascist-sympathizing Jew should be treated like his Catholic neighbors, it's that the least patriotic, pacifistic, pro-Zionist Jew should be. Those who can't trace back their lineage until the 1500s. Like his wife. Aldo says he and his children are Italian through and through. She? She was born in Patmos in 1907 and moved to Rhodes at age four. The Italians took Rhodes from the Turkish empire in 1912. She could not, in short, have traced her Italian credentials back before her fifth birthday. Italian was her fourth language.

Frequently, when speaking of the war years, Rachel says, "I did everything." She demanded the bank give them their bonds when they were desperate for money, she found food when their ration cards weren't renewed, she found people to hide their jewels, she had a wall built around the valuables in their apartment, she found hiding places in Florence. She took charge. Of course, it was much more dangerous for Aldo to be out and about, to make a nuisance of himself. Men in the street were instantly under suspicion, after the German occupation in September 1943. They could be deserters from the Italian army, they could be spies, they could be Jews. Much of what women did, therefore, they did because it was safer for them than for their men. But it was also easier for them to disobey. Rachel had never made an oath of loyalty to the King, she had never met him. She had never fought for her country, never received medals, commissions, promotions, or a sense of achievement from it. Her talents were not officially recognized by public institutions; her career was not supported by grants from the state. Between the time she started learning Italian in high school in Rhodes and that moment when she had to give up her Catholic maid in Florence, Italian officialdom affected her only indirectly. So she could lie to that officialdom, hide from it, confront it, hate it.

Aldo could not. When it came time to protect himself and his family from the system he had embraced, he hesitated, ignored the danger, tried to continue a normal life. To act otherwise was to admit betrayal, was to admit that Mussolini was not going to come to his senses and the King was not going to come to their rescue. To act otherwise was to be disloyal.

Rachel says they had two opportunities to leave before the Germans came. The first was an offer from a friend, the historian Cecil Roth, at Oxford, who promised Aldo a 90-percent chance for a position there. Rachel said that when they packed their bags to spend the summer of 1939 in Fiuggi Città outside of Rome, they were planning to go. But then, she said, war broke out between England and Germany and they couldn't go. Another offer was from a former pupil from the summer courses Aldo taught in Perugia. She was from Buffalo, New York, and arranged for him to have a house and a job there. He went to the American Consulate in Naples with an affidavit to this effect and they told him he needed proof that she had available funds to pay him. But once he relayed this message to her and she replied, America had entered the war.

Aldo doesn't mention either offer in his diary. Why? Why doesn't he write about his efforts to leave the country and how they were foiled by poor timing? Maybe in hindsight, he realized he could have tried harder to go, maybe he really didn't want to leave his country, maybe he believed, as so many others did, that things would get better.

In *All Our Yesterdays,* Natalia Ginzburg said that before the Germans came "all you had to do was pay a little and the police left you alone." But Aldo was not capable of bribery. Even after the Germans had arrived, he hesitated to take the necessary illegal steps to keep his family alive. In January of 1944, his family was still in Florence, though round-ups had begun in November. Rabbi Cassuto had been telling community members to leave for months. But how, he writes, can they go, how will they eat? "Everyone's advice was the same: get a false identity card. The hesitations of the professor, whose moral uprightness wasn't accustomed to compromise with his conscience, were at last won over by the spontaneously offered opportunity to perform a good deed of patriotic charity, and that was to help the 'rebels,' that is the patriots, by handing over a large sum of money, receiving in exchange a blank card, for himself and his wife, with the stamp of the Municipality of Catanzaro."

A good deed of patriotic charity, as if he bought an expensive raffle ticket to save the bald eagle. And he emphasizes the words "patriotic" and "patriots," from *patria*, fatherland. *Compiere*, to perform or fulfill, is the same word he used in the short story he wrote five years before to describe his military duty. Fulfilling his duty, carrying out his oath, performing a good deed of patriotic charity. Responsibility, uprightness, citizenship. He is not selfishly and illegally saving himself and his family, he is helping his country.

Discrimination

O N   N O V E M B E R   11,   1938,   five and a half years before the Neppi
Modonas were forced to escape from Florence, they read about the racial
laws in *Il Corriere della Sera*, Milan's daily newspaper. Under the glaring headline,
"Laws for the Defense of the Race Approved by the Council of Ministers," was
another, smaller, subheading, "Discriminations." This did not refer to discrimination as we think of it, discrimination *against* a certain people the official approval of which was first page news. This referred to discrimination *for* people—
setting certain Jews apart from Jews who were set apart from Italians, Jews who,
on the basis of merit (most often military service), were somehow not as dangerous as other Jews. These Jews had to apply for the label of *discriminato* or discriminated, which, if received, exempted them from many of the racial laws
(they still could not attend or teach school). They were praised by those who
damned their community, their friends, their family. They were in the first ranks
of second-class citizens.

Philosopher Hannah Arendt believed this "discrimination" effectively let
everyone off the hook.

> When Mussolini, under German pressure, introduced anti-Jewish legislation in the
> late thirties, he stipulated the usual exemptions—war veterans, Jews with high dec-
> orations, and the like—but he added one more category, namely, former members
> of the Fascist Party, together with their parents and grandparents, their wives and
> children and grandchildren. I know of no statistics relating to this matter, but the
> result must have been that the great majority of Italian Jews were exempted. There
> can hardly have been a Jewish family without at least one member in the Fascist

Party, for this happened at a time when Jews, like other Italians, had been flocking for almost twenty years into the Fascist movement, since positions in the Civil Service were open only to members. And the few Jews who had objected to Fascism on principle, Socialists and Communists chiefly, were no longer in the country.[18]

Indeed, Aldo wrote that these exceptions left veterans and honorees with "a glimmer of hope," but that, in reality, once the exceptions were interpreted by various ministers, "they ended up reduced to a pretty nothing." He applied to be discriminated. "How many visits to the Minister, how many times did I insist . . . Meanwhile, the concessions of discrimination happened with enormous delay and after a series of quite lengthy investigations, and often they never arrived in hand."

Memo Bemporad writes in his memoirs that "the much-extolled 'discrimination,' let us understand each other, showed itself to be little more than a piece of paper. In fact it was an 'administrative' provision and could be (and was) annulled at whatever moment by whatever prefect or provincial Fascist secretary, or even by the humblest official or hierarch."[19] Bemporad calls discrimination "useless."[20] But of course it was not useless. What was the regime to do with Jews of unassailable patriotism, Jews who had served their country so well that they were respected and admired by their Christian neighbors for that service, Jews who were so far from being Zionists or anti-Fascists that they could raise a clear and compelling voice against the "logic" behind their oppression? The answer was simple. Assure them they were different and set them to work filling out papers to prove as much; fill their days with mind-numbing bureaucracy. They will be so busy securing their own livelihood, they will not realize that they are contributing to their own oppression. It may have been useless for the Jews, but discrimination was essential to the regime; it was, says Bemporad, "a trap that there and then seemed a life preserver."[21]

In other European countries, Jewish councils formed by the Nazis helped organize the deportation of their people. This was not the case in Italy, though some Jewish leaders surely acted foolishly—failing to warn their congregations or their communities of the Nazi threat in an effort not to spread panic. But that some Jews grabbed at the "life preserver" of discrimination, while fellow Jews were drowning, certainly contributed to what Hannah Arendt describes as "the totality of the moral collapse the Nazis caused in respectable European society—not only in Germany but in almost all countries, not only among the persecutors but also among the victims."[22] In offering Jews this seeming life preserver, Fascist officials showed that they had learned something from their Nazi counterparts.

The categories had been accepted without protest by German Jewry from the very beginning. And the acceptance of privileged categories—German Jews as against Polish Jews, war veterans and decorated Jews as against ordinary Jews, families whose ancestors were German-born as against recently naturalized citizens, etc.— had been the beginning of the moral collapse of respectable Jewish society. (In view of the fact that today such matters are often treated as though there existed a law of human nature compelling everybody to lose his dignity in the face of disaster, we may recall the attitude of the French Jewish war veterans who were offered the same privileges by their government and replied: "We solemnly declare that we renounce any exceptional benefits we may derive from our status as ex-servicemen" [*American Jewish Yearbook*, 1945].) Needless to say, the Nazis themselves never took these distinctions seriously, for them a Jew was a Jew, but the categories played a certain role up to the very end, since they helped put to rest a certain uneasiness among the German population: only Polish Jews were deported, only people who had shirked military service, and so on.

What was morally so disastrous in the acceptance of these privileged categories was that everyone who demanded to have an "exception" made in his case implicitly recognized the rule . . .[23]

Aldo was the perfect candidate for this ploy, since he loved hierarchy and could not shake his image of himself as an upstanding citizen. And, indeed, it is hard to blame anyone for trying what he could to keep the racial laws from affecting his family. But Aldo could not have kept his job in any case—since he was a teacher—so all that would be left him was, perhaps, his "Aryan" servants, his access to the libraries, and his right to publish books. Perhaps. He himself asks what it's really worth.

What was it good for practically? To be believed something different from the others, for some people, to get into certain environments, to penetrate the libraries and be able to borrow books, and that's all. What a difference from the Duce's highfaluting declarations in the famous and so noisily applauded Trieste speech!

And in the end, of course, it got him a "pretty nothing." Perhaps he wished he had not applied, that he had protested by refusing the privileged category, like the French Jewish war veterans. But he does not say that that was so, he merely rebukes himself for having faith in the "understanding of our government." He is angry because he does not get what he was promised, and he is embarrassed to have expected it. But he is not embarrassed to have sought to be "discriminated" from his fellow Jews.

"What Painful Months Those Were!"

.... ☀ ....

Aldo had to stop teaching. And he made arrangements to do so, he worked harder than ever to arrange for his own poverty, for his own professional humiliation. And yet what else could he do? He had no choice other than to play out the ending of his career—forever, as far as he knew. Today, looking back, it was seven years of persecution; then, 1938 must have seemed the beginning of the end, the unraveling of their lives.

So too public servants [exclaims Aldo in the Red Book], away with them! Only with an extension until March 30, an extension of which most people took advantage, happy to be of some use until the last. And what strength of spirit it took to continue to fulfill all your duty, knowing that zeal and maximum scrupulousness meant nothing. Such was the case of Prof. N. M., who in the afternoon worked as head of the publications and filing departments at the Institute of Roman Studies, enjoying the full trust of its president, Galassi Paluzzi. What painful months those were! Aside from the usual incessant work, long reports, and memos, he had to prepare to leave his successor fully up-to-date on every work in progress. And as if that weren't enough, the threats of sanctions and punishments against philo-Semites, the *pietists*, rendered even colder the relationships among superiors and inferiors. Jewish employees were received almost in secret, avoiding encounters and conversations with outsiders; at first there were promises of work at home, of intervention, then less and less, to the point that it was understood that even visits at home weren't much appreciated, that it was better to thin them out.

Ah, what dreadful months, this feeling ever more estranged from active life in which one was once involved . . . This feeling oneself dodged, avoided in the street and in public offices, even by those who felt affection and sympathy, but fear for one's career surpassed—as you could well understand—every other feeling, even that dictated by a sense of profound humanity.

What would it be like to go out to buy the paper I had bought for years and read headlines like: JEWISH INFILTRATION OF TURIN or DANGEROUS INTRODUCTION OF JEWS IN THE INSURANCE SECTOR? To know that my neighbors are being taught to suspect me, and not to be able to ask if they had learned the lesson? How can I ask such questions? With my neighbors I discuss the chance of rain, the price of milk at the corner store, perhaps some gossip about another neighbor's illness. If the pleasantries have ended, do I want to press the point, force my neighbors to confirm what I don't want to believe? If they continue, if the blessed and bizarre normalcy continues, do I want to break it off with an awkward plea? No. I let myself fade, sink into silence, I begin to watch them while they talk. I feel I have barely noticed their faces before. Between us there is knowledge, a fact, two facts: I am a Jew and Jews are supposed to be dangerous. And depending on what they think of the government and of me, there is sympathy or there is suspicion. As if, on the one hand, they know I have cancer and, on the other, they know I'm a thief. Either way, there is no way for the subject to be broached, no way for me to find out which. Or perhaps it's both—perhaps it's as if I had syphillis, and they both pity and suspect me; I am both pitiful and wicked. And I'm not sure I want to know what they are thinking, but I am amazed I can stand here on the street with this newspaper in my hand and not know. Waiting for a word of pity or solidarity that will not come, cannot come.

Primo Levi wrote in *Periodic Table*:

A few months before, the racial laws against the Jews had been proclaimed, and I too was becoming a loner. My Christian classmates were civil people; none of them, nor any of the teachers, had directed at me a hostile word or gesture, but I could feel them withdraw and, following an ancient pattern, I withdrew as well: every look exchanged between me and them was accompanied by a minuscule but perceptible flash of mistrust and suspicion. What do you think of me? What am I for you? The same as six months ago, your equal who does not go to mass, or the Jew who, as Dante put it, "in your midst laughs at you"?[24]

Mutual suspicion grew, fostered by everything from subtle propaganda to bald threats. Embarrassment may have prevented many non-Jews from making their support clear; fear prevented many others. Perhaps some actually believed what they were reading in the papers:

Jews and Jew Lovers

We won't be melodramatic, because we will be pitiless; and it is precisely without pity that we speak of these poor fools and enemies of themselves who set themselves up as friends of this or that Jew . . . That fellow is a Jew? Before being this or that he is a Jew; it's worth saying he's of another race, he cannot have the rights of an Italian . . . They are of another race. They don't have roots in Italy. They are foreigners here. They live parasitically on a plant that has no reason to feed them.[25]

Aldo writes:

It's clear that would-be Aryans should not have had any contact with the Jews, so let's not speak of notes bearing best wishes for the New Year or Passover and Easter, which were naturally suspended on both sides, but even if on an occasion of a sorrowful or a joyful event, a Jew sincerely felt the need to console or congratulate with a simple line, it was useless to wait for a response!

And that's what happened many times to our Prof. N. M., who would not have believed such a silence on the part of colleagues with whom he'd had such cordial relationships for years! There were, of course, exceptions—those who had a solid consciousness of moral values and their superiority to any other opportunistic reasoning. This difference in judgment is clear also in other particulars. On the one hand, for example, was the president of the Institute for Roman Studies, who immediately gave the order to suspend the mailing of the bulletin and of every other invitation to Prof. N. M., for fear that his name would figure in the mailing list, and on the other hand was the rector of the Royal University for Foreigners in Perugia, who had the university's bulletin continue to be mailed!

Rachel also mentioned this bulletin, twice in fact, as if this were a mark of real courage, of heroism, that the University in Perugia left Aldo on the mailing list. Perhaps at the time it was; perhaps that list could have been dangerous for them. But how little must people have been doing and saying, how few gestures of humanity must have been left for a mailing list to be so important. Those little fictions of everyday life—condolence letters, letters of congratulation, the sense of being part of a community—these are what Aldo can't stand to lose. The pleasantries that imply that we are all knitted together, that the death of my mother means something to you and the birth of your son means something to me—to lose these was to realize that people don't really matter to each other. And therefore Fascism could do whatever it wanted to the Neppi Modonas, and their neighbors would go along with it. "Much has been said of the persecution," said

Bemporad. "But only very few select souls, among those not affected, have truly understood. Those affected, yes, they know what it is. And mind: not only in the most known or felt excesses, in the most terrible tragedies, in the most vile atrocities, in the most subtle deceptions, in the most hypocritical practices, but also in the symptoms and in the minor particulars, those that eluded the not affected, or seemed insignificant to them."[26] A greeting on the sidewalk, a tip of the hat, a polite inquiry—these, as any traveler knows, are what separate the natives from the foreigners, those who belong from those who do not. Slowly, magnificently, Fascist propaganda was turning Jews from the natives they were to the foreigners Mussolini claimed they were.

Aldo writes very little, comparatively, about this time in his life: a hasty summing up, about one quarter of the Red Book, to cover three quarters of the time. He wants to write about the war instead, about the occupation of the Germans. In the fall of 1943, Mussolini's government crumbled, the new one declared an armistice with the Allies, and Germany occupied Italy. That's the time Aldo wants to write about, when the bad guys were invading foreigners and the very bad guys were the ones wearing skulls and crossbones on their epaulets. He wants to write about going incognito into the countryside as a Displaced Italian, when no distinctions were made between him and all the other Italians trying to survive. When Aldo and his family finally left Florence, he was relieved and happy no longer to be recognized as a Jew—not because it was safer, but because it was less lonely: "[A]t least they were accompanied by courteous strangers, for whom they could be 'Aryans,' and it didn't give them misgivings to speak to each other," he wrote, ". . . and so, a word with this one, a word with that one, and their souls felt comforted."

He never describes his life in detail until he could be mistaken for an "Aryan"; he rails about the indignities he is forced to endure when the racial laws are passed, but he does not describe, day to day, how he lived. Daily snubs are far more interesting than daily bombings, but also probably far more painful. This is perhaps why, though his memoirs eventually ease into first-person familiarity, they begin in rigid third-person formality. How much easier it is to reveal the naiveté, the vulnerability, the suffering of "the professor" than of "me." How much easier to keep those five years at a grammatical distance.

Leo kept a diary too, as Rachel wrote to tell me. It was amusing to her, proof of her son's precocity, but she did not take it seriously as she did Aldo's book. Yet Leo is clearly a born writer, and with a writer's instinct he focuses on what his readers will want to read—those daily interactions that his father finds too painful or too humiliating to record. Secure in his family (which, since he never had a career or went to school before the racial laws, is the only thing that matters to him), Leo is willing to tell us anything, even when he looks foolish or selfish and he knows it. His book is as marked by honesty as his father's is by gentle self-delusion, and that is what makes him a writer.

But during the occupation, the bombings terrify him, as does the possibility that his parents could be snatched away by the SS at any moment. He puts down his pen and refuses to write; he does not think he will live.

When Leo writes of his life under the racial laws, his father hovers in the background, deluded, disillusioned, hopeful, despairing. When Aldo writes of the occupation, Leo is there, mute, disobedient, anguished. You can peek at each trauma through the other's words; they cannot write about what pains them most: Aldo does not have the courage and Leo does not have the hope.

Rachel and Lionella were there too, of course. They were survivors. In a way it seems appropriate that they are still living, while husband/father and son/brother are not. Talkers and copers seem to live beyond writers and sufferers. They are comforted by their contact with people, they are energized by pragmatic concerns, and they are carried on by their own hard strength. Rachel and Lionella were frightened and hurt and upset, and for Lionella at least, the pain reached to the core, but it did not twist or torture her.

When Leo's story begins, on September 2, 1938, they are all—Rachel, Aldo, Leo, Lionella, and Aldo's mother, Ada—living in an apartment in Rome, where they had been for four years. Aldo taught in a high school for the classics and worked in the Institute for Roman Studies, and the children (Leo, 6, and Lionella, 7) were tutored at home, though Aldo and Rachel agreed that they would soon begin public school. Sometimes Aldo would take the children on walks to the Forum where he would teach them about architecture and ancient civilizations; Lionella says she has never forgotten what he taught. They attended a small synagogue on Via Balbo; it was the closest. Mamma Ada and Rachel tended the home with the help of Erminia the cook, and there was a nanny to take the children out to play.

Apart from a few lapses, Leo calls himself "Andrea" in his book, his sister "Milena," his mother "Lucia," his grandmother "Mamma Alice," and his father "Alessio." He chooses the family name "Nola." He did not rewrite and probably did not reread carefully—names and spellings change as the tale proceeds. I have changed them back, because I thought the mistakes were more confusing than revealing. I have also cut some chapters because, although none of Leo's writing is boring, some is less relevant to his life as a Jewish child under the racial laws, some is full of relatives' names and family history, and some takes us

Leo and Lionella (1939).

on yet another summer vacation, making it harder to remember the one before. I also interrupt him with commentary by the rest of his family. His mother's and sister's comments are from interviews and letters, his father's are from the portion of the father's journal that overlaps in time with Leo's.

Leo wrote on lined newsprint in cursive (Italians, in fact, do not learn to print), in heavy black ink, in straight-up-and-down letters that tend to collide with the ones above and below.

PART TWO

Leo's Diary

Barbarians in the Twentieth Century

·············· ☀ ··············

CHAPTER I. EXTRA! EXTRA!

THE SKY OVER Rome was covered with dark clouds when a Roman news-paper hawker (the kind you can spot from a half mile away for their poverty and slovenliness) popped out from who knows where into the clatter of trams and automobiles. He was shouting with all his breath, and people milled around, while some windows opened and immediately closed, since it was right in the heat of the afternoon.

The little red trucks of the *Messaggero* ran through the city carrying with them the news: "Special Edition! Special Edition!"

A few men bought it, read it, and then shook their heads in disapproval; oth-ers instead, though few, seemed pleased by the news. Most of those were fanatics who let themselves be deluded by Fascism, dreaming of who knows what.

At that same moment, a professor came out of the Institute of Roman Studies. The president of the Institute was a master at sitting on the fence, keeping a leg on each side just in case. He had sent away an employee for not knowing that a certain day was the Birthday of Rome [a Fascist holiday], but when it was in his interest, he knew quite well how to smile and ask forgiveness from that poor em-ployee—Professor Nola, Jewish by religion, very Italian by sentiment. In the pi-azza lined with linden trees, Nola stopped to talk with another professor who had just then gotten off the tram, Professor Di Castro, of the same religion.

The hawker crossed the noisy street and stopped to sell his papers in front of the Institute where the professors who were coming out would be sure to buy them.

The piazza, in fact, had become animated: the professors and the employees usually came out in small groups, said goodbye to each other, and headed home. That day they stayed longer to discuss the news written in large red headlines on the special edition of the newspaper that, by now, everybody had in hand. The news: the removal of professors of the Jewish race from every chair and post. The two professors said goodbye to each other, preoccupied by the news, which, with no illusions, many people had expected.

The tram stopped at a busy intersection: the one between Via Manzoni, Via Emanuele Filiberto, and Via San Quintino; the big four-story house facing it was on the corner of Via Manzoni, Via Emanuele Filiberto, and Via San Quintino, which was narrow and full of houses.

On the corner of Via Emanuele Filiberto stood a cart loaded with tasty bananas in front of a newspaper stand; then many stores with various goods, one next to the other.

Professor Nola, having bought a kilo of bananas, crossed the square and entered the four-story house marked with the number 100; two children with their faces to the window cried, "Papa! Papa!" and drew back from the window. They were a boy and a girl; the boy was called Andrea, the girl, Milena.

Half an hour later, the whole family was at the table: the papa at the head, the mamma and the grandmother to one side, the children facing them.

While the cook was serving some exquisite roast potatoes, Leo whispered to his mamma, who was across from him, "What's making you so serious?" But the grandmother didn't allow whispering, especially at the table.

"If you have something to say to us, say it out loud," and the attempt stayed there forgotten, on account of the perfumed flavor of the bananas which the boy started to eat à la "Indian," as he called it, that is, in bites, without a knife.

Having eaten their bananas, the children were dismissed, "as the grown-ups had something to discuss." Behind the door, they tried to hear, but understood nothing because "the grown-ups" were speaking French. Then they got tired. Andrea ran to the curtain that divided the hallway from the other rooms and started to wrap himself up in it so his big sister wouldn't see him—"Where am I, Milena?" But instead, the cook (who had been in the house for three years), Erminia, passed by. "No, Master," she said, "you're ruining it—the curtain will tear!"

"Oh, all right!" And having emerged from the yellow satin curtain, he ran after the cook as far as grandmother's room; but Erminia didn't pay him any attention, and so, discouraged, he sat down in a chair.

That room was like the children's kingdom. In one corner, behind the little bed table, a tribe of dolls, little and large, each with its own name, was scattered

This building in Rome (1993) was the Neppi Modonas' home
at the time the racial laws were enacted.

on the bed, which was covered with yellow cloth like the chairs and the armchairs. Every evening, poor Mamma Ada had to remake the bed, completely undone by the children's rowdiness. There was also a table, dirtied by Milena's watercolors. Last of all there was a dresser with its drawers all hanging open clumsily.

The room's two large windows opened onto the square, on the corner of San Quintino alley. Tired now of sitting on a chair and watching his room, Andrea got up, stuck his nose to the glass, and looked curiously about the street.

There was much less movement in the lunchtime heat; the great milk trucks that came by full in the morning passed by empty now, some carts went by, then a crowd of people arrived followed by the noisy carts of porters who were bent over by the excessive weight they shouldered. Who knows why those people carry such weights on their shoulders, thought Andrea, who didn't know about the unhappiness of the world. And he asked himself many other things he didn't know the answers to: he asked himself why they didn't have a terrace like the one upstairs where one could look at the street from up above, and why he couldn't go to that lady upstairs and say "I want to go onto your terrace to look at the street from above." But then he remembered that Erminia had told him that "I want" grass doesn't even grow at Boboli. And so, thought upon thought, he got hungry and therefore thought that maybe it was time for snack, even though Beppe, who started selling bananas at 4 o'clock, hadn't yet come, and even though the fat priest who at about 3:30 crossed the piazza to go to Santa Maria Maggiore to pray, hadn't yet passed by.

He opened the door softly, softly—he wanted to be the first to get the milk and cookies in order to claim the larger cup and the crunchier cookie, so Milena mustn't hear him going into the dining room. He crossed the hallway softly, softly, so as not to wake his mamma who was sleeping; he pulled back the dining room curtain, but he found nothing prepared. Funny, he thought, and knocked on Erminia's door, but no one answered. Then he called "Papa! Papa!" but instead his mother woke:

"What do you want Andrea?" Andrea gathered his courage, opened the door, and entered the room.

"I want my snack! That is, I would like my snack, because Erminia said 'I want' doesn't exist, not even at Boboli. What's Boboli?" He had already forgotten snack.

"Boboli is a beautiful garden where the King lives."

"And Papa, where's he gone?" he asked, not seeing him anywhere. "Did he go to Boboli?"

"No! He went to see a professor."

"What professor? Professor Gotti-Puzzi?"

"Gotti-Puzzi?! Galassi-Palazzi!"

"Gotti-Puzzi is shorter! Why?"

"Oh, stop asking why!" She didn't want to say that he had gone to talk over the racial laws.

"And snack? Snack, Mamma?"

"It's now 4:00; Erminia should be making it for you."

But Milena had already been in the dining room and she had left for poor Andrea the smaller cup and the staler cookie.

"Oh well," he said; he was hungry and he ate, and then he left for a minute, then he thought of washing the dishes himself, but he carried them into the kitchen and left them there. "Erminia will take care of the washing."

He started off toward his room to look at some pictures in a book when the bell rang; he ran to answer it, slipped, got back up, started to run again, but his papa had already opened it with his key. Why does he ring when he has keys, thought Andrea, but then he remembered Mr. Gotti-Puzzi:

"Papa, what did Professor Gotti-Puzzi say?"

"Professor Gotti-Puzzi?! I went to take a walk."

"I don't believe it, in this awful weather!"

"I had an umbrella!"

"And you went alone? You should have taken me with you!"

"Oh, stop asking why. If you must know, I went to see that professor at his house. Are you happy?"

"Yes." But he wasn't.

Aldo had been saying goodbye to his career. Headlines in early September 1938 read, JEWISH TEACHERS AND STUDENTS ELIMINATED FROM FASCIST SCHOOLS, and in smaller letters beneath, "Belonging to Academies, Institutes, and Associations of Sciences, Letters and Arts Forbidden to People of the Jewish Race."

And so, goodbye school, goodbye Institute of Roman Studies . . . *[writes Aldo in his journal]*. And from the Academy of Italy—National Academic Union—two large packages were returned to Prof. N. M.: the manuscripts, already type-set, of the Pisa volumes of *Forma Italiae* and of *Inscriptiones Italiae*. And from the Minister of National Education were returned to the professor the voluminous bundles with the publications presented at the competition for the chair of archeology at the Royal University of Naples . . . What were they worth, all those long, rigid, tiring days spent cataloguing and organizing the Museum of the Estruscan Academy of Cortona, which at the time had procured for him an appointment as honorary member of the Academy itself and honorary citizenship of the ancient city? Away from there, too, and from the Colombaria Society and from the Anthropology Society and from the Italian Society for the Progress of the Sciences . . .

LIONELLA: *In Rome, many many Jews were baptized. Many, many . . . Even very noted Jews . . . the president of the orphanage, the president of the community, entire families, all the acquaintances. And I, I understood that there were these people who were no longer Jewish, but then, above all, I was stunned, because—there was a boy that I saw, an older boy, but he invited us sometimes with other children to parties, among which was his* bar mitzvah—*a few months later, a package arrived with lots of books, like the story of Moses as a child, the life of Samuel, Joseph and his brothers, all books for children, not books printed for Jewish children, but books that spoke of the Bible, of the Old Testament characters. I was happy . . . I looked at the pictures at the beginning and a few months later I knew how to read.*

But I didn't understand how come Enzo gave them away . . . Mamma said, "You know, he's grown up now," something false like that. "Why don't we go play with Enzo?" "Nooo." Quickly I understood that he was among those who had moved outside, who were no longer Jewish, and so therefore, the family absolutely did not want to see any Jews, understand? They became Catholics, as they are now.

RACHEL: *There was a professor called Calò. Calò is a Jewish name. He was an imbecile, this professor . . . when the racial things came, he put in the paper . . . he wrote, "My name is Calò. But I'm Catholic." Understand? "I'm of the Aryan race."*

So he was afraid for his career?

Yes, of course.

2

"What are you doing Erminia?" asked Andrea, hearing packing noises in her room.

"She's leaving," said Milena, who was passing Erminia's door. And both of them widened their eyes: there was Erminia with a handkerchief at her eyes, slowly putting her things in her suitcase. When it was full, she took a bag and filled that too. "She's really leaving! But—why?"

"As usual, you didn't believe me," said Andrea. And he returned to his book.

But Milena stayed there, gathered her courage, and entered the room.

"You won't tell me any more stories, Erminia? No more stories?"

"No, I'm going."

"Why?"

"Because that's the way it is . . ." And she cried, the poor cook who had loved that house. She couldn't tell Milena why she had to go.

"Tell me . . . come on!"

"Because I'm old!"

This time the answer satisfied her, and she ran to her brother. "Erminia is going away because she's old!"

"Really!" But he was hardly convinced that from one day to the next she would forget how to make those exquisite roast potatoes.

Erminia was pleased to have found a plausible lie: in fact she was getting old and her hair was getting whiter and whiter. However her head and her hands were still working fine—the truth was that a new racial law prohibited Jews from keeping non-Jewish servants.

For a few days something had been going on in the house, thought Andrea, and he mourned the good things that Erminia would no longer make.

Having opened the door, Erminia took her suitcases and sadly went down the stairs. In front of the main door stood the surly doorman. "Ah! You're the maid for those Jewish folks; it's time you were gone already—the decree came out yesterday."

"I'm the *cook*, and we were given twenty-four hours."

"Yes, yes, too much." And muttering, he disappeared again behind the glass door; then with a broom he started to clean the stairs thinking, how evil they are to send away the servants! Because he was one of many who was obliged to act enthusiastic while inside he wasn't at all. And yet to keep his job and to have enough to buy bread, he had to say "Long live Fascism!" Or if not, into the poor-house—there were two options!

And the children knew what was happening . . .

RACHEL: *Everything.*

With the racial laws . . .

Everything, everything.

You explained everything?

Of course, yes.

How did you explain these things?

Oh, they were very upset.

Did you speak about these things all together?

No, no, no, no.

And so?

We still didn't have our false documents, we had, let's say, all the racial things, for example, we no longer had kosher meat, we no longer had schools for the children, we didn't have maids, understand? And so, it was difficult. They understood. They knew.

LIONELLA: *My parents explained very little . . . They were subjects for grown-ups, for adults . . . it was like a forbidden subject, we couldn't talk about it.*

I listened. So I heard the conversations and I knew more about it than they thought . . . My hearing is still quite sharp . . . I was able to make myself reasonably aware of what was going on . . . I slept in the study, and so I heard everything perfectly well, even the conversations. It was stupendous. At night, I pretended to sleep, but . . . then our parents' door was open, and our parents continued to talk, talk, talk, talk, hours and hours, and I listened and listened until my eyes closed and I had to sleep . . .

I think [Leo] did the same thing. He slept in my parents' room, so his position was even more convenient.

Then grandmother took the two grandchildren and brought them outside.
"Where are we going, Mamma Alice?"

"We're going far, far away."

And in fact they walked and walked and it seemed like forever, but grand-mother liked to walk whenever possible. Then finally a great stairway appeared with many old houses on each side—this was the place "far, far away."

They rang a great brass doorbell and the ring echoed through the large, poor, austere, silent houses. A poorly dressed girl came to open the door and led the grandmother into a long dusty hallway dotted with many worn-out doors gnawed by woodworms.

Way in the back there was a black door, the only one with a little white sign, half-torn, where one could barely read "Ramorino." The girl opened the door on its rusty hinges and showed the grandmother in, leaving the two children outside. A weak oil lamp feebly lit a flight of stairs step by step, filthy with peels and cigarette butts, which led to another gloomy hall strewn with doors. Halfway up the stairs a rickety door marked "Restroom" sent a pestilential odor through the building. Andrea was entertaining himself by running through the hallway when the black door was half-opened to let out a ragged baby of a little less than a year, just able to toddle a few yards, who sat on a dirty step on the staircase. Then a mangy cat followed the little baby out the door and the two of them sat on the stair in perfect harmony.

Andrea and Milena compared their clean and ironed little clothes with the tat-tered clothes of the baby and thought themselves very fortunate. Meanwhile the grandmother came out and while they were crossing the hallway they saw out of the corner of their eyes a bony dog who had come jumping down from the floor above and had joined the others, forming a strange group of friends. Of all three the cleanest was the cat.

Around evening a prolonged ring of the bell announced the arrival of the new housekeeper. Jewish of religion, fat like the women of the Roman working class, unkempt and shabby like her daughter and her little baby boy, her fur coat clashed with the rest of her; she wore two mammoth earrings and her lips were colored fiery red. She entered the kitchen with heavy steps and the odor of cheap face powder spread through the house. The children were left at home searching for their mamma; they were the ones to be pitied.

RACHEL: *Look, when this woman came, I saw that she was very dirty. I gave her*

*money, because we didn't have a servant's bath and I said, "Please, go—" because
there were public baths—"go, take a good bath, and then come back."*

*She came back, and ... because I doubted that she had gone to take a bath, I said,
"By the way, could you please lift your dress a little to see?" She was all dirty around
the knees, etc. So, what did I do? I gave her the money again, I said, "Go take a bath
and bring me the—" you know they give you a little paper to get in, etc.—"and bring
this to me."*

So she did it.

She did it. (Chuckles)

ALDO: Sad months, those of the winter of 1938–39 for Prof. N. M., although he
was still very busy, both because he was still working at the Institute of Roman
Studies and because he'd been made responsible for Latin and Greek at the Jewish high school instituted in Rome under the aegis of the National Organization
for Secondary Education. And Prof. N. M. found great comfort in that atmosphere of study, being able to continue his own work, and among very studious
youth. But with the remuneration from the Institute of Roman Studies termi-
nated, without the payment yet of the pension, with only the compensation of
the lesser job at 1,000 lire, the first serious financial worries began: to live in
Rome with a growing cost of living, with a family—mother, wife, two small children—how was it possible to go on?

And meanwhile, how painful to see his own spouse waste from day to day
from the excessive housework! Relatively accustomed to all the eases allowed her
by a solid, certainly not brilliant economic condition, with the help of a full-
time maid, who helped with special services (deep cleaning, laundry, etc.) and of
a young lady who took the children out to play, and now she had to burden herself with continuous toil! As for cooking, it was a joy for the whole family to
taste the flavorful specialties prepared by expert hands with an affection that
only a wife and mother can add. But washing the vegetables and cleaning up
after was the trouble, with an insistent hint of arthritis in her arms, for which
immersion in the frigid winter water is most pernicious. And it was useless to
hope for help from Jewish domestics, not being a class adapted to such services.
In fact, where are maidservants hired? In the country. And there aren't Jews in
the country in Italy, they're all concentrated in the cities on account of their oc-
cupations. And so, various experiments turned out very badly, so much so that it
was better to give them up. And so Prof. N. M. had to watch his old mother
make the beds and sweep all the rooms, and his wife spend three quarters of the
day in the kitchen, and the children help, the one and then the other.

LIONELLA: *Then, in short, the cook left, the maid, the nanny. Cries, hugs, scenes. At the time, I didn't do any chores. So in twenty-four hours I had to learn how to make beds, sweep, help with the housework, help Mamma in the kitchen . . . We used to eat separately, all prettied-up, my brother and I, half-fed like babies, but no, now we eat at the table, and it's up to us to set the table. It had an extremely brusque impact.*

3

That evening the house was in an uproar. Besides the departure of Rosa, the housekeeper who had been fired after a few weeks, Flora Sabatini (a more willing worker than the fat widow) had arrived and preparations for summer vacation were being made: they were going to Fiuggi.

Flora was tall, brunette, and wore a black dress on account of the loss of her parents, but Andrea and Milena didn't know this—they were always asking her: "Don't you have a red dress?" But Flora didn't answer.

The whole corridor was full of suitcases and trunks and to make everything more confusing, the young lady who gave lessons to the two children came to say goodbye.

Miss Lidia was very kind and had brought the girl, who was the better of her two pupils, "The Vowel Box," a cardboard house where the vowels appeared in the windows, one after the other.

The young lady's farewell was moving, and after kisses and hugs she left, carrying with her many memories that would never again return.

4

The little train of the Latian line ran through the open countryside after abandoning the last suburbs of Rome; every once in a while it let out a whistle and stopped; then behind the tiny flowered stations appeared little Latian hamlets, hidden until that moment by the other hills. The engineer shouted out the town's name and Milena echoed it, and the sleeping gentlemen grumbled, but then fell back asleep, the dogs barked at the noise of the train; everything followed in monotonous but solemn succession. And finally: Fiuggi, with its woods and its baths, half on the high plain and half on a pleasant mountain.

ALDO: Where and how to spend the summer? Staying in Rome wasn't good for the children, and so immediately after their exams at the Nino Bixio school—both for admission to the third grade—the professor's family went to Fiuggi Città and stayed in a house rented for the season, which sat along the avenue that descended from the fountain; it was composed of two apartments, the first and the second floor—this last was inhabited by a nice family from Naples (Marigliana) who were easy to get along with, since they were just and understanding. Other summering families were also ready to make friends, and this was a comfort in those two months, so heavy with worry.

LIONELLA: *They told us that we had to take an exam to get into the third grade . . . It was in Rome . . . So we went, and they put us in a room on the ground floor, very dark, with a grate on the window. It was terrible. You know those chain links? They were tight, tight, under the window, so the room was dark . . .*

And then they left us—they locked us in, practically, to do our problems for the exam. Such small children, for goodness' sake.

Were you frightened?

Well, in short, it left a very unpleasant impression of public school. And also, to understand that we were alone because we were Jewish. I had understood this well: I wasn't with the other children who took their exams in large classrooms. My brother and I were closed up in a minuscule little room because we were Jews.

The little house of which the Nolas had rented the third floor was in upper Fiuggi; it had a gracious garden amid immense spaces of fields and meadows scattered with brown spots—the sheep who went to pasture with their shepherds, huge flocks of fat and woolly sheep, with a horned bull (a bell jingled at his neck) and a sheepdog as their trusted guardian.

This calm didn't seem to instill itself in the grown-ups, who were worried by the news they read in the papers. The racial laws came out in number and many things were prohibited to the Jews; they knew that in Germany and in Poland even worse had happened, and that Germany was preparing powerful forces for the next war. They didn't know anything else because a muzzle stopped the mouths of those who wanted to speak.

Across from the Nolas' house there was another even smaller house with two little windows and a little door on which "Caroli" was written. The Misses Caroli were two sprightly old spinster ladies who quickly made friends with the tenants in the house across the way. Every evening, the tenants went punctually to see them; the words they exchanged were almost always the same:

"Good evening, Miss Caroli. Miss Caroli."

"Good evening," said Andrea and Milena more hesitantly, downcast because they had never before been in such a sad and dull house.

"Good evening," the ladies responded, one after the other. "Come in, come in and listen to the radio."

"Might I offer you a little candy?" said the older, taking the box and offering candy that was who knows how many years old.

They stayed a half hour in chilly silence and then:

"Good night, and have a nice dinner."

"Good night, have a nice dinner."

And so on, every evening in wind or in rain, they never missed their visit to the Caroli ladies—that is, in three months they missed it only twice.

One morning around eight, the Neapolitan tenants of the ground floor arrived in a car: the Lussurgiùs with two children, Antonio and Frido, one three years old and the other five. At once all four children became great friends; Milena especially, who liked little children, started to play with Antonio. That was one of the two days, not counting the day they arrived, on which the daily visit to the Caroli ladies was missed; that evening the radio was silent and the candies got even staler. The Lussurgiùs invited the Nola family to a concert, and the idea of riding in a car appealed to Andrea much more than the concert did. Milena stayed home with her grandmother.

The concert was very beautiful, but Andrea saw only an enormous crowd and remembered the taste of an orangeade drunk with a straw, and gentlemen in black jackets with golden trumpets under their arms. When he woke, everyone was getting up, the gentlemen with the golden trumpets were gone, and mamma and papa were dragging him away while his head was spinning like a top. Then he went home and fell asleep, and the next morning they asked him:

"Was the concert nice?"

"What concert? Yesterday we stayed home."

Then he remembered, but he wanted nothing more to do with concerts, not even going in a car!

The second time the rule was broken was one evening when a dear cousin from Rome arrived by car. He was the engineer Angelo Camerino, who had a sister in Florence, Dora, married to the lawyer Benedetto Sadum, and an old father who was more than ninety. He was so kind that he played like a child, without saying anything but still taking part in the game; Andrea came with building blocks and started to play a primitive doctor! And so on. That evening they had an adventure because halfway along, the car sank in the mud and there was no way to go on; so they left the car on a little street that ended in the middle of a lonely and majestic wood.

"It would be wonderful if we got lost in the woods now, Angelo! Then we could sleep under the trees like those coffee-colored people and eat bananas like they do, with our hands."

"But there aren't any bananas!"

"Oh, yeah. I didn't think of that. Well, we'll fast."

So saying, they crossed a contorted pile of thorns, bramble, branches, and stalks, and a magnificent plain opened up in front of them, with a lone lake in the middle. Many sheep bleated and nibbled and a girl was singing a mountain song; the verses raised themselves up across the valleys and mixed with the songs of the birds and of other shepherds, and with the unique and rhythmic sound of the zephyr wind.

They stayed there a little to drink in that immense peace, and then they went toward the car.

They arrived when it was almost dark.

"Mamma, I'm hungry."

"Didn't you say you were fasting?'

"Oh, yeah . . ."

And the days passed slowly, quietly, the grape started to fatten, and deep underneath, the world started to agitate for the next war. The men were nervous and their eyes understood that something was happening in the governments and in the kingdoms. They thought about an inevitable war and jumped when they thought of the terror of that war to which sky, earth, water, air, man against man, deceit against deceit would all contribute.

ALDO: Meanwhile one felt the European war with all its consequences approaching . . . you had to foresee the possibility that Italy would enter the war, to think about keeping the family safe, to find a less expensive place than the capital, to find some way of earning money, under the circumstances.

5

One day in October the grandmother left; she took lodgings in Florence for a few weeks, invited by Aunt Giulia Cassin.

Mrs. Giulia Cassin was a little old lady so small and thin she had the stature of a fourteen-year-old boy. She carried a cane with a silver handle as a faithful friend. She was pleased when she gained a few grams, but her favorite subject was her special food. Widowed for many years, she lived on a modest private income, and it would give her great pleasure to have her dearest relative as company for a few weeks.

After a little while, papa left too, and the two children remained, unhappy and very alone. But papa had to go because Rome would be dangerous if war broke out and so he had to find a place on the outskirts of Florence.

He found a nice one in the middle of the countryside near Galluzzo, he came back, and everyone left for Rome to put the house in order.

ALDO: The offer from Florence to entrust the professor with the responsibility of Latin and Greek at its Jewish middle school was opportune. That way he could return to his native city, to relatives who remained there, and find in that incomparable atmosphere, collected and peaceful, a little calm for himself and his family. Fortune assisted him that time and in a rush he was able to rent a nice house, modest but charming, situated between Due Strade and San Felice a Ema, in beautiful Galluzzo, with a little farmland and some nice tenant farmers: just in time! The same day war was declared between Germany and England, as was the nonbelligerence of Italy. Although in Italy nothing was changed then and there, in a wartime climate it wouldn't have been very wise to stay on in Rome, with the "crescendo" in the application of the racist principles, while a country residence on the outskirts of Florence suited perfectly. And so, all the practical matters settled, our professor's family moved definitively to Florence.

RACHEL: *And then, when we came to Florence . . . we went to a house in Galluzzo, partly because Mussolini had written in the newspapers that it was better, on account of the bombardments, to stay in the country outside of the city. So, we went to Galluzzo, and we were settled very well.*

6

"Keep going! Keep on going driver!"

The driver kept going, though he was convinced that the house where he had stopped was the first and the last on that street, when behind the flourishes of yellow daisies and the green iron gate appeared a short graveled driveway and a graceful little villa with only one floor and little windows, green as well.

"Look, look. It looks like the cottage of the Blue Fairies!"

"Blue Fairies?! Don't you know that Pinocchio and the Blue Fairy never existed?" said Milena, who hadn't believed in fairies for a while now.

"I know that . . . so it looks like the cottage of the Seven Dwarfs."

"Those didn't exist either!"

"What, beautiful Snow White didn't exist? Or Grumpy? Or Sleepy? I don't believe it."

"Don't believe it, but it's true."

"O.K., so it looks like the cottage of the Black Witch, but without the witch."

"Oh! That one didn't exist either! Gullible!"

"So you're saying Erminia told me just a lot of tall tales. But didn't you like them too?"

"Yes, but I knew that they were made up, stupid!"

"You keep calling me names: stupid, gullible, all right—Mamma . . . Mamma!"

"Hey, cut it out, come see what a pretty little room!"

"Even 'cut it out'! You're in charge?"

"O.K., stay there. Goodbye!"

But he followed his sister—after all, he wanted to see his room. They went from a pretty living room with a sweet little wood-burning fireplace, an antique desk decorated with inlaid flowers, and two large divans covered with grey cloth, then through a hallway/dining room.

The children's room was white with a large window onto the garden; it was next to the larger room with two windows, the parents' room.

Milena was looking dreamily over everything when a new voice made her jump:

"Good evening, Miss."

"Good evening . . . who are you?"

A girl Milena's height stood in front of her; you could see from her coloring that she had been working in the sun. She wore two long tangled braids and a Sunday dress put on for the arrival of the tenants. With her calloused peasant's hands, burned by the sun, she looked like a cabbage at tea in that dress.

"I'm Liliana."

Milena decided to leave the inspection of the things in her room until a better time and looked the newcomer up and down.

"Where do you live? How old are you?"

"I live down there," and turning to the window, she pointed to a cottage higher up in the middle of a field. "My mamma is Venice."

"She was born in Venice?"

"No, no, Venice like the woman that rents rooms down the avenue, Venice di Raimondo."

"Funny. And your father?"

"Ferdinando."

"That one's not so funny . . . And now you're leaving? Open the door, I'm going."

"Yes, I'm going to do the grass."

"What? Only God can make grass."

"Yes, but I cut it."

"And then you eat it? Erminia says that unwashed grass gives you . . . umm . . . typhus."

"No! I give it to the rabbits!"

"Oh! Rabbits! Where are they?"

"There in front!"

"And how do you get there?"

"How? You open the door and you go!"

"But no, I have to ask Papa, Mamma Alice, or Mamma Lucia if I can! You don't have to ask? You're lucky!"

"But tell me—you have two mammas?"

"No, one is my grandmother, the other is my real mamma, but I call my grandmother 'mamma' too. You don't?"

"Me? No. But I'm going now, and then I'm going to help Papa cut sunflower stems and gather their seeds, then I'll show you the rabbits and my doll."

"But sunflower and pumpkin seeds give you a stomach ache, according to Erminia, and Papa says so too."

"Not me! Goodbye!"

"No, wait, I'll introduce you to Andrea, my brother!"

"No, no, another time. If not my mamma will worry. Goodbye!"

"And what's your doll's name?"

"Regina . . . a!" shouted Liliana as she ran and disappeared behind an avenue of dahlias just as she had come.

Happy, Milena ran after Andrea, but he didn't notice her, busy as he was taking the petals off a daisy: you love me . . . you love me not . . . she loves me madly . . . she loves me until death . . . she hates me until death . . . she loves me . . . she loves me not! "Look, your friend Liliana that I heard you talking to, the daisy says she doesn't love me!"

"Of course not, you didn't even say hello to her, and she's supposed to love you! Stup—"

"It's a good thing you stopped in the middle, or else!"

A few evenings later the terrible war that men had foreseen started between Germany and England: it was 14 September 1939.

7

"Pretty, pretty rabbits. Look at this white angora, and this grey one. Watch how they eat the fresh grass I give them!"

"No, no, for heaven's sake, fresh grass will make them sick!"

It was Ferdinando who said this, the farmer who was working in the other room.

Milena and Andrea tore their eyes from the angora rabbits, and having crossed into another large room lined with cages, they saw a shortish and stocky man with a wrinkled forehead, who was holding a rabbit tight between his legs, in the middle of whose beautiful angora coat the rosy skin showed through; evidently it was all shaved.

"Poor rabbit! Are you killing it?"

"What are you talking about—it's healthier than I am!"

"So what are you doing to it?"

"I'm shearing it because they pay me a mint for its wool, my dear Miss?"

"And then they make scarves and jackets with the wool?"

"Of course—not for poor people like us, but for rich folk like you who can afford to go into stores and buy anything you like."

"But the other day I wanted a Japanese doll on display in a store in Via Cavour and Mamma said that we couldn't buy anything we liked."

"Yep! These days no one can buy as much as he wants!"

"But . . . where's Andrea gone? Andrea! Andrea! If something happens to him now, there's just the maid in the house, so I'm responsible!"

"Good day."

"Good day, Ferdinando!" And she ran off: "Andrea! Andrea! Where are you?"

"Ha . . . ha! ha! ha! Here I am!"

"Where?"

"Looking for grass snakes!"

"But where . . . where?"

"Behind the woooood!"

"But where . . . !"

"Behind Liliana's house!"

Then she got her bearings, looked for the place Liliana had showed her, saw the cottage in the middle of the field, and ran in that direction until she got there.

"What are you doing? May I ask?"

"Look, we were looking for this green garden snake, we heard it rustle . . ."

And Liliana raised Andrea's hand where the snake was pierced with a stick!

"Oh! Throw it down, don't you see how slimy it is?" said Milena, and she pulled his hand away from it.

"Liliana, come see my dolls, did you know I had three? Dedo, Enrico, if you think rubber's nice, and Elena!"

"I only need one doll, I'm thirteen years old by now, and when I finish school in two years, I'll be a seamstress. Yes, I'm coming."

They walked silently holding hands, the taller one having already clearly marked the way of her humble life, the other lost in the mysteries of the future. They took a narrow path surrounded by patches of tomato plants and still-unplowed fields where traces of the cut grain remained.

LIONELLA: *Giuliana [whom Leo calls "Liliana"] was my first real friend. From morning to night I was with her. She taught me many things—how animals are born, and thus children, how things are planted . . . I practically lived with this girl. She had a great hunger for sweets, so she ate glue. I taught her to cut out pictures and make compositions, which I'd learned from my grandmother or a relative of hers. We spent hours doing it, and I always cut, and she glued, and she ate some glue. She was a little primitive, but so nice, and there we were together. In short, she was a constant playmate.*

Liliana took a just-ripe tomato, dusted it off with the edge of her dress, and put it in her mouth; only then did they start talking:

"Raw like that, without washing it? You'll get typhus!"

"Come on! We peasants never get typhus!"

"Well, city folk do get it! My Uncle Benedetto's mother lost her daughter and her husband to typhus and then she died too!"

Walking nearly barefoot in worn-out clogs, Liliana got a little thorn stuck in her foot, which didn't bother her at all, and she kept walking.

"Don't you see that you're bleeding? If you don't disinfect it right away, you'll get tetanus."

"We peasants never get tetanus from a thorn! My great-grandfather Alessio died of tetanus when he was just five months old [Rachel notes that "clearly the child doesn't perfectly understand the meaning of the word 'great-grandfather,' or at least makes some sort of error here"], but because he cut himself carelessly, with a salami knife! No one has ever died from a thorn—as long as I'm not the first!"

"So peasants are very fortunate!"

"Other than health, we have nothing but misery, Miss!"

"But Papa says health is the most precious thing," interrupted Andrea.

"It's true, but when the boss wants the grain, wants the potatoes, wants the wine, it's awful, you know, to see everything that was harvested with our sweat leave in his car! At the least we should sharecrop, but then what does a pile of money do for you? A dress and a pair of Sunday shoes and that's it . . . instead we live in the fields and have to go to town to buy flour, and it's all like that, except for a few things. Even the rabbits, we're in the rabbit kingdom, and we have to go to the butcher in Galluzzo on Saturday and spend 30, 40 lire to have a little boiled meat on Sunday, since Papa says Sunday's for the family. Doesn't that seem very miserable to you?"

"Yeah! Really, I had no idea!"

So saying, they entered the room where the three dolls were lined up on an ironing table, well dressed and refined. But after a bit, the door opened and two boys, brothers, boldly entered the room.

"Hello, Liliana!"

"Oh, hello Duilio, hello Carlo Vittore!"

"Who are you?" asked Andrea courageously, since it was up to him as the man.

"And who are you?"

"Andrea Nola."

"All right, Mr. Andrea Nola, I . . ."

"But I'm a child . . . not a mister."

The two brothers laughed hard and the older, who was nine years old, continued:

"All right, Child Andrea Nola, I . . ."

"Yes, now that's fine!"

"But let me finish. I'll introduce myself: Carlo Vittore Cavalcanti, nine years old, my brother Duilio Cavalcanti, eight years old, sons of the proprietor of the present house, Azelio Cavalcanti, engineer."

"So we treated you like guests and instead you're the owners! How embarrassing," said Milena.

"But for the moment, things are different: we are guests who come from Viareggio and you are like the owners of the house you're living in. Get it?"

"Not really, but it doesn't mat—"

"Fine, I'll repeat myself—"

"No, for heaven's sake, don't go back over all that—"

"Fine, all right, we'll talk about something else. Let's talk, for example, of going up to the dungpit to play stones."

"Great!"

8

Up on the little tree-lined street was the dungpit: it was a large cemented underground cistern used to store manure. Farther back there was a well and the little electric motor that pulled up the water to send it to the house and the farmers. You couldn't go beyond the buried cistern because three strands of blue barbed wire marked the end of the Cavalcanti farm.

On the meadow, they each placed a stone standing on end, and they began to play a game like ninepins.

"You killed me!"

"My stone fell."

"One more and I've won!"

"Resuscitated."

"I killed myself!"

"Alive! I won!"

A break, and then they started shouting again, even more than before. But around noon someone called them.

"Duilio! Carlo Vittore! Come home!" And then again: "Hurry so we don't miss the tram!" It was the father who, done with giving orders, called his sons to go to lunch at their Aunt Beatrice's. Then he called Ferdinando.

"You said there was a sick rabbit, bring it so tonight we can eat it with the chicken you gave me."

Liliana elbowed Milena. "You see? They'll eat two kinds of meat and I'll have to go to Galluzzo tonight to buy a rabbit. We were planning to eat that sick rabbit before it died, and instead . . . and the chicken was ours, he took it like a gift . . ." Milena laughed and thought that Liliana was right.

And when Milena told the story to her mamma, even she said Liliana was right.

All these things were new for Lionella and Leo?

RACHEL: *Of course. We had never been in the country, like this, peasant country.*

And it also seems that they hadn't been with poor people much.

No.

Because he is always surprised.

Surprised by any old thing. Because we were in Rome, no? And we had our apartment, we had our friends, but they were all high-ranking, understand. And then the children always had their young lady, they always went out with their young lady . . .

And do you think that it was good for them to meet . . .

These farmers? Yes, very good.

9

With her usual silver-handled cane, Mrs. Giulia Cassin entered the cosy living room where, for the first time, with the cold coming, the red-brick fireplace was lit.

"Hello, dearests, I have two—no, three—wonderful pieces of news to tell you about."

"Let's hear, Aunt Giulia, let's hear; I bet the first one is you've gained a hundred grams!"

"You're wrong, dear Alice, I've gained half a kilo, and guess in how long."

"A month."

"Wrong, two weeks! In two weeks, half a kilo, think of it!"

"And the second piece of news, let's see if I can guess it . . . you found a way to make a good dish?"

"Wrong again: it's about recipes I found in the back of a drawer. Listen to the first one, I'll tell you in the proportions you need: you take two eggs and beat them; six spoonfuls of semolina, nutmeg, lemon juice, and when the broth boils, throw it all in and work it for fifteen minutes; what do you say?"

"It would come out delicious, Aunt Giulia."

"Now listen to the other one . . ."

"It doesn't matter, tell it to me another time!"

"Yes. And the third surprise is for Milena: I got a good deal this time because I found a very well-supplied stationer's in Via dei Benci."

Milena who, as always, was waiting for this sentence, came out from behind the door and took the package Aunt Giulia had brought her.

"Thank you, Aunt Giulia, you shouldn't have bothered!"

Inside the pretty package, there was a drawing pad and a package of candy.

"Look at that candy; I found it for Andrea in a store on Via dei Neri, it's made of egged marsala and orange juice. I bought two kilos for myself."

"And it's delicious, Aunt Giulia."

But she ran off so she could make all the faces she wanted at that awful sour taste that reminded her of the Caroli ladies' rancid candy!

Aunt Giulia spoke for a half hour about her delicacies, explained a quick and practical system for conserving tomato sauce, emphatically championed a new nutritional autarchic chocolate product which she ate with white rice, praised the stationer's in Via dei Benci again, and then, having gathered her cane and put her black purse on her arm, she got up to leave.

"By the way, now I remember that I haven't told you my menu for today—wait till you hear—a bowl of broth with the mixture I described to you and a plate of Neapolitan potatoes like my cook used to make—ah! Yesterday I was with my cook and he gave me two dessert recipes . . . I thought of you right away since you like to make them; listen . . ."

"But Aunt Giulia, it's time you went to enjoy that nice lunch you described . . ."

"You're right, but first listen to this recipe," and she delivered, by the sheer force of her words, an endless rambling talk. "Wait," she said, "now I'll write it down." She took a slip of paper from her purse and wrote down everything she had said.

"Thanks, Aunt Giulia, it's too bad we don't have much milk and as for butter! So . . ."

"Yes, yes, it's true—wait, I'll give you another recipe with ingredients you can buy here, listen . . ."

"Aunt Giulia, excuse me, it's 1:15, I won't ask if you want to help yourself to lunch because I know that you don't like chard dressed with garlic or eggs or the other things we have, but . . ."

"Ah, of course! But actually, speaking of chard, I'll tell you I was at my niece Settimia's house and she had some delicious trifle and then little alkermes cookies that I found in Via San Jacopino, in a little store that sells chestnut-flour polenta. If you find yourself in Viale dei Mille, there next to the tram depot, just before the coal-seller, chestnut-flour polenta, what a treat!"

"I'm sure it is. Anyway, I was saying that they'll certainly be expecting you at the pensione in a little while . . ."

"Yes, yes, you're right. Yesterday I got back late and the potato gnocchi were cold; I ate a nice pigeon thigh with some eggplant that Mrs. Lear gave me, because she had found some sweet potatoes—wait, do you know where to find them? In Via Romana before the dyers. Well, I'm going now, goodbye Alice!"

"Goodbye dear aunt!"

Then she turned around before opening the gate.

"Remember: Via Romana 41, before the Liviari dyeworks."

RACHEL: *In Fascist times we had to make everything in Italy, not taking anything from abroad. Everything was "autarchic." So much so that Lionella, when she was a girl and didn't know how babies were made, one day said to me, "Mamma, mamma, but babies, poor things, do they also come autarchic?" (Laughs) Because, when it was autarchic, it wasn't very good, understand? Chocolate that should come from Switzerland but instead is made here in Italy . . . it wasn't good.*

And this was for the entire time of . . .

Of Fascism, not all of it, not at the beginning. When we were quarreling with England.

10

"Well then, Miss Andreati, we're agreed, severity and precision!"

Miss Andreati, retired elementary school teacher, was over fifty years old, dressed in an old-fashioned way with long grey pleated skirts and a red wool bonnet. Unable to go to public school because of their religion, the Nola children would study the third grade privately.

LIONELLA: *And after this famous exam, prisoner in this room with my brother, I came to Galluzzo. At Galluzzo, what do we do, what don't we do? They discover an ancient teacher, with a hundred-year-old mother. It took place in a little house near the church of San Leone . . . Then there were only fields and this isolated house. So these two ancient women—decrepit, in my opinion—dressed always in white, shawls, with an odor of stuffiness, of mildew.*

"Naturally, Professor Nola. We will have lessons, at least for now, Tuesdays and Thursdays; the other days are all spoken for. Toward the end of the school year, I will teach them the rudiments of music," she said, caressing the shiny brown grand piano.

"Yes, yes, we'll see. They're not much interested in music, though."

"I wouldn't have believed it. All right, goodbye children, until Tuesday; look over your grammar a little."

"Good evening, Miss."

They went down the short staircase and approached a graceful little garden where a large tortoise rested quietly, protected from the sun, then another steep dusty staircase and finally a white gate, which a man with a ladder was repainting from top to bottom.

"But Papa, Liliana goes to school, why don't we?"

"Because you can't; Jews aren't allowed to go to public schools. In two years, if we're in the city, you'll go to a Jewish private school."

ALDO: Meanwhile for students: exclusion of foreign Jews from the universities, prohibition of Jewish registration for elementary and middle schools of every level and of the matriculation of new Jewish students in college. Poor souls, young and innocent, what a profound first sorrow, what an unheard of surprise! "But aren't we Italian like all the rest? But my father, my brother, didn't he serve his Fatherland, isn't he decorated, isn't he wounded, didn't he die in the war?" Deep within himself, each one asked question upon question, and felt a discomfort inside, an agony he had never felt; it seemed like an awakening from a lethargy. But then was it all a trick, bad faith to call us Italians, an on-going fiction since birth—parents, relatives, everyone complicit? But no, no, this is the fiction, a fictitious construction, just to take it out on someone, and naturally, on the weakest, on he who has no one of his own, on he who can't react to such an enormity.

Aldo was teaching at the time at the Jewish school that was too far away for his children to attend.

Amid the scholastic responsibility, some rare lessons and some editorial jobs, the winter of 1939–1940 and the following spring went by peacefully enough, and if there hadn't been growing financial preoccupations, life, day by day, would have been tolerable and sometimes even pleasurable, with the frequent visits of family and friends, the apparent stasis in the application of new racist norms, if only because of the sense of human understanding on the part of the local authorities above all regarding the concession of the "Aryan" domestic.

The professor also had the job of compiling some writings for an abridged edition of the *Enciclopedia Italiana,* since even in a racist regime the scientific value of the Jews continued to be appreciated, only their work had to be used on the sly: one of the editorial staff officially gave the responsibility to the Aryan professor Such and Such, with the tacit agreement that his responsibility of ———— would be fulfilled by his friend Such and Such . . . But how to prepare using the original edition from which the summary compilations were in part derived? Can one go into the libraries, yes or no? In certain periods, it was conceded as an exception to the *discriminati* . . . however with what state of mind could one work in surroundings where he is known, where every face would look at him from all sides and would put him in a spirit that was everything but favorable to working with tranquility? On the other hand, if the compilation was done in secret, he couldn't work in a public place.

Luckily, the kind Mrs. Edmea Lurini [whom Leo will call "Garlini"], well known for her spirit of Christian goodness and understanding, put at his disposal her drawing room with her son-in-law's entire collection of the encyclopedia, and there, in a peaceful and reserved atmosphere, the professor could, at his ease, dedicate himself to this work. Meanwhile at his own house he worked on a little dictionary of Latin syntax which—certainly not under his name—was to be launched in a new revised and corrected edition. Contemporaneously, a trusted childhood friend, a valiant university professor, entrusted our professor with the commentary on a few passages of a Latin author for an anthology.

And so working in the shadows, taking no satisfaction in compilations that meant nothing compared to the works of serious scientific value he had already published, he cheated time and made a few pennies . . . oh, how few! Yet he was very grateful to those who found him such work, a greater proof of friendship than any other. Even a few pennies were gratefully accepted in that time of poverty. Indeed, it seemed at first that some way of earning a living would be assured to the *discriminati!*

11

A few minutes before, the first lesson with Miss Andreati had begun:

"Miss, do we do this problem?"

"Yes, now I'll read it to you: 'A haberdasher sold 18 pieces of 38 meters each—'"

"Miss, why are there 18 pieces and 38 meters?

"Because the one has nothing to do with the other. Let's go on, 'at 53—'"

"So each piece isn't one meter long?"

"No, no. I said 38 meters apiece. O.K., 'at 53 lire per meter—'"

"Expensive! Miss, I paid 60 lire per meter for the cloth this dress is made of—"

"So, you paid more, if you paid 60 lire per meter!"

"Yep, it's true—so I should cross out 60?"

"No, no, let it go since we're the only ones to see it."

"I've already crossed it out."

"All right, then you cross it out, too, Milena."

"But it's ugly now . . . oh God! He made an ink blot."

"You hadn't crossed it out before?"

"Well truly . . . truly . . . truly no, Miss, I only *meant* to cross it out!"

"What a mess! Well! Tear out the page and I'll tell it to you again; done? All right, let's go, pay attention: 'A haberdasher bought 18 pieces—'"

"Just a minute, Miss!"

"You tore out your page too, Milena?"

"Yes, because I wrote pies instead of pieces."

"You could have corrected it."

"I didn't want to . . ."

"All right: 'A cloth merchant sold 18 pieces of 38 meters each at 53 lire per meter—'"

"I wrote 60 again."

"Write a 5 over the 6 and a 3 over the 0, O.K.?"

"Yes, I did it."

"But I already wrote 53, do I write it again above? It'll be a mess."

"No, Milena, let it go, or you'll really make a mess. So, at 53 lire per meter; how much did he make?"

"I wrote cubic meters; it looks nicer, doesn't it, Miss?"

"No! Cubic meters are something else, cross out 'cubic' and go on: Then, if he spent 84 lire, how much would he have left over?"

"I'll write it here nearby: he would have, for example, 20 lire left."

"But aren't you doing the problem?"

"Oh! That's right! Miss Lidia did it like that too."

"Write: 'Solution' and then it's up to you, we'll see who's quicker."

"But yesterday Papa sent me to the pharmacy to ask for a solution and they gave me a bottle full of alcohol. What's that? A symonim?"

"No, it's called a synonym."

"But what's left for the haberdasher he divided among the clerks and his sons, right?"

"No, no, he was alone in the store!"

"What are you saying, Milena! What questions! You can tell that he's a first-born bachelor; it's a good bet he was also bald as a pumpkin."

"You think so? I on the other hand want to get married."

"Of course! Have you ever seen an old maid?"

But the last two words he whispered because Milena gave him a hard pinch. "There's one right in front of you," she whispered.

"Come on, children, the hour will be over and you won't have finished yet; whoever does it first will get this toy puppy as a prize."

"I bet I'll win it!"

"But the problem has to be perfect!"

"Yes, yes; and what would he do with a toy puppy anyway! He would surely give it to me or throw it away!"

"When is the last—no, the first answer coming? Milena!"

"It's coming, it's coming . . . oh! I haven't done it yet, I'll do it now."

"When you've got it, tell me."

"Here it is: it comes to 41,553."

"You're wrong! For me, it came to 8,003,420."

"Really? Which is right, Miss?"

"Hm? Give me a minute to do the math: 3 times 412 plus 20 . . ."

"Meanwhile I'm correcting mine; there it is, there's the mistake! But no, it doesn't come to more than 8 million, it comes to 41,552, a much different number. Look Miss."

"One minute: 35 times 270 times 2140 . . . All right, let's look at the messes you've made. Milena, you deserve the toy puppy and a perfect 10 with honors, but Andrea, oh Andrea! Your work would make stones laugh: 8 million and then some . . . But the other question? We'll do it again as if we hadn't gotten there yet, but next time pay attention . . . Here's your papa. Goodbye, children!"

"Goodbye, Miss, thanks for the toy puppy!"

"I promised!"

LIONELLA: *She was very patient. However, she certainly didn't encourage ties of af-fection. I remember very strongly only this musty smell. And then the only thing that I remember, she taught me something beautiful, it was part of manual labor, to con-struct a house of cardboard in miniature, with all the tapestries stuck on. With paper tapestries, flooring, walls, then with all the little furniture inside. An incredible thing. I later tried to do it with my daughter, only bigger.*

We studied together, my brother and I . . . My brother learned to read with Mamma, he had a mastoiditis, an inflammation of the mouth, pretty bad, then there was otitis, in short he was in bed a lot. And Mamma taught him to read, he had a great facility. And so I was there still doing "ba ba bay bee bo boo," and he was al-ready reading . . .

But he recovered slowly, so toward spring they put us together, we studied together. He was sixteen months younger than I. I started late, six and a half, in school, because I was born in February, so I enjoyed this extended childhood. So, I was behind and he was ahead. And we studied well together, because he was wonderful at reading, not as good at understanding math problems, and so, in short, I helped him in certain things and this worked perfectly.

12

"Mamma, where are you going with your suitcases?"

"I'm going to Venice with Papa."

"But Venice is at her house; you don't need suitcases to go see her."

"No! Venice the city!"

"Oh! The one with Saint Mark's lion, from the book that opens and closes, where 'Pax Tibi' is written."

"Yes, that one."

"And me?"

"You stay here."

"Take me with you!"

"No; tickets cost money. And you have to study, too."

"So will you write me every day?"

"Of course."

"And what will I do all alone?"

"You will be the knight in shining armor for Mamma Alice and Milena."

"And not study?"

"On the contrary, you will study even more than before, so that when I come back, you will know many new things."

"But Charlemagne's knights didn't even know how to read."

"Those were uncivilized times."

"I see. These days knights study?"

"Yes, but Charlemagne's knights are gone now."

"But those from Malta are still there, right?"

"Right." And Mamma left.

RACHEL: *It was my first visit to Venice. Aldo had said, "But really, we've gotten this far, and I haven't yet taken you to Venice." Now he knew that the war was coming, so he says, "Let's go now." And so we went to Venice.*

13

Bent over the desk in the study, Andrea was intent on a great labor: he was writing a letter to his mamma.

"Dear Mama," he had begun, but everyone knows how to write this, and he didn't know how to go on.

Then he added:

"How are you?"

Another pause.

"Andrea, you're not writing?"

"I don't know what to write."

"Don't be silly!"

"'Is Venice pretty?' It that O.K., Mamma Alice?"

"Of course."

"'Have you given breadcrumbs to the pigeons?'"

He wrote another thought or two and then filled the other piece of paper with an endless squiggly signature that was supposed to represent a river.

"Read it, Mamma Alice."

The letter said this:

"Dear Mama, How are you? Is Venice pretty? Have you given breadcrumbs to the pigeons? Have you started to write to me? Have you been in a gondola.

This morning I wrote a wonderful essay.

p.s. Bring me a nice photograph."

"Good, you've only made one mistake; find it."

"Maybe pigeons, it's spelled without an 'e'?"

"No, no, that's right."

"O.K. then gondola is spelled with a 'c'?"

"No! Mamma with two 'm's!"

"What a fool! I didn't see it!"

"Have you finished, Milena?"

"Yes, yes, but I already put it in an envelope and gave it to Liliana who was going to Galluzzo."

"Who knows how many mistakes there'll be, since you had to be so clever! How could you send a letter without having me read it?"

"I didn't think it was necessary!"

"Well, what's done is done! It just means you're going to look bad."

"I could write another to apologize."

"No, let it go. Did you at least put the address on it?"

"Of course! What do you take me for!"

"And a stamp?"

"Naturally. I put a two lire stamp on it, airmail!"

"What were you thinking?"

"That way it will get there sooner, don't you think?"

"Yes, but think about it: between Venice and Florence the mail arrives quickly anyway."

"I didn't think of that!"

"As usual, Milena: 'I didn't think of that.'"

"Be quiet, Andrea; I'll worry about your upbringing, not you."

"But I was saying . . . I said . . ."

"But nothing: children like you should busy themselves with what concerns them and nothing more."

"Yes, yes, children . . . don't count for anything."

"It's like this: until a certain age, children don't know how to judge and think."

"After a certain age, they do?"

"Then, yes. But you'll see how you'll miss childhood."

"I should say not!"

"You'll see . . ."

LIONELLA: *Practically speaking, Grandmother gave me my development. She supervised our learning. And she taught me precision in problems, which stayed with me all my life, how to put mathematical operations in columns, to write "solution." Indications, calculations, all this. This served me well, this rigidity, the explanation of every operation. I maintained it my whole life . . .*

I think really I owe the fact that I succeeded in mathematics to this foundation of great order and precision—which I was then unable to inculcate into my children. But which my grandmother, a very precise woman, gave to me.

14

"Dusting . . ."

"What is it, Pasquina, come in!"

"Dusting, I . . ."

"Dusting, you broke something?"

"The back of a chair came unstuck on me . . ."

"Oh well. It just means that on your way home, you'll go to the carpenter at the tram gate and send him over."

"Yes, yes, I'll take care of it."

Around 4 P.M. the carpenter came.

"Look, Carlino, the back of this chair came unglued."

"Oh, that's nothing! I'll glue it back right away."

"Carlino, you don't happen to know of a girl who wants a job as a maid?"

"Hm! I'll see. Maybe in Galluzzo there's the kind of girl you want. Tomorrow

I have to go there for my wood supplies at Carrai's; I think Dina Belinghi lives above Carrai's."

"In any case, it'll be in a month, because we're Jewish and I have to ask permission from the Commissariat."

"Hmmph! Another spiteful law that won't be forgotten!"

"Indeed!"

RACHEL: *We couldn't have maids. We had to ask permission from police headquarters . . . They gave it to us.*

And you had permission because you were . . .

Because my mother-in-law was old . . . But in Rome they didn't give us permission. We asked in Rome, too. Here, on the other hand, the officer said to Aldo, "Yes," he says, "You see, we are better here in Florence."

15

"Do you know?" Grandmother had said, "Your mamma wrote that she is coming back tomorrow."

And in fact, Mamma and Papa returned the next day.

"Mamma! Mamma! Did you bring me a photograph?"

"Certainly, it's beautiful!"

"The present?"

"The present is for Mamma Alice . . ."

"Mamma Alice, you got a present!"

"A present? It must be for you, you must be mistaken!"

"No, no, it's for you. In fact, see, it's a little package. In general you take big packages of chocolates and candy to children."

"Oh! It really is for me, poor things! It's a beautiful little black and white collar. Look!"

"And let's be clear, we were also thinking of you two."

"But you said not!"

"You were wrong that children have to have large packages, because look what a little package I brought you."

Inside there was a lovely tie for Andrea and a little green brooch for Milena.

"I wanted candy!"

"I wanted a doll!"

"And instead I brought you this, hard to please as you are."

"I'll wear my tie February 16, for Milena's birthday."

"Of course. And I'll wear my brooch. But what's today?"

"Today's the 12th."

"All right, so tomorrow we go with Angelo to buy toys." Because it was the custom of the family that a few days before each birthday, Uncle Angelo took the two children to a toy store and got them plenty of presents.

16

Three days later was the big day, one of the two anticipated all year long.

After 2:00, Andrea disappeared into his room and got all dressed up: he took an ironed silk shirt, with a monogram, the new tie from Venice, the light-colored trousers with the man's pleat. Finally, at 3:30 he presented himself in the sitting room.

After a little, Liliana arrived in an ironed red dress and a big white bow in her hair, happy because her father had let her off work until 8:00.

Then Mrs. Serani arrived breathless from the heat of the trip with three children: six-year-old Serena, four-year-old Alina, nine-year-old Pallante.

They had just begun to play bingo when little cousin Maria Grazia arrived; since she came from a mixed marriage, she could go to public schools.

"And now you're all together! Come have a snack!" said Mamma.

"Yes, yes, we won't make you wait any longer!"

After they'd eaten in silence, they began to talk again.

"Andrea, always the last!"

"I taste everything and chew it well."

"And us?"

"You gobble and swallow so you can go play and you don't taste anything."

"Liar! It's you who are famous for being a slowpoke."

"And you, who don't hear Mamma when she calls you because you're reading stories?"

"What's that have to do with anything!"

"A lot—you accuse me of something so I throw something else back in your face."

"Alice always finishes last too!" said Serena.

"Enough, Serena! The doctor said to eat slowly in order to digest well!"

"You see, Milena?"

"There's a limit to everything."

"Where are you, Serena, in the history of the Risorgimento?"

"Far behind!"

"We are too, because Mrs. Andreati doesn't make us do much of the oral stuff; tomorrow we'll have a lesson with Grandmother, because if we don't . . ."

"I've gotten to Mazzini."

"From the day after tomorrow we'll have gym class with you every Wednesday."

"If I can, I'll ask Miss Becaccioni to put you next to me, but it will be hard, because Pia Serani, the girl next to me, is so touchy."

"Who is this Pia Serani? That way I'll recognize her at synagogue when I go Saturday."

"She's dark and has lots of black curls. Her brother's called Luvy, he's fat like I don't know what, and he also has little black curls like an African."

But in the sitting room next door the grownups were very nervous despite the happy day; it was Mrs. Salmi who had brought the bad news: French radio continued to say "Rien à signaler dans la ligne Maginot," but German radio had announced a strong offensive on the European fronts for the spring.

17

RACHEL: *Oh, oh, gymnastics, my son, poor thing . . . He was always messing up gymnastics. (Laughs)*

In the midst of the big tall boys and the little girls already with little purses and suits, the Nola children, accustomed to private lessons, felt like fish out of water.

"Nola, stand up straight!"

"Yes, Miss!"

"Nola, right . . ."

"Yes, Miss."

"Nola, arms crossed behind, like this: at ease!"

"Yes, Miss."

"Nola, legs open wide, hup!"

"Yes, Miss."

"Right-line . . ."

"Miss—"

"One minute: Right-line, hup, march!—Nola, don't interrupt, would you tell me what's wrong?"

"That girl with the cough kicked me."

"Kick her back. And you, Donate Guetta, don't bother these children."

"All right: Left-line, hup, forward, march! One two, one . . . two . . . one . . . two . . . mark the step, halt! One . . . two . . . one . . . two."

"How do we mark the step, Miss?"

"Like this, don't you see?"

"Yes, yes."

"Nola, Andrea, you're out of step."

"It's a pleasure."

"It's a pleasure?! You're out of step! Are you deaf?"

"Ah! You mean I'm lifting my right first instead of my left first, then the left after, instead of first, then the right before the left after . . . but it's getting all messed up, Miss!"

"So go over to the entrance and wait."

"Yes, Miss."

Having left the dark and badly equipped little gym, he entered the little foyer of the Jewish school, once the private home of the learned Rabbi Margulies. To one side, a narrow staircase led to the upper floors, a little locked door carried an enameled sign: "Principal." Then there was a sign, a few months old, with a list of enrolled students. Andrea started to read it:

"Anyone who wants to enroll in the Jewish school of Florence . . ." but it was too long.

RACHEL: *It was newly organized. When the Jewish children couldn't go to school, the community put up a school. There was even a high school, a middle school, all the classes.*

And your children didn't go to this school, because it was too far.

Mine didn't, we were at Galluzzo, and to come all the way down . . .

At that moment, a short, thick little woman emerged from the steep and narrow stairway.

"Being punished?" she asked.

"No. I'm small."

"But you like to read?"

"Of course."

"All right, come on."

They took the stairs back up, and then farther up, up to the third floor. There, Andrea saw another enameled sign: "Entrance to the School." The white door creaked on its hinges, and they entered a great white-and-green-tiled entranceway, with an austere desk in the middle, where a gentleman with glasses was bent over, writing quickly on a sheet of paper.

Andrea was very afraid of that man, and turned his eyes so he wouldn't meet his gaze.

"Good evening, Principal." But the man with the glasses was too absorbed in his work to respond to the custodian. Andrea recognized in that gentleman the name on that enameled sign and was even more afraid. A stern pendulum clock sounded 4:30; then the principal raised his head from the manuscript, which he put back in a large drawer: "The young ladies have come for their Latin syntax lesson?"

"Yes, sir." They were there as usual. She added, "Shall I send them in?"

"Precisely."

"If you would wait a minute," she said to the boy, and went to call them in.

Alone with the principal, Andrea broke out in a cold sweat and hid in a corner of the room. Behind him there were coathooks and there was a stove that gave off the last bit of heat from its half-cold ash. Facing him high up, the head of the Soldier King seemed to watch him. Around the room there were many doors; each one marked with a little number and the number of the class that used it: 1— Sixth grade, 2—Seventh grade, and so on. But since it was evening, not a single voice resounded in the room, except for the chattering of the children from the nursery school on the ground floor.

Impatient, the principal got up from the high-backed red leather armchair, closed his fountain pen, polished its golden surface with a handkerchief, put it back in his breast pocket, and started, with great relish, to smoke a Tuscan cigar.

Then he turned toward the stove, nervously poked the last piece of wood, and leaned sadly against the wall.

Meanwhile the custodian entered the room followed by six young ladies.

"Belforte is absent."

The principal, nodding his head to show he understood, threw the cigar butt into a glass ashtray, and gestured to the young ladies to follow him into a room off the entranceway.

Before entering, he came back and asked the custodian to light the stove again. Having done this, she finally remembered Andrea, relegated to that dark corner.

"Come with me," she said to him. They returned to the stairwell and entered another large room where there was only a dusty grand piano, several chairs, and a little rickety table with a stack of music books on top. Chiarina opened a drawer and took out a loose-bound book, *Are You There, Wolf?* Andrea thanked her and had started to read when the door opened and in came a blond young woman followed by three tall girls.

The girls sat down on the chairs, the teacher on the little bench in front of the piano.

"Miss, I should go . . ."

"No, no, stay." But the clock struck 5:00 and Andrea, thinking that gym class would be over, put back the book and went downstairs.

18

Passover came with the sun and the first roses.

Passover lasts eight days, in which only matzoh and no leavened bread is eaten, in memory of our fathers who fled from Egypt with unleavened bread.

But that year, like the two years before, it was a sad and nostalgic Passover. Until 1937, on Passover evening the candelabras were lit on an elegant table and in every house gathered twenty or so Jewish people who couldn't celebrate in their own houses; the head of the family said a long prayer and then began, according to tradition, the meal with hard-boiled eggs. From '38 on, Passover evening was usually quite different because such large gatherings of Jews could attract the attention of those who stood spying on the streetcorners. And many families had emigrated, some to Palestine, some to America and England.

LIONELLA: *Giulio was very important for me . . . because he was the only presence of a boy in the house. When he came to visit, I was seven or eight and he was ten or eleven, in short, he was older. He organized games, messed things up, made noise—*

exciting things that didn't exist for me except on Saturdays when Giulio came to get his sisters . . . So I always looked forward to his arrival, and he became an important figure.

And then he was bar mitzvah, and then, meanwhile it was '39, and his father said he wanted to send him to Israel. Given my curiosity, I heard this big discussion between my father and his father . . . And I heard that relatives were blaming him: why are you sending Giulio, just fourteen, to Israel? And you'll stay here, then there will be war, and this boy will be all alone. And he said—clearly he was very sharp—"At least one member of my family will survive."

Things got even more serious, in Germany and Poland they were already very far ahead, there were already ghettos. In short, it was crazy that we didn't know. Indeed, some of us did know, *because this man sent his boy away. Against the advice of all the relatives. And I found it a very beautiful thing . . . and so this boy who left was always very special to me. And after the war, his sisters joined him . . . When his sisters left, I would have gone very willingly too . . .*

For me, this boy was very important, in order, let's say, to understand how you could save yourself, that it might be necessary to leave Italy to save yourself. So I would have gone very willingly to England or America. Papa studied English, right? But it never happened, because we stayed here. I knew this was another way. Just as this boy left, we should also leave if we couldn't go to school in this country, if this country didn't want us . . .

It was after Passover that the great German world offensive began. The world watched and became alarmed, but said nothing; even the Italian people, muted by twenty-two years of Fascism, said nothing, but there were some who thought: their hour will come! All the European Jews martyred by German bullying were thinking this.

You knew what was happ . . .

RACHEL: *What was happening, yes.*

In Poland?

No! Nothing! Nothing!

Nothing?

Nothing! Nothing! Nothing! Nothing!

You knew nothing . . .

Nothing!

about the Holocaust?

About the Holocaust, no, no, nothing!

Really?

Really, really.

Until what point?

After the war.

Your mother said that people didn't know anything about what was going on.

LIONELLA: *It's not true. You could put cotton in your ears. You could play deaf . . .*
There were thousands of refugees who came through. Italy was a transit area. They
came, they went. Many families left; in Florence many friends went to Israel. All those
who had the money.

We didn't have the money. Maybe we could have had the courage to sell every-
thing, to get the money, but for that, it's necessary to have a lot of courage. To sell the
house in Florence, it wasn't a large place, we would probably have had to sell the
jewels, the silver . . .

There were people who moved, who didn't wait it out. When Mamma says "Ah, we
were going to Oxford, but there was war with Germany, and we were afraid." No! . . .
I didn't know this, for example, I learned it now . . . I knew that there was this friend
at Oxford, who says to us, "Come." But not that there was the possibility of going, and
Mamma said no, there are bombings. Because I would have rebelled at this had they
told me. Because here too there could be bombings, here too . . .

In short, it's a solution, painful as it may be, but it was the right thing to do, in-
stead of waiting . . .

The Maginot line was broken through the betrayal of an engineer, and the
newspapers broke the important news in great gaudy headlines:

"The Maginot line is broken and by now the British Empire has fallen. The landing on the isle of Great Britain is imminent."

But Chamberlain and his ministers naturally laughed to themselves, looking at their country's impressive defense, with extremely powerful coastal cannons and factories preparing marvelous materièl for the future counteroffensive.

And Chamberlain must also have smiled in a humiliating way, as his King must have too, when the papers trumpeted the German hunger blockade against England.

You're taking Belgium, France, Austria, Denmark, and Finland for yourself? But we have the colonies, and soon you'll have to face us!

Our King is about to flee? But he's healthy and thriving in Buckingham Palace, if you really want to know!

But Germany, sure of winning, sent its forces throughout the world without considering the consequences.

"Luftwaffe has bombed London with many victims . . ."

It's like this: the German people are gratified by blood, death, destruction. But the Allied forces also possess powerful airplanes, like the swastika-marked airplanes by Luftwaffe, and, having crossed the Channel, the terrible flying Allied fortresses furrow the German sky—it's terrifying—and their mortal cargo of punishment falls onto Berlin, grand and beautiful city and birthplace of famous men, but also, often, of barbarians.

The Nazi German people begin to see that Anglo-American factories have built sound instruments of death, without which modern war could not be waged, but they will soon see worse.

And the humorous Italian papers print ridiculous jokes—for lack of anything better, they help people laugh, but still people know they're foolish.

And finally, when the threshers are about to cut the grain, the true wealth of Italy, war broke out between Italy and the Allies.

"We're ready; we'll declare war on the most powerful nations on earth and brag about it."

Chamberlain and Roosevelt certainly laughed heartily.

19

The burning sun beat against the closed shutters of the parlor; Mamma and Papa had gone into the city. Andrea, sitting in front of the radio with the headphones on, listened to the Balilla [Fascist youth group] meeting.

All at once, the story Andrea was listening to was interrupted: "Attention! Attention!" shouted a male voice, "In ten minutes, the Duce will speak! Attention!"

And the regal march sounded majestically.

"What's happening, Grandma Alice?"

But Grandmother had already understood what it was about and put the radio to her ear; Andrea took the other headset, but Milena wanted to listen too, so they each took an earpiece.

After a few minutes, all Italy resounded with the decisive speech and a shiver of terror ran through all the families.

With a tormented face, Andrea looked out and thought; he thought about the war and finally asked his grandmother:

"But Mamma is out . . ."

"And so?"

"The war's there. Don't they fight in the streets?"

His grandmother calmed him by explaining that one fights at the front, and so, happier, he returned to his games.

That evening Mamma and Papa returned with two pieces of good news: they got permission to have a servant and they got a postcard in which Grandmother's cousins, Susanna and Livia Almansi, said they wanted to return to Florence as they had the year before.

It was June 10, 1940.

ALDO: June 10, 1940: Italy's declaration of war! Not that life was peaches and cream before, but certainly from this point everything became more difficult and the problem of living became even more serious. The total blackout kept anyone from taking two steps after dinner, except on moonlit evenings, and Italy's ever-closer ties to the Axis increased the fear of further renewals of the racist laws. And so the second year of the stay in Galluzzo was very sad, and the trips to Florence, to school in the morning, in total darkness because of daylight-savings time, the returns in trams, out-of-the-way and crowded beyond measure, made living far from the center of town exhausting.

20

Immediately Mrs. Alice began searching for lodgings for the two ladies who were to arrive.

Finally one day she decided to enter a large white gate with two bells, but only one worked, the one with "Garlini" written on it.

A little while after she had rung, the gate opened electrically and an aged lady dressed in black came to meet Mrs. Alice. Her pearl necklace stood out against her black veil.

She led her up a stone stairway to a little annex of the house which once belonged to a Frenchman from Nice. Two nice spacious rooms with a bath were available.

Everything settled, Mrs. Alice made as if to go, but Mrs. Garlini wanted to show her the pretty, shady wood where her daughter, married to an employee in an office at A Orientale and mother of a young twenty-year-old, kept a flock of geese for their precious feathers.

Then, being a great philosopher, she invited her into a disorderly parlor full of books and started one of her endless lectures.

"Life, my dear lady, is a long chain of steel. Each ring is a piece of our mortal life . . ."

After an hour, dazed and exhausted, Mrs. Alice found herself at the fork of the two streets. When she turned onto the road, a fat man in a white shirt ran to meet her.

"I've got good stracchino!"

Mrs. Alice thanked him, she didn't need any.

"I've got exquisite provolone!"

Just to humor him, she entered the store that smelled of wine and bought 50 grams of provolone.

"And do you want some spumante?"

"No! We don't drink."

He was always like that, that Toscano Batti!

When she returned, Dina, the woman sent by the carpenter, had already come to work. She was tall and brunette; every minute she brought up her fiancé—my fiancé does this, my fiancé doesn't want, my fiancé says this . . .

2 1

While Milena was passing by the stationer's, a tall woman, dressed in black voile, stopped her all of a sudden:

"Tell your grandmother that those ladies have arrived." Milena nodded yes, she would, if she remembered.

"Oh, yes, of course you will remember, little one, because listen, life is a long chain, every link of the chain is a part of our mortal lives. Woe to those who forget certain things necessary to form another link; because, little one, life is composed of many parts . . . woe to those who take life with sadness without studying it with methodical philosophy. Philosophy harmonizes and gives life to depressed souls; philosophy makes those souls think that all the world is already predisposed by God, and therefore in this very elevated philosophical thought those souls are comforted. I was telling you that life, this life, which is an unreal dream, given that man lives the real spiritual life up there, is a chain of iron with many links, hidden in the hands of God. Every once in a while one of those links slides into the uninformed sight of man, and then another, and another, until the chain, longer or shorter, plays itself out and man returns to dust and mud while his soul, almost flying and invisible, rises to the impeccable justice of God.

"This, my little one, is life as it unfolds in the earthly period of our stupid existence, but it is the soul, the soul alone, that is worthy of divine justice, given that man sins every hour, every minute, for his profanity, his ambition, his pride, his arrogance, and especially for the mania that everyone has to decorate and retouch their bodies with rouge and luxuriant clothes not worthy of the human body, so indifferent to the respect it owes to its Creator.

"Therefore, when you become a young lady, for moral decency don't corrupt your body with that sort of thing, and you will be honored by everyone."

"Yes, ma'am, of course."

"All right, goodbye little one, until tomorrow."

RACHEL: *Edmea Lurini [whom Leo calls "Garlini"] lived in Galluzzo, at Due Strade, understand? She was a lady . . . (laughs) . . . you've read what Leo said, yes? . . . She was very good. Aldo went there often to study the* Enciclopedia Treccani *because Professor Bianchi Bandinelli, who was an archeologist, a good friend of Aldo, knew that Aldo wasn't allowed to work. So he gave him some articles that he had to do himself for the* Enciclopedia Treccani, *and Aldo did them. Understand?*

Leo made fun of her all the time.

Yes! She'd start talking and talking . . . And she never finished! Never, ever, ever. (Chuckling) She was a special woman. A very good woman, poor thing.

---

2 2

A few days later, with war declared on the United Powers, Italy sent her first forces to the French Alps, and after some fighting occupied Mentone.

The forces were still drunk on the order given by the Duce to win, and still hopeful, naturally, about the victory of their Fatherland. On the 25th of June, the war with France ended. But many mothers were already shedding their first tears and the first men were sacrificed to the Fatherland.

Around August, the number of heads in the Nola family chicken coop grew because the hens had borne offspring of a choice race; a sumptuous and large cock named Doge helped with the work of his hostile and crippled companion, while the hens who had produced neither offspring nor eggs ended up roasted. Each hen had its name and every day Venice patiently checked which hen had laid eggs during the day, so that the unlucky one who hadn't produced for a long time and wasn't breedable came to a bad end—as did poor Brizzolina, as Milena called her, who, after she was finished off sadly according to the sentence of the jury (for the benefit of Andrea's birthday lunch), was found to have four half-made eggs in her body. From that moment the very sharp knife that Papa used only after he said a prayer, was used less—he was slower to pronounce hens worthy for the mortal knife which, as prescribed by Jewish law, cut their tracheas.

LIONELLA: *[Papa] was a* shochet. *I was a strong woman, you know. It was I who held the chickens for the* shochità. *It wasn't Mamma, it was I. Turkeys too, and geese. (Laughs) Enormous animals (laughs) . . . I had to do it, since we came to Florence. But not before, in Rome. In Rome, there was a kosher poultry store. Here in Florence we were in the country, so we had our chickens, our animals. Papa had his knife, he cleaned it, they were solemn moments. He explained the words . . .*

Meanwhile, after the war, I wanted to get a shochet diploma—I'd held the animals for five years, I knew everything. It's a nice memory. The Rabbi at that time said that when there's a man, the female shochet isn't needed . . . Later they told me it's not true, a woman can be a shochet for her family.

It was around the beginning of September, while Italy was invading British Somalia, that the visits to Villa Garlini thinned out. With the end of the heat, the Almansi cousins began to learn their way from Mrs. Garlini's apartment up to the Cavalcanti house [where the Nolas were staying]. The final visits to the

Lionella and Leo tending the coop in Galluzzo (1940).

Almansi ladies were terrrible since the last great heats pierced even the shadows of the wood. They returned home tired, sweaty, stopping every minute because they were known by now—over there was Toscano who offered his extra rare cookies (in parentheses, don't tell anyone), then Ricca, the young seamstress, recently married, came to the window: could the young lady come to try on the dress?

"But could it be done this evening?"

"Right away, because this evening Mrs. Ricca has to go out with her husband."

Milena fretted and grumbled; she was hungry, but there was no remedy.

Having completed the long fitting, with corrections and misunderstandings explained, it was Andrea's turn: he wanted a drawing pad with smooth paper.

But Masina, the stationer, has only rough paper. What to do since tomorrow is Sunday?

Finally it is decided that he will ask Liliana; she has a smooth pad, she will give him a sheet. Then there is Andreina, the washerwoman, who has two extra fresh eggs, so Andrea might recuperate from the little flu he's had (but he must keep them in his pocket, because she swore on her life to Gigi, the shoemaker's helper, that she didn't have any).

There's Gigi, the shoemaker's helper, who has Milena's sandals ready; also Mrs. Lucia's shoes are resoled.

Unfortunately, he saw the eggs through a cranny in Andrea's jacket pocket and he started to make a little scene so that, lie upon lie, they had to confess that it was Andreina who had sold them. Finally he decides that he will stop greeting her when they pass each other and he hurls the washerwoman's slightly broken shoes into the street.

The old woman to whom Mrs. Alice gave a little wool to spin lets her know that she has lost one of the two already-spun skeins, and she humbly apologizes.

Then they have to read a little sign that announces the rationing of bread; Miss Andreati comes by, greets them, and asks about the math problem in which the dry cleaner has to wash twenty skirts if he can. Then, not having her glasses, she is informed of the gist of the notice and despairs to think of the consequences.

Dinella, the older and better seamstress, though a very slow worker, asks if her daughter the embroiderer has to embroider an edge on the tablecloth; Mr. Nola implores her for his shirt, it's urgent; but it won't be done until next Friday.

When finally they are about to enter their driveway, here comes Mrs. Garlini from San Felice a Ema, asking if there's any news. They tell her about the rationing of bread.

"You see, you see! Life, my lady, is a long chain, each link . . ."

2 3

From the end of May, a terrifying date was etched into Andrea's and Milena's minds: June 15, exams.

But there was a moment when the date no longer seemed terrifying: around mid-June a high fever put first one, then the other child in bed and a postponement of the exam was considered. Later, though, once their fevers were much lower, it was decided that they would go—and in a taxi, no less.

They arrived half an hour late at the Queen Elena School—Jewish Section, but no one said anything because the Jewish section was very poorly organized.

Behind the taxi stopped a closed carriage out of which emerged a boy named Frido Finali, his highly elegant mother (wife of Giacomo Finali, the industrialist and proprietor of fabric factories in Prato), and his Swiss governess in her elegant brown cloak.

Frido, who was already friends with Andrea and who was also convalescing, had a freckled face like his father's, wore elegant tortoiseshell glasses and trousers of the finest cloth with a five-centimeter-thick belt of real leather; the shirt, finely monogramed in red, was of purest linen.

Wrapped in a blanket of green cloth, he set out with Andrea into the school, but Miss Curiel came to meet them, saying there was a half-hour to wait.

"But . . . what about the other children?"

"What children? You're the only ones!"

The two boys turned to the window and stayed there, elbows on the windowsill and hands in their hair; they were thinking about the exam. Milena took the history text and went over the curriculum.

Under the window there was a grand avenue of plane trees that led to the school, girded by high walls and a green gate. All of a sudden, a swarm of kids came out of a door: they were the examinees, more or less satisfied with their efforts, exchanging their opinions as they left the frightening place. Those who knew they had failed calmed their parents: you'll see, I said this, I corrected . . . The others, happy as larks, only laughed.

Since the Aryan examinees were finished, it was the Jewish section's turn.

"Frido, will we pass?"

"Andrea, will I fail?"

"Frido, will I know the poem, 'The Two Lads'? It's the longest."

"Will *I* know it?"

"Listen to me say it, since you have the book. *It was . . . sunset: at their games . . .*"

"No, *garrulous games.*"

"What does 'garrulous' mean?"

Frido didn't know. So what should they do? They asked a passing teacher.

"Miss . . ."

"What is it?" she answered coldly.

They wanted to know what "garrulous" meant. But they were unlucky, because they were dealing with the extremely severe teacher Beatrice D'Ancona:

"You'll find out later what 'garrulous' means." With great strides she entered the classroom of the Jewish section and collared Miss Curiel:

"Annie, listen to this." And, softly, softly, she told her something.

"What would 'garrulous' mean, Milena?"

"I think: childish."

Satisfied, they went back to studying the poem:

"*They were intent in the silvery peace . . .*"

"No, golden."

"*From the shady avenue the two . . .*"

But Miss Curiel had already opened the leaves of the classroom door, and, the poem abandoned, all three entered the classroom, covered in blankets to stay warm.

Everything went fine until after the essay, but Andrea and Frido left the math problem blank, and as for the poem, there were troubles. To start it was Andrea's turn and, the poem was, of course, "The Two Lads."

"What does garrulous mean?"

"Childish . . ."

He was immediately sent back to his place and to Milena who was about to get up he blurted out softly:

"Miss D'Ancona is a spy . . ."

From that moment until Andrea stopped going to that school, he whispered his decree to all his friends:

"Miss D'Ancona, spy . . ."

And every time he heard her name mentioned, the memory of that poem made him say:

"Spy!"

Halfway through the lesson, the custodian came in with a pack of cookies and an orange juice for the sick children.

Andrea and Milena drank, ate, and offered cookies to Frido. But when they left they had to apologize because they had offered Frido cookies that had been brought for him!

And for that year, the school closed behind them. Everyone was ready to leave for the countryside and the seaside, and Frido, in his great green blanket and with his Swiss satchel slung over his shoulders, got in his carriage and the fluttering corner of his handkerchief disappeared at the corner of Via Benedetto Varchi.

LIONELLA: *There was a Jewish section, however we took the exams by ourselves. Here too we were closed in a room, but this time we were grown up, we had already done it once. And this time there was also another Jewish boy taking private lessons— he was called Alfredo Forti. He was full of complexes, isolated and full of complexes. And so we took the exams with him, if I remember. There were three of us.*

ALDO: In this too, how many humiliations! The written tests, possibly in separate classrooms, and the oral one all at the end, after nervewracking days of waiting. Thank goodness good sense and fairness triumphed in most examiners, many of whom did not hesitate to give the grades deserved, even a 10, to the candidate. But there were also some explicit declarations that it wasn't possible to give the highest grades to young Jews . . . another way to get in good with your superiors and get ahead in your career . . .

So the Jewish children could take exams?

RACHEL: *Exams, yes, yes, yes.*

After the others.

After the others. Also the high schools had to, after the exam was over, put out a sheet with all the names . . .

With the grades?

Not with the grades, but with "passed," or not. But they did it just for a year, because all the Jewish students passed, while some Catholics didn't. And they had done the list of the Catholics separate from that of the Jews, and so everyone could read, "But these have all been promoted, and these, no." And so, the next year, they mixed them all together instead . . .

---

2 4

Summer passed quickly and winter came, the second spent in Galluzzo.

The battles in East Africa were the only topic of discussion in all of Florence, and when the Italian troops were winning, the newspapers also talked only of that, but when they were losing—quiet, and keep your mouths shut!

Minister Pavolini had put a huge map of Africa in Piazza Signoria, but after the Italian retreat, the map suddenly disappeared.

Around October, the Almansi ladies left; Mrs. Garlini bade them farewell with her philosophical discourse: life is a long chain . . .

And in November they took up their lessons again with Miss Andreati, only more frequently, since Milena wanted to take an exam to skip the fifth grade.

Oil, butter, pasta, sugar, cloth, and linens were rationed, to everyone's dismay, while the resounding defeat in Greece made Mussolini say:

"We weren't ready, we were forced to go to war," contradicting his June 10th speech.

Around June, the Almansi ladies returned, but the daily visits dwindled: Andrea and Milena had been quite bored ever since they lost a favorite piece of their game, "The Soles." On the branch of a laurel they had attached a sign that said this:

LOST: THE BLUE HEAD OF A SOLE. REWARD 1 LIRA

It was followed by the drawing of a sole missing its head.

One day, returning from a melancholy visit, the stink of something burning reached them suddenly, followed by cries and shouts.

"Liliana" they asked the girl who was running up and down, "what's happening?"

"The wheat! The wheat! "

Perhaps because of internal combustion, or because of someone's carelessness, the towering heap of wheat had gone up in flames and now, after much effort to put it out, only ashes remained on the ground.

Ferdinando was between sobs and tears when the postcard ordering him to report for service sent the family into its greatest turmoil.

"Poor things, Mrs. Lucia! Poor us! Without a man! Wretched as we are! Damn whoever invented war!"

"Come on, Venice, calm down! These days, everyone goes to war!"

"Well I know that it's an ugly invention! And we, we are wretched, and the field burned too, good and sainted God!"

But Ferdinando's call to arms was a joke:

After a few days he was working his fields again in civilian clothes.

"Weren't you called up, Ferdinando?"

"My uniform's supposed to arrive tomorrow."

After a week, uniformed, he was there again. The suit was awkward on him—such was the scarcity of cloth, there wasn't a size to fit his build.

"I asked leave to thresh, eight days."

After two weeks, he was still at home.

"Why haven't you left yet?" They had tripled his leave since the marshal was a schoolmate of his.

He left again and soon returned home again; this time he came to say goodbye because he was leaving for real for Russia.

"Do you understand, Mrs. Alice, that they're sending him to Russia in the cold, with just that cotton suit? That my girl and I will be left here alone?"

That evening they had a grand "farewell" dinner, with tears bursting forth in desperate sobs as soon as anyone said that word.

The next day, Ferdinando was peacefully beating his grain.

"And Russia?"

"Oh! I got leave to thresh."

But after three months he was still on leave:

"What can I say, I was discharged."

It was clear that the Italian army wasn't well organized.

25

One day Mr. Cavalcanti arrived at the house and gave notice that by September 15, that is, two months later, he wanted the house free.

Meanwhile Andrea, who had shown a marked ability in Italian, wrote a short story on a certain lion of gold, then sent it to a little Roman paper, "Little Red Riding Hood," which a few weeks later published a short feature evaluating the story. But publication wasn't possible for lack of illustrations.

And so, the project went no further than that.

RACHEL: *I told you, no? He did crosswords when he was seven, and he won those two medical dictionaries . . . He was very good.*

And did you read this story on the Lion of Gold?

Ah, of course. Of course, yes. But I don't remember it anymore, it's been fifty years . . .

Of course.

"So, that's where the project was left." It means that he didn't write anymore, he didn't send anything. (Laughs)

Did Leo write in front of everyone, in public?

No, no, he went into his little room.

But you knew that he was writing, or not?

Yes, no, we didn't know much. Only when he reached the upper grades, he was always at his desk, always at his desk, so much so that my husband Aldo had a high book rest made for him, so that he would stand up.

So it wasn't that you read what he . . .

Oooh, no, no, no, no, no, no. Not at all, not at all. The first time we saw it was then, understand?

When did you first see this book? After the war?

After the war, yes. You know, when we were at Galluzzo, we spent, as Aldo said, a nice time, a wonderful time . . .

So he didn't say that he was writing.

No, no, no!

So, you didn't read this until the war was over?

Yes, yes, yes.

And then was he embarrassed when you read it?

No, no, no, no, no, no. He was happy.

He thought that what he had written was good?

Yes, yes.

Then in August two children arrived with their parents, dear acquaintances, Grandmother's relatives, they were going to spend the summer in their house in Marignolle, at the home of their maternal grandmother, eighty-year-old Enrica Funaro, and at their aunts'.

The two children, Pia and Anna Paola, often came to visit Milena, and Andrea and Milena often returned their visits.

The Funaro-Amedeato villa was enormous and in front there was a little garden where the old, but slender and graceful Mrs. Enrica and her daughters were accustomed to sit since many years back; Mrs. Dora Sadum and her husband (who rarely left his office, however), the grandchildren of the smiling old lady, and sometimes besides the great-grandchildren, even the Nola family used to gather in this little garden surrounded by oranges and rhododendrons.

Among the children there was a delightful baby of about two years named Berto Modigliano, son of Mrs. Anna-Milena, who had been in a very serious condition on account of his birth, and of Mr. Fritz Modigliano, who suffered, on certain days, from stomach problems.

On January 5, 1941, Berto's second birthday, Mrs. Anna-Milena had invited Mrs. Nola and her husband to her pretty house in Via della Cernaia; all the numerous aunts met there, cooing over the fat and thriving baby who was enjoying himself amid his toys, both old ones and new.

"Look, look, Lucia, what a nice wind-up truck! And these chocolates!"

His papa watched him and could have eaten him with kisses; in fact his pain had left him in peace for a long time now.

But around 6 P.M., Mr. Fritz became pale; his yellowish face showed signs of suffering.

"What's wrong with your husband?" asked Mrs. Lucia.

"Hmm! Nothing. In fact, for the past month he's eaten with quite a healthy appetite!"

26

But Mrs. Lucia was right.

That same evening, Fritz Modigliano went to bed with a high fever which was thought to be the flu. The next day his stomach pains increased, well-known doctors and physicians were called, and he was taken to a famous doctor in Bologna who said it was a matter of a small stomach problem, x-rays, medicines, shots.

Around June, Mr. Fritz felt better and to recuperate they settled in the annex where the Almansi ladies had stayed the year before, in three rooms of the apartment. Some days Fritz felt better and played with his baby, picked him up, and perhaps thought of a time sooner or later when his baby would ask:

"But where's Papa?"

On days when his father didn't want to be with him, Berto said:

"Papa got a booboo! Papa not want me!"

And everyone smiled sadly.

When he didn't see his papa, he was restless, wandered around the woods, ran up and down, with Milena following close behind so as not to lose sight of him.

Then Mr. Fritz got worse again, there were more x-rays and consultations, until a minor ulcer was discovered: medicines, cures, and then he got better: Mr. Fritz is cured, Mr. Fritz is cured, Doctor Messi is a genius.

To recuperate, the mountains were prescribed: Vallombrosa? Too low, it must be three thousand, four thousand meters!

2 7

Also around June, admission exams.

Milena was quite displeased that the mathematics exam was on none other than a Saturday, day of repose for Jews, but there was no help for it; so she wouldn't have to ride the tram on the sabbath, the good Mrs. Dora took Milena to sleep at her house.

The teachers at the Michelangelo School saw right away that she was an intelligent girl, and well disposed to her, they asked her questions almost jokingly.

Saturday, all disturbed at having to write on that day, she answered her problem right, but when she was at the end a boy (who certainly wasn't a genius) said in her ear: "you're wrong, it's like this" and showed her his last operation.

Milena quickly, quickly corrected her number, in a great hurry since the professor had said to turn in their work; she wasn't thinking that the calculation might not be correct.

When she left she found out from her classmates that the correct number was the one she had put before. She was quite upset but the examiners must not have thought it mattered, because the grade that was written on the school lists was "Excellent."

2 8

Mr. Cavalcanti pestered his tenants, saying he wanted to come to his house around the first of October, but the Nola family still had to organize the house that Uncle Angelo had rented them.

ALDO: The offer made by the professor's cousin, the engineer Leone Ambron [whom Leo calls Angelo], to rent to him a nice apartment at a low price right in the center, was accepted with utmost joy. And life in the city offered the possibility of giving lessons which, thanks to the goodness and the concern of two colleagues to whom the professor will always be grateful, were, in some months, numerous enough, and gave a little material and moral relief.

29

Up on a high alpine mountain, Fritz Modigliano seemed, as if by miracle, to recover from his illness. In the stove of the high wooden refuge, his wife happily burned all the letters in which doctors and scientists had written of her husband's grave state, along with those in which her husband told his wishes in case he passed away. Mrs. Anna-Milena thought of reserving a car in a few weeks and of returning triumphant, with Fritz healthy once again, to Bologna, where her baby boy was waiting for them.

Eight days passed; the doctor who came daily to see the patient pronounced him cured.

"Your husband is in perfect health—more than I; he needs only to recover. From this day on he has to eat two raw eggs each day."

Mrs. Anna-Milena wrote immediately to her relatives and also a long postcard to Mrs. Nola.

"Dearest Alice.

You can't imagine how happy I am at the thought that Fritz is cured, better than I thought possible, of that awful sickness he got in Africa.

This morning I found two very fresh eggs and he drank them with gusto. Just think, dear Lucia, with what joy I wrote to my family and to my boy that his father is cured and will be able to hug him all the time. I've burned all the sad letters that made me cry so much; now I want only to be happy, to come home, and to celebrate Berto's third birthday in January.

Until we see each other again in Florence, then—all of us. Fritz, who was up and around all day yesterday, after so long, says hello.

Anna-Milena."

This postcard was written and mailed Sunday.

But at two o'clock that same night painful cries echoed through the silent walls of the Alpine refuge: it was Fritz Modigliano, whose tremendous pains had started up again.

At noon Anna-Milena was still there, pale and sweating, watching over her husband.

"Take me away, I can't die here . . . it's cold . . . Berto."

"Yes Fritz."

A taxi from the closest town was called urgently—but hurry for heaven's sake, the patient is about to die!

The automobile arrived covered by the first snows of the mountain. The sick man with his wan face, mortal sweat dripping down his bluish forehead, teeth chattering from the cold, was loaded on, and the taxi set out again, taking off at breakneck speed.

Later, Anna-Milena, wild-eyed and shaken, found herself in her in-laws' sitting room in Bologna.

She said it had been a terrible trip, but she remembered only the snow that wrapped around the car, the deserted street where the taxi almost skidded, the rapid curves that receded and Fritz crying out, crying out from the tremendous pain, while she tried to calm him. And then, then, oh the excruciating scene when the mother, that mother who had spent everything for her son, went to embrace him thinking him cured and saw his waxen face which just barely recognized her.

Anna-Milena wails, cries, her boy comes in and, miracle that mothers can perform, she smiles, kisses him, jokes with him, and a large tear, one alone, falls on Berto's hair.

"Why are you crying, Mamma?"

"Nothing, Berto."

"And Papa?"

"Papa? Papa is far away . . ."

The last operation on his stomach did not succeed and the next day Berto had no father.

"And Papa?"

"Papa? Papa is in America."

"And we're not going?"

The response was a kiss on his blond curls; Berto thought about the big tear of the day before and didn't understand.

30

In early September the Nolas moved into the new house in the center of Florence. The Almansi ladies returned to Rome and left the Garlini house forever; and so did Anna-Milena, with her brother Lucio, who would see to the boy's education, and her grieving mother-in-law.

A few days later another tragedy struck poor Fritz's family: another son, a doctor, died in a motorcycle accident on his way home.

Liliana had cried a lot when Milena left, thinking that friends from school in the city would take her place, but Milena had promised that she would never forget her. Thus calmed, she said goodbye once and for all.

Then school started and Miss Andreati's not-so-conclusive lessons ended.

Milena and Andrea had come to Galluzzo as children and now as little adults they left it, leaving behind their childlike innocence.

Milena got up at an impossible hour in the morning and often returned around two, while Andrea went to Jewish fifth grade for three hours in the afternoon.

LIONELLA: *My grandmother wanted to accompany me the first time I went to school . . . Mother never went out early in the morning . . . Out in front of the school, I said, "Goodbye, Grandmother!"*

"But—what? You don't want me to—"

"No, no, no, no!" She respected that. I saw the other girls went in alone, I didn't want to be accompanied. Even if I didn't know anyone, since it was a new school.

So I went alone. When I returned, my grandmother said to me, "For the first time, you have hurt me. You never made me suffer before. I was so upset. I wanted to go up and see your class, see your teacher. I was so disappointed." It's easy to hurt someone you love dearly, isn't it?

Grandmother, however, respected my wish. She was good, wasn't she? But she told me how she felt, because we had a very beautiful relationship, very honest. We had to tell each other. If we were hurt, if we felt good.

At the Michelangelo school, I took the exam to enter sixth grade. There we were all together, Jews and non-Jews. However, the Jews all in a row in the room . . . Oh! This enormous room! All these girls! (Sharp intake of breath) What terror! First it was the terror of isolation, then the alarm at finding myself with so many girls!

Leo, instead, went to fifth grade at the Giotto . . . He had to go from Via dei Banchi to [school] on tram no. 6 alone; they sent him alone so that he would mature, grow up. Who could say to a child, "Grow up! You're big, grow up! Take the bus, and go alone"? He was a raw youth, sensitive, lost. For him it was a trauma to go to school alone.

· 3 1

For the first time, after a month of school, Andrea goes alone, armed to the teeth with courage. He sets off on the broad Via Vecchietti flanked by high buildings and boards tram no. 6.

"A 50-lire ticket, please."

"Here you go." But the ticket flies out of the ticket-seller's hands and falls to the ground; people walk over it, crush it, carry it off with their feet.

"A 50-lire ticket, please!"

"I gave it to you, little one! Here's another."

When the ticket-collector comes, the same thing happens: he doesn't find the ticket. He looks here, he looks there, and finally he sees it deep in a pocket where he didn't remember putting it; meanwhile Simon Salmi gets on and starts laughing at Andrea's embarrassment.

At school, Andrea finds himself embarrassed around all those kids; Renzo Bemporad, who shares his desk, whispers a few words to him, but Andrea turns red at the geography examination and mumbles some words.

That evening the family received warning telephone calls from Miss Curiel, but that was the only "insufficient"; from that day he took private lessons from Miss Walenchstein to catch up. It was the only "insufficient" that Andrea had all year.

Soon the classmates became friends and, at Milena's birthday party, Liliana cried to see that she had other friends; this time she was truly jealous!

LIONELLA: *Mamma insisted on inviting her to my birthday parties. Because we had our birthdays near each other, hers on the 18th, mine on the 16th. She was very unhappy, because they were more sophisticated girls. Mamma didn't understand that we should have had a separate party for her. If we'd had a party alone, that would have been a party. I saw that she was suffering, and I suffered for her. I understood that she was simpler, you see?*

When I was bat mitzvah, Giuliana [Liliana] came to the party, she was really isolated, poor thing. And she brought me a book on canaries . . . I always kept it on my night table; for many years, I always carried it with me. It has a very particular value for me, this book on canaries . . . It was a book that had nothing to do with anything, but she knew that she was coming to a family with books and everything . . . So she brought me this book. For me it has great value.

One day Miss Curiel showed her pupils a loudspeaker that was installed next to the room's great blackboard, white with a beige framework in the middle.

"Woe to whoever takes or touches the plug; everything would be ruined," the young lady had said before giving a math problem, and everyone obediently nodded.

32

Around April Miss Curiel's heart problems began again and so she came to school very agitated, determined to examine her students pitilessly on their history to get it over with quickly and get home as soon as possible.

Bemporad, who usually got by with a "good," started off by getting an "insufficient" marked in the register, underlined in blue, then one by one the others got the same bad grade; only Andrea had "sufficient" and Franco Modena "good." Franco Sorani was lucky because when he was about to say that he hadn't studied, someone knocked at the door:

"Come in!"

The door flung open and Biancalani, the director of the school, came in, fat and robust in her black smock.

"Fascist salute, children!"

All arms were raised but many would have liked to salute in another way; in fact Bemporad put his hand on his cap.

"Bemporad, Fascist salute!"

The arm rose sadly.

"Miss Curiel, at four the Duce is speaking, turn on the radio; don't forget the Fascist salute; explain the Mare Nostrum to the children."

Miss Curiel nodded her assent and, once Biancalani had gone, began reluctantly to explain the question of Mussolini's declaration on our sea.

"Italy is a maritime nation and because of this, the Duce . . ."

But her words fell on deaf ears; no one was paying attention.

"Pay attention!"

"But the Duce doesn't interest us much, Miss."

At that moment Miss Biancalani appeared again:

"It's four, Miss Curiel. Have you explained the question of the Mare Nostrum?"

"Yes, yes! My kids were very interested and they did nothing but say 'Long live the Duce,' begging me to have them do an essay on the subject."

"What fine children; now stand at attention."

"At attention, children."

"Salute to the Duce!"

"Eia, eia, alalà!"

"Louder: Eia, eia, alalà!!"

"And to the King?" someone whispered.

"Yes, yes to the dear little King too, if it makes you happy."

"Long live the King!"

"Must you shout like that?"

And Miss Biancalani, with her Fascist badge, disappeared.

"Now stay quiet," warned Miss Curiel and turned on the radio.

"Italians, the solemn hour . . ." But no one was paying attention.

"Listen, Andrea, let's start a club."

"No, no, Ferrari, I don't start clubs just to get in trouble later."

"Mo, do you want to start a club then?"

"Yes, yes."

"A war club; Andrea will be a soldier, I'll be the head of the male band, you females," he said, turning to the other side of the classroom, "will be the enemies; our motto—"

"Children!"

"The motto will be Blood or Victory; tomorrow I'll bring you the badges."

"Good, good. And when we're ready—"

"Children, try to listen."

"When we're ready?"

"Then we'll have a battle in Piazza Oberdan—"

"Children, really!!" And in a nervous outburst, she pulled the radio cord from the jack; the radio stopped talking as it murmured the end of a proud 'Conquer!'"

"But, Miss!"

RACHEL: *Poor thing. He was used to life at home, relatives and friends who came to our house to play. But at school like this! They stole a lot from him! Poor thing. Yes, yes. He would come and say, "Mamma Rachel, they . . . I can't find this anymore." And sometimes when Luisa met him on his return, she found him downcast. "What happened?" "Oh, they stole this from me." "Come, come, come. Let's go and I'll buy you another."*

He was so good, so good . . . it was the first time that he'd gone to school with so many children, and the teacher said to him, "But, no! Don't be so good that you get 10's all the time . . ." But he, poor thing, stayed that way . . . His teacher told me to tell him to be bad. "I don't want to give him 10 in conduct." (Laughs) . . .

Aldo said to me right away when the children had to start school, he says, "Listen Rachel, I did the elementary grades at home. I don't want our children to do the elementary grades at home. You're agreed we'll send them to school?" I say, "Of course."

Instead, we taught them at home on account of the racial laws, understand?

So Aldo had this problem too?

Yes! Poor thing. And that's why he wanted his children to go to school.

LIONELLA: *He was a very timid, very private boy, who grew up too much in the family circle, before he ever made friends. Already at the Jewish school, he was isolated. Maybe he was too far ahead . . . In any case, he was isolated, he didn't have friends, so this was very serious. He was eager, maybe, and green, but it's not easy to become part of a group that's already formed, is it? He joined a class who had been together from the first grade. Nobody made an effort to get these children to make him welcome . . . He came home and they'd stolen his kepah, they'd stolen his watercolors, they'd stolen his pen, they'd stolen his schoolbag, they had his notebook . . .*

33

The next day the children from the Jewish section arrived to find the door to the classroom still shut; they turned the key in the lock, and once inside, they began to go wild. Traces of the previous day's outburst were still there: chalk on the ground, radio wires in the air, benches crooked. A few seconds after they had entered, schoolbags full of books were flying through the air, and fights, cries, scratches, and bursts of laughter were exchanged along with a whole mess of stuff that flew and broke, bits of plaster loosened by tremendous yells, windows and doors that slammed, a massacre of chalk pieces that ended in original drawings by Franco So and armored warriors by Franco Mo. Amid all this confusion and pandemonium, something happened for which the windows and doors were closed again silently and—no longer flying through the air—everything returned to its place: the entrance of Miss D'Ancona. Everyone's face went pale, breathing became noisy, legs trembled, school books were opened immediately and mouths that pretended to read attentively instead spread the word: "We're in for it! Miss Beatrice has the math book under her arm! Pass on the awful news with telegraphic speed."

Halfway through the room, the message sent by Andrea was changed into a note written by Pia Servi and continued to be passed until Sergio Ferrari rewrote it, because the first, written on the back of something, was hard to read. Gaddo Orvieto, the last one to learn the bad news, tore it up just as he was instructed to in an addition to the second note.

Immediately the books closed again to make room for the math books which everyone wanted to review.

"All right, what was that mess? I see how Miss Curiel disciplines you; I've always said she should be retired."

The whole class dragged itself to the first grade classroom where Miss Beatrice taught.

And contrary to expectations, the math problem didn't go so badly. Miss Curiel, who had been absent on account of her pains, returned the next day and chided them for their behavior.

"Miss D'Ancona, spy!"

At the end of the school year, there was the battle declared by Ferrari in which only Frido and Andrea didn't participate, and which ended terribly because they were spied on by the director, who from the cellar of her house saw even Serena Dalmi hitting Sergio Ferrari with her schoolbag.

3 4

At the beginning of the summer, Mrs. Lucia, Andrea, and Milena left for Cavi di Lavagna, a hamlet of the town of Lavagna, where they had arranged for a room, thanks to the goodness of Mrs. Dora, who had given them a small sum for their vacation.

Grandmother had said that on their way back she would come to meet them at La Spezia and they would stay for a week, after which they had to declare their race: whoever was of the Jewish race had broken the law if he didn't request permission—which would be granted or denied who knows when.

They found a very charming little room in Lavagna, a little annex of the Central Hotel, and there they settled; they had lunch in the hotel's great hall, lit in the evening by large candelabras, and the fat and kind Giuseppe Baffo had hidden pieces of roast or exquisite steak under innocent leaves of lettuce on days when meat was prohibited. To one side was the radio with a little card surrounded by long Fascist insignia: "STAND TO LISTEN TO THE BULLETIN" and someone had written next to "bulletin," "OF THE DEFEAT."

At the next table there was a Jewish lady with long earrings who always ordered large bowls of rice; then there was a long table with three people, a woman and two men, fat as barrels, who brought salamis, hams, and sausages every day. Their likenesses, little resembling the originals, appeared in the letters that Andrea and Milena wrote to Mrs. Dora and her brother Angelo and to Grandmother and Papa.

From Lavagna, they took long walks to Chiavari, a pretty place on the sea with big modern buildings, luxurious shops, and richness in everything, and they were having a wonderful time when . . .

3 5

Dina, who had been back for a while already and had summoned a girl named Iolanda from Fucecchio as extra help, had prepared for that evening a delicious custard and Mrs. Alice, like her son, enjoyed it immensely and even had seconds. Professor Nola's dearest friend, Rico Della Torre, came over, and Mrs. Alice had more custard. After going over the accounts with the cook, she went to bed. Around eleven, a long ring of the bell calls the cook, who gets out of bed frightened. By the weak light of the bed lamp she discerns the very pale face of Mrs. Alice who is about to vomit, with a terrible headache.

Her son gets up and goes to help her, and in the morning Doctor Taormina diagnoses a strong indigestion which had passed. In the evening the illness gets even worse, but with miraculous strength of will, Mrs. Alice is able to write two lines to her trembling and confused grandchildren.

"Dearests," she wrote,

"You should know that I've had, as a consequence of my gluttony, a terrible indigestion that has disturbed me for two days, and now I'm better.

Kisses.

Alice."

"That's too bad; she was so well," said Mrs. Lucia, never dreaming what would happen.

The next day Mrs. Alice lost even more consciousness and just barely succeeded in writing, "Kisses, Alice."

Professor Nola wrote, "I called Doctor Camalli," but actually a real consultation was done, in which Dr. Camalli said she was in danger of dying. Then she completely lost consciousness.

3 6

Seven days of their stay had passed; only then did Mr. Baffo declare to the authorities that Mrs. Lucia had just arrived. But it wasn't enough, because as a Jew she didn't have permission to stay in Lavagna, and the mayor sent for her.

RACHEL: *So what did I do? I put on lots of powder so that he wouldn't see that I was dark from the water and from the beach . . . Because as a Jew, I tell you, not even when I wanted to go take the waters for the pains in my arm, I couldn't go to Padua. Because it was full of Germans, and the headquarters here didn't give me permission.*

The mayor was tall, brunet, young, and from his high walnut desk he studied Mrs. Nola.

"You're Jewish?"

"Yes."

"Why don't you have a permit?"

"Hmm! What permit?"

"The visitor's permit. You must not read the papers."

"In fact, my husband reads them all the time and he hasn't told me anything."

"What this means is, you have to go get permission now in Genoa."

"Genoa? I can't possibly go there."

"What this means is, I'll go there myself and have them give you an answer—not today, tomorrow."

But the answer never came.

Two weeks went by and Mrs. Nola left. They arrived in Florence late in the evening and everything was dark already, lights were out because of the war. Mr. Angelo and his sister were at the station with Professor Nola, who took Mrs. Nola's arm.

"Lucia . . ."

"What's happening?"

"Mamma . . ."

"Yes? Well?"

"She's not well."

"But she wrote me that; a bad indigestion."

"She's in agony, she could die any minute . . ."

Mrs. Lucia was thoroughly confused; she entrusted the children to Mrs. Dora who had kindly offered to keep them at her house and, stumbling up the stairs and pushing against the black shadows in the dimmed light, they arrived home.

Mrs. Alice was immobile in bed and her whitened face rested mute on the pillow; she probably barely recognized people.

"Mamma!"

But she didn't hear, she didn't understand, and the nurse shook her head, dissatisfied.

When Mrs. Lucia left the room, terrified, she found Dina, the cook, leaning on the dining room table.

"Ma'am . . ."

"What is it?"

"I'm leaving."

"Now, at this moment?"

"Yes, because the lady has typhus."

"Typhus?! It's an infection in the meninges, but it's not contagious."

"Yes, infection—You tell me that to convince me not to go, but I'm going—and with Iolanda too."

"But Dina!"

3 7

Andrea and Milena lost sight of their parents and didn't understand anything. They would have liked to find them, go home with them, but the tram didn't stop, it ran and ran, so that Andrea just managed to see his mamma and papa entering the house.

[At the Sadum home on Via Cavour,] Mr. Benedetto ordered the maid to bring in dinner and they headed toward the beautiful room where the massive silver flatware was neatly aligned.

After dinner Mrs. Nola came back to sleep with the children and, speaking tête à tête with Mr. Benedetto, she told him that Mrs. Alice was getting worse and would have a second consultation the next day.

The consultation did, in fact, occur, and both Dr. Taormina and Dr. Camalli agreed that death could occur within a few hours and oxygen tanks would be necessary for her to breathe.

When the two doctors left, Dina entered the room.

"Do you see?"

"What?"

"It's typhus . . ."

"Come on! It's unfortunately what I told you it was."

"Well, I want to leave."

But she never actually decided.

One morning, the patient opened her eyes and looked around.

"Mamma!"

She said she wanted to see the children, she asked if they had returned, she said she had suffered a lot; she felt better.

At the third consultation she was declared cured by a miracle; she needed only a long convalescence. Arturo Coen, a cousin from Milan, came to Florence and she wanted to invite him over; the next day she closed her eyes and slept the entire morning.

"I don't know what's wrong! I've got sleeping sickness."

Then she went back to sleep and her mouth closed; she lost her appetite and speech. Meningitis had reached the central nerves and the seventeen-month-long battle between life and death began, as long as her heart could take it.

Did you suffer much when she died?

LIONELLA: *A lot when she was sick. She lost, she couldn't speak anymore . . .*

So she was already gone in a way.

It was as if she weren't there anymore. And I didn't see her almost at all, because I knew that she suffered, because she understood.

She suffered . . .

She suffered more to see me than . . . Her tears fell . . . So I tried, I didn't go, not even to say Good morning, Good night. I knew that when she was sick, she didn't want me in the room anymore . . . And also she didn't want to be sick around me, understand? I respected her wish, I think. I stayed very little. I knew that she understood, precisely because if not, she would not have cried. It was terrible.

---

3 8

Then school began: Milena was in seventh grade. Andrea was in sixth grade; again he saw the man bent over his desk writing, his hair now completely white. But he was no longer afraid of him and greeted him politely as did everyone; the man responded, but perhaps reflexively while he was thinking about who knows what.

Except in Italian, Milena had the same professors as Andrea, and she was the best in her class: she always got "excellent" on her homework.

Often the lessons were interrupted by long alarms and the whole school met in a vast shelter under the synagogue.

3 9

Mrs. Nola felt a little knot next to her breast; she showed it to her husband and then she called Doctor Grimaldi and requested an evening visit.

That evening, when the doctor saw what it was about, he was worried.

"We must operate tomorrow."

"Is it serious?"

"It might be; it could as easily be deadly as nothing."

Mrs. Dora thought it would be good to take the children away from Florence and they left for Pisa. They stayed five days, during which, to please Andrea and Milena, Mr. Angelo was constrained to climb to the top of the leaning tower.

They wrote a postcard from the Pisan seashore, and on the tower of Pisa they wrote "We were up here!" to which Mr. Angelo added "Unfortunately!" After going to Viareggio they returned home because Mrs. Lucia was well, since the little tumor wasn't malignant, while Mrs. Alice's sickness was by then chronic.

4 0

That summer Mrs. Lucia arranged for two rooms at Consuma where Mrs. Salmi, her sister-in-law, and Professor Rosselli's sister were vacationing.

Consuma, a noted vacation spot, is dotted with graceful bungalows, more or less luxurious according to whether you had more or less money at your disposal. The Lapi pensione was a low one-story white house on the bright paved road, while Mrs. Salmi's bungalows were up on a knoll, like little Swiss chalets.

As soon as the Nola children arrived, the Salmi children came to look for them and led them, along with Mrs. Lucia, to their house.

The bungalows rented to the two families were next to one another with little gardens around them and sloping roofs with little windows in the center.

In the grand dining room, Mrs. Lucia made the acquaintance of Miss Fortelli, who, however, strongly supported Fascism; of Mrs. Morlani, mother of a young lady, Anna, and a big robust boy, Beppino; of Mrs. Masiero, wife of the rich engineer Masiero Masierò with her son Luigino, daughter Maria-Luisa, and sister Margherita—but they didn't have lunch together with everyone else.

"Come play in the garden—I've made such a lovely little house with the stones!"

"Yes, yes, Serena."

"If you saw how ugly it is!"

"Quit it, Pallante!"

Five days later while everyone was still in bed, Angiolina came to bring the morning's hot water.

"Happy?"

"About what?"

"About last night. I am."

"But what, Angiolina?"

"Didn't you hear the radio? Badoglio has taken the government and Mussolini . . ."

"Mussolini . . . is dead?"

"No! He resigned."

"How wonderful! Terrific!"

Andrea, in the comic outfit of a robe and slippers, ran down to listen to the eight o'clock broadcast. "His Excellency Benito Mussolini," the radio was saying, "has resigned. His Majesty the King has accepted his resignation. His Excellency Badoglio has formed a new ministry."

"Mamma! It's true!"

In Florence someone had already anticipated the news and it was Rico Dalla Torre who telephoned Professor Nola immediately to tell him; people ran through the streets hitting anyone who had praised Fascism the day before, the stucco fasces fell from the workmen's clubs and Fascist headquarters. The people, free at last from the oppressive government, didn't know how to express their joy.

Right away Professor Nola wrote to Mrs. Lucia.

"Dearests.

It's truly a shame that you're not in Florence these days: everyone runs, shouts, punches. Here as you will know from the papers, there's curfew at nine and night draws rifle shots against windows that aren't closed tight. The night of July 25th even Lucio Gallichi went to demonstrate and he heard them yelling through the streets "Long live *us*," "Long live *us!*" Also, as you know, we can't circulate in groups or have meetings . . .

Andrea—Miss Rosselli has said that you should prepare homework for mid-September . . .

Alessio."

The next day, word spread of an unconditional peace, but the radio immediately contradicted the good news. In his next letter, Professor Nola enclosed a newspaper clipping in which one writer banished by Mussolini wrote to another: "Also we must see the shame of the racial laws removed."

ALDO: And so life in Prof. N. M.'s house went on passably until the unforgettable summer of 1943, when on the 25th of July, the Fascist regime was declared deceased and Marshal Badoglio assumed the presidency of a military government. Many exulted at such news, many others worried, and justifiably so, realizing immediately the grave consequences of such a change while Italy was full of Germans.

Certainly there and then, a Jew could not but be comforted to think that racism practically ceased magically, or by reading lots of pretty anti-racist articles, or by seeing the names of so many top-grade writers, hidden for so many years, return to the light of day, or by hearing talk of liberty! But fear that Germany would react and take greater root among us than before, consequently applying to us its own racist laws, much more severe and inhuman than ours—this fear, I say, was well justified, and it didn't take much to guess that a high price would be paid for the momentary enjoyment. And so it was.

Until the famous day of the appointment of Marshal Badoglio to the Head of the Government—July 25, 1943—there weren't substantial changes in the regulations on race except for a few renewals more apparent than real: Jewish names were suppressed in the telephone books and on store signs, and radios were confiscated on the basis of the Commissariat's incomplete lists, on account of which many radios remained unsequestered. With the 25th of July it seemed to breathe, when in the night between the 25th and the 26th, the streets in the center of town echoed with patriotic songs unheard for some time, a sense of astonishment seized everyone and from half-closed windows they called to each other: what could this mean?

When they found out, their faces lit up with joy to hear that for which no one would have dared hope so soon. And reading the newspaper the next morning one asked oneself why a transition that was apparently so simple, so legal, could not have happened earlier . . . but one didn't know yet what had happened nor what was coming to a head. And until the 8th of September Jewish hopes grew; no one paid any attention to the application of the racist laws, although not one counter-regulation had come out yet. But in practice many laws were let slide, and as far as they could, the local authorities showed that they didn't take any notice of orders that were now given hesitantly. So even Prof. N. M.'s mother's crystal radio was returned to her after it had already been deposited with the Commissariat—as if one could find prohibited stations with a crystal radio!

RACHEL: *We learned [what was happening] from newspapers, from others, from people, like that. The Catholic people who could have radios listened to them at night. For example in Milan, my sister was in a house of the modern type, which had walls like this [she shows an inch between her thumb and forefinger], where one could hear the news from the other side.*

After the war, the Fascists, were they embarrassed?

RACHEL: *Of course . . . Everyone said that they weren't Fascists . . . They disappeared. And then, on the street, one found the pins, the badges of Fascism that everyone had here (points to chest). Then after the war . . . one couldn't find a single Fascist (laughs) right from the day that Mussolini fell.*

In '43.

'43. Yes.

And so after the war, one pretended not to . . .

Not to, yes. Or they said, if they joined up, like Aldo for example, he joined because if not he would not have been able to compete for a teaching position, and so on. Everyone said, if you don't join, how do you eat?

The real Fascists said this too?

No, no, the real Fascists often went with [Mussolini] to the Republic of Salò.

41

"I'd like to see what the children will do this year when they can't go to camp," said Miss Fortelli, who must have enjoyed many things during the Fascist period. [Rachel explained that, "With Fascism, Mussolini had put up a commission . . . to take the children who couldn't go to the sea or to the mountains, and so they took them to a camp."]

"Oh! You can't be serious," everyone responded.

Meanwhile, because of the continuous aerial bombardments around Florence, Mr. Nola didn't think it was wise to keep the family in the city when they returned, and, profiting from an apartment rented by the Sadum family at Impruneta which they put at his disposal, he went to get it ready, planning to bring Mrs. Alice in an ambulance to the Villa Camerino at Bellosguardo.

"It's a lovely apartment," he then wrote, "on the ground floor of a bungalow, with three rooms—kitchen, two bedrooms, and a bathroom, and I liked it a lot . . ."

When they returned from Consuma, they did in fact leave again for Impruneta in a very crowded bus which reminded them of the M.P. 1 or the C.P. Red of Rome.

When they arrived, Impruneta with its white town hall and the yellow tower of the ex-Fascist Party had just awakened from the night and the first wayfarers slowly crossed the grand piazza where the first shutters opened up one by one. There was a street to one side, Via della Fonte, and there were two workers loafing in front of Town Hall. Next to the grey stone fountain, there was a large pile of rubble.

"What's this rubble?"

"It's the statue of the brigand Mussolini, may he suffer the same misfortune as my chickens."

"And?"

"And, lots of people came, with pickaxes, stones, rocks, and they knocked it down."

4 2

For two or three weeks Professor Nola came to see them but then the bus schedule became so impossible that he gave up coming and once arrived on a bus to see his family and, without getting off, went back on the same one.

There were moments in which Mrs. Alice's condition was very serious but then she would improve on account of the extraordinary strength of her heart and her constitution. Doctor Taormina shook his head:

"If there isn't another miracle . . ."

Then he cut down on his visits because by now the patient's condition was chronic.

The summer seemed to end nicer than the one before; people prepared themselves to bear anything, but were happy about the freedom won.

Then the world shook again, something terrible happened in the long boot, and where they could the people shouted, "Foreigners, get out!" and the verses of many patriotic songs were reborn quietly, since the muzzle and the bandits had come back.

43

Milena, who wanted a half-kilo of yellow squash, pushed into the crowd that filled the green-grocer's.

It was soon dark, and the greedy grocer, old vixen, fat and feeble-minded, did not turn on the light of course, but weighed and did everything gropingly until, exhausted by the crowd, she started to yell.

"Everyone out, I'm closing! Outside—you too, girl; who knows how many things you've stolen!" And the shouts spread through the courtyard of the narrow little street, Via dei Cavalleggeri.

Mrs. Lucia was very offended;

"My daughter isn't a thief! Woe to you, Milena, if you buy something from that rude woman." And they went into the shop next door where there was a kinder little woman.

"*They're* the thieves! But one day they'll have to say: 'What can I do for you, Madam?' That day will come too, Mrs. Clarice."

"Of course; those up there have made money these twenty years. You know why? Because the daughter joined the Fascist Party from its beginning; but now they should hang their heads! The other day, that is, four months ago by now, she came back from Florence in [the Fascist bigwig] Tamburini's car with a fur that you don't see much around here, of ramuschino. She came here to my place: 'You know,' she said, 'Tamburini was very kind, he put his car at my disposal and in Florence I bought this fur for 80,000 lire; do you like it? What do you say?' Then they ran off on July 25th but they came back after a little."

The next day Mrs. Ferreira and her husband invited Mrs. Nola to go for a walk toward the wood.

"You know what, Andrea? Tomorrow I'll make a kite, then we'll go to the plain under the cemetery and fly it," said Sergio, but on their way back a young man stopped Mrs. Ferreira: "Happy? There's peace."

"What peace!"

"Yes, don't you know? Badoglio has signed the armistice and has said, 'We're ready to fight against any enemy.'" It was true.

The immense square was crowded with people who yelled, drank, played the violin, and discussed the news.

In the middle of the crowd, a woman moved forward, broke the chain of people who were blocking the way, and reached the church: "Mrs. Lucia! Mrs. Lucia! That day has come."

That evening there was a great joyous dinner at the Ferreira house in which the Nolas took part, and the mountain lit up all at once with little luminous bonfires: it and its inhabitants were also showing their joy.

But the Germans, the barbarians of the twentieth century, were prepared, and, on cue, they came out of their dens and invaded the barracks. The Italian army disbanded; it was catastrophe.

Long columns of men began to pass, some on horseback, some on foot, who were returning to their houses with their clothes torn and their feet often bare.

"Is this the way to Naples?"

"Huh? This is the way to Florence."

"Yes, and then to Naples; I'm going to Naples."

"Poor men."

And the horses set out again at a trot.

ALDO: When, on the evening of September 8th, he [Prof. N. M.] suddenly heard on the radio the announcement of the armistice and the invitation to take up arms against the resistance "whoever it came from," far from rejoicing, he immediately started to worry. He calculated to himself the enormous trap that was now closing, with many thousands of Germans in Italy, not to mention the consequences for the Jews of Italy. And when the next evening he heard silence on the Roman radio station and then on all channels came a voice with an angry accent in a fiery German speech (he later found out it was Hitler's) he felt his blood chill and glimpsed ruin before him. But how is it possible, he asked himself time and time again, how is it possible that a man like Badoglio had not perceived the very evident danger represented by so many heavily armed Germans among us? How is it possible that they won't consider us traitors and won't put Italy under the yoke they have already—even without any betrayal—forced upon other European states?

RACHEL: *Everyone was happy because they thought the war would end. But Badoglio said that the war would continue. We were at Impruneta when this happened. We were out taking a walk, Aldo wasn't there, he was in Florence to be nearer his mother, and we were there because the Germans weren't rounding us up yet, understand?*

Then did you feel betrayed by Badoglio, or not?

No, no, no. Nothing, nothing.

You didn't have any hope?

Everyone was happy, etc., but Aldo, who thought better of it, wasn't happy, because—happy, yes, but he didn't hope that the war was over, understand? Because he said that the war would continue, and meanwhile all the soldiers escaped. At Impruneta, we saw all these soldiers, etc., there were no more buses, there was nothing, understand? It was all upside-down.

44

In Florence, Professor Nola was giving lessons to a university student in his study, when the student, who had good hearing, interrupted the reading of the *Aeneid*.

"What's the matter?"

"Nothing, I thought . . ." and he started to read again, "'To the fields that from the name of Alba . . .'"

"Well, don't you know it?"

"Yes, but I hear a song . . . '. . . were later called Alban. Then King Latinus had his great stall there,'—do you hear?"

"But what do you hear? I—" But a very loud song interrupted his sentence:

"*Brothers of Italy, Italy is awake, her head is girded by Scipio's helmet, where is . . .*"

The song moved farther away.

"It must be some fool."

The student, unconvinced, continued his lesson: "'When he stopped and looked back in vain for his lost friend.'"

"*Farewell, my dear, farewell.*"

"Professor, allow me to look out the window."

"Please do."

As soon as he looked out, he let out a cry: "Come see, professor!"

A long parade with an immense tricolor flag at the front was moving through the old street and all the old memories seemed to live again in those songs of the ancestors while people appeared at the windows and cried sincere tears.

"*Farewell, my beautiful, farewell, the army is going, if I don't leave too, it would be cowardice!*"

"*Red shirt, burning shirt, in Milazzo I'll be a sergeant, red shirt, burning shirt!*"

"*The tricolor flag is the most beautiful that there is!*"

"Professor, allow me to join in the demonstrations."

"As long as it's clear I didn't send you."

ALDO: That same night, he was in Bellosguardo, where he could be with his ailing mother, guest of some cousins. He had gone there from the 12th of August, following repeated aerial strikes, even more than one a night; and every time the alarm was accompanied by anti-aircraft cannon fire, it was wise to descend into the cellar, to shelter. To do that they had to transport his mother too, who was affected by advanced encephalitis, which kept the poor thing from speaking and expressing her own desires and needs. They had to set her down gently on a blanket and carry her down with four or six people on a very steep stairway, and neither the nurse, who easily fell prey to fear, nor the professor, with the help of other people, was strong enough to bear too great an effort. So after a night of double prolonged stays in the cellar, the professor asked permission of his cousin to move immediately into the villa, where the patient was transferred in the Misericordia's motor ambulance.

Soldiers beat on the door; they had been given their freedom by their respective divisions and they were looking for shelter and refuge, fearing, hour by hour, the arrival of the Germans. They requested civilian clothes, which the peasants gave them, and they hid their arms and packs among the plants in the garden. What an effect that nocturnal apparition had, what fear of bullying and trouble! Luckily they were educated young men and behaved themselves worthily.

That night as usual, Professor Nola went to sleep at Bellosguardo, to be with his mother. Around midnight there were two knocks at the door.

"Tapum, tapum!"

Iolanda, frightened, went to open up.

"We are escaping from the Corridoni Barracks, give us lodging or fight," and he showed his musket, knowing perfectly well that it was empty.

"Come in, come in, I'll call the professor."

"Yes, yes."

"Professor, professor: there are two men here looking for lodging."

"What men?"

"Two soldiers."

"Tell them that at this time of night, one does not wander about the streets."

"But they're escaping from the barracks."

"There's no room here, tell them."

"But they've already come in and they're drinking."

"What?"

"They're already drinking wine."

"I see: if I don't get up . . . ," thought Professor Nola.

When he arrived in the sitting room fifteen minutes later he found five of Mrs. Dora's candles lit one behind the other on the good table, now completely ruined by the hot wax, and two flasks of wine were already empty.

"Hello," said the soldiers, red like poppies.

"Hello," responded in chorus the other twenty soldiers who had entered.

"I'm infantry corporal Giorgio Candeli."

"I'm sailor Beppino Maraddi."

"I'm artillery soldier Giulio Strani."

"Well, it's a pleasure to meet you all. And the uniforms, how come they're all the same?"

"We stole them: there was a Fascist fool with a lot of pins and decorations and he wanted to command; he had about a hundred uniforms under his arm, I killed him with the last cartridge—and what a shot! Right in the heart! And we took the uniforms and disguised ourselves."

"Fine. All right, Iolanda, make them leave as soon as possible and close the door with that double padlock; I'm going to bed."

But Iolanda already had a big crush on the little corporal Giorgio Candeli, with his big black eyes and blond whiskers, and the nurse had her work cut out to convince Iolanda that you don't make love to the first man who comes along.

The next night Professor Alessio was forced to take his mother back into the city so that this kind of thing wouldn't happen again, but the crush Iolanda had on Giorgio Candeli didn't end just like that, and every minute the little corporal would come to mind.

"Iole, set the table."

"Words!"

"Iole, there's a handkerchief missing."

"Words!"

RACHEL: *Poor thing, she died, she threw herself in the Arno. We had sent her away because we didn't like her conduct, because . . . she stood at the window and sent notes to her boyfriend.*

To the soldier?

To the soldier.

To this one?

Yes, or another. I don't know who it was. So we didn't want to take the responsibility, so we sent her away. And then she went into another house, and then it happened that she threw herself . . . we read it then in the paper. That she had thrown herself in the Arno. For what, no one knows. (Laughs)

ALDO: Meanwhile the professor called to invite his family, which had evacuated to Impruneta, to return as soon as possible to the city, and his wife was very alarmed about the news reported by several peasants of having seen German columns marching on the Cappello Bridge on the Chianti road. And in the morning in Florence cannon shots were heard from Futa [an Apennine pass between Bologna and Florence], and around 10 A.M. one of the first groups of Germans had arrived and installed itself at the garrison in Piazza San Marco, hoisting a great German flag. Alas, what a terrible effect this sight had, though it was foreseen! And when Prof. N. M., going down into the city, had to cross the Carraia Bridge and saw the two entrances protected by two large cannons, he exclaimed to himself, "Poor Italy! Poor Florence!" And immediately he turned to the task of finding a way to get his family back in, but the taxis didn't want to have anything to do with him, for fear of being requisitioned, so much so that very few even risked parking. So he looked for the driver of an aquaintance, who had even dismantled and hidden his car. But he pointed out a garage where, after much insisting and negotiating, the professor arranged for a car that would arrive at Impruneta at 6 the following morning and go by secondary roads into Florence. The driver would risk the trip for 300 lire.

45

Mrs. Lucia phoned her husband every other minute: "Look, the Germans are about to come, isn't it time to go?"

"No, wait. Everything's calm."

"But look, the buses aren't running anymore."

She was right: the Germans were rapidly descending from Brenner and soon would be at the gates of Florence. Wherever they went they mercilessly took vehicles, livestock, food.

Finally Mr. Nola decided to look for a way to have the family come.

"Sorry; without a permit from the German Command . . ."

"Sorry; for less than 1,000 lire . . ."

"Sorry but I can't risk my car."

One man alone, for 500 lire, risked his beautiful black car and picked up Mrs. Nola and her children at Impruneta.

"You have a permit?"

"Yes, yes."

And it sped and sped, crossing the little-used roads like lightning; the poor driver trembled when the ugly mugs in khaki uniforms passed with machine guns at their shoulders.

Through a hidden little street, they came out at Poggio Imperiale, decorated with a great sign: "Deutsche Command." They went down the avenue of the Medici at top speed, passed Via Romana like a flash without paying attention to the cries from people who almost got run over, grazed the tails of dogs who fled, terrified, came close to knocking someone off the Santa Trinità bridge, and took Via del Moro, startling the high buildings which seldom saw automobiles in the narrow street. When he arrived, he said: "We didn't have a permit!"

And under the noses of the not-so-shrewd German cops, he returned to his garage.

ALDO: How the children were alarmed to see the streets full of German soldiers and all that flurry of trucks, cannons, motorcycles . . . what a sense of subjection to the foreigner, "Axis" aside! And then the special occupation currency, the bullying on the tramways, the traffic limitations, the meddling with the street police . . . university locales, the pretty garden connected to the Semplici house, all was occupied . . . But at least in the beginning private life went on calmly for everyone. The divisions of the "SS" (Schutzstaffel) hadn't yet arrived, to the point that even kosher butchering, prohibited by the racist laws, and immediately allowed again after July 25th, continued for several weeks without any difficulty. So did services at the synagogue, although wisdom counseled the directors to limit their officiating to a minor sermon and to suspend it on the day of the great fast of atonement (Yom Kippur), to avoid the substantial crowd that usually showed up for such an occasion.

46

Outside, after sabbath services at the temple, Jews gathered in groups to discuss some bad news.

"Do you understand?" says the principal Sonnino nervously to his colleagues, among whom are Professor Nola, Professor Viterbo, who had suffered poverty for many years, and a very worried Professor Cassel. "In Rome the Germans have blackmailed the Jewish community for I don't know how many pounds of gold, and then arrested many, many families and taken them who knows where."

"It's just talk."

"No, no, it's like what happened in Poland."

"Well! We'll see about that."

Even Master Angelo laughed about that. "Just imagine! Now, of all times!"

ALDO: Rumors began to circulate of the imminent arrival of the "SS" squads, who had already operated round-ups of the Jews in Rome, where the price of 50 kilos of gold had already been imposed on the community, on pain of the execution of various hostages. It was collected in a few hours, with the help of the Holy See, which promised to make good the difference, but then it was discovered that the community was able to put together the 50 kilos requested on its own.

Mrs. Lucia, on the other hand, was very worried, and thought about barricading herself in her house, hermetically sealing the doors and the windows, and sending Mrs. Alice to a nursing home. But one needs air, food—how to do it? The impossible idea of barricading was abandoned, although Andrea came up with a mountain of solutions, not very feasible practically speaking; the idea of sending Mrs. Alice to a nursing home was, on the other hand, considered. But it was very difficult to find free rooms and only after many days was a room found in a nursing home called Villa Faward in Rovezzano.

Poor Mrs. Alice left the house she had prepared and yet enjoyed so little; smiling, she succeeded in saying "Goodbye" under her breath, but from that day on, without the affectionate attentions of her family, she never again improved and, little by little, gave in to the disease. The next day Mrs. Lucia went with the children to see her mother-in-law.

"Mamma Alice! Remember when you held me and read me stories?" asked Milena, but she got no answer.

4 7

Not long after that, Uncle Angelo, his sister [Dora], and her husband [Benedetto Sadum] decided to go live with their dear friends in the Mugello in order not to be hunted, and they put their house in Bellosguardo at the Nolas' disposal. The Nolas took advantage of this and closed their house in the city, saying they were going to Impruneta.

The first families began to disband. Mrs. Anna-Milena's mother withdrew into a nursing home; Lucio, his sister, and the baby boy, took an apartment around Pian dei Giullari. But these were merely precautions, no one imagined what would happen that famous [November] Saturday.

ALDO: The autumnal Jewish festivities were celebrated quietly, when lo and behold on November 6, a sabbath of unhappy memory for the Jewish community of Florence, a round-up of Jews began early in the morning in the zone around the temple and the Santa Croce quarter, with ambulances and other vehicles. Prof. N. M.'s family was at Bellosguardo, where it had returned October 14, faced with the alarming rumors coming from Rome. But since that address could be dangerous too, given that the villa belonged to Jews, the professor had booked a room at the home of the good Mafini family in Via Borgognissanti, which they had completely furnished.

Mr. Alberto Orvieto, living around the Campo di Marte, closes house, gets his things together, and sets off toward a little apartment where he has put his family. It isn't wise to stay at home.

A few hours later, Mr. Lucio Gallichi has occasion to pass by there and turns, from behind a tree, to see a terrifying scene: a small truck with the markings of the famous Schutzstaffel (Security Staff, SS) was stopped in front of the Orvieto house and two of the SS, with skulls on their epaulets, kick the main door, closed just a few hours before by Mr. Orvieto, and after breaking through the bolts with pliers they enter as if they own the place.

Master Lucio already understood what this meant and, having taken the first tram, arrives at Porta Romana, crosses Viale Petrarca, and gets to Bellosguardo heated and out of breath.

"Lucia, Lucia, the round-ups have begun!" and closing the door with a thump runs away to warn the others.

Mrs. Nola paces up and down, dismayed; then it is decided: they will go to the little room she has arranged in Via Borgognissanti. She packs the suitcases and bags and when her husband returns with the children, she alerts them. They close the house and set off toward the unknown.

ALDO: And when the professor returned to the villa, he found his wife and children in the grip of a great fervor, with suitcases ready and a bag packed with the most urgent provisions. There was a moment of uncertainty as to whether they should eat lunch or abstain, but the professor, endowed by nature with a calm and faithful character, said that they should stay there to eat lunch, which was, moreover, made with unusual speed, and then immediately off to the city, by different roads, to the prearranged room: from this moment the real and particular odyssey of the family begins, which will not pause, one could say, if not momentarily and precariously, for more than a year!

48

In the immense expanse, the grass alone, damp and rotten, was the only witness of that precipitous flight across the fields with bags, suitcases, and every kind of garment.

Andrea fearfully crosses the border of the two fields with a shopping bag heavier than he in his hands and a pile of four raincoats on his arm; Papa comes behind, worried, with two suitcases; then Milena, braver; and finally Mamma, who in the hurry left her dressing gown on under her overcoat. They walk with the fear that one of the SS is shadowing them step by step; they cross the large street of Marignolle. At Porta Romana it begins to rain, they put down their cases, put on their raincoats, and continue slowly down the avenue—every tree is one more piece of ground they have put behind them. At the last oak tree, Andrea breathes a large sigh, and they are in the great Tasso square where the German trucks pass by quickly. One of them stops, and Mrs. Lucia immediately envisions herself in a concentration camp.

"Street . . . Arezzo?"

"Ja." The truck left again and everyone starts off hopefully down the little San Frediano street, then Nazario Sauro square; there they split up so as not to be conspicuous, to meet again in Via Borgognissanti.

Mr. Nola arrived first and a minute passed, and then two, ten, fifteen, and no one appeared from the other corner.

"Have they been taken? What could have happened to them?"

Finally they appeared at the curve; they had met Mr. Eugenio Arlib, who had told them that the SS had been at Mrs. Costanza Salmi's house and had ruined everything.

The little room in Borgognissanti rented from a couple without children was large enough to accommodate four beds organized as best they could, no room to spare, twenty centimeters squared off to turn around in, and a series of suitcases destined to become a table. The minuscule window looked out on a filthy courtyard where the cry sounded, "Water! Water, Caterì!" since water arrived on the upper floors only when it wasn't being used below.

There all four of them burrowed for eight days, but on the ninth, while Milena was going down to buy bread, the door of the first floor opened and there appeared the terrible face of a man who looked like a gangster.

"Who are you? The girl from upstairs?"

At the end of her typed and bound version of Leo's book, Rachel wrote:

My Leo was not able to continue his Diary! We had many frightening vicissitudes, going from one hospitable house to another!

Then after many scares and much wandering we went to Anghiari until the end of the war . . .

R. N. M.

PART THREE

Aldo's Journal

A Tale of Life Lived

·············· ❁ ··············

Aldo kept careful notes in tiny pads throughout the war and later expanded them into a journal/memoir. In it, he refers to himself as "the professor" and to his family as "the N. M." I have edited his journal for length.

We pick up in Aldo's journal where his son's journal leaves off: on November 6, 1943, the round-ups begin in Florence, and the Neppi Modonas rush to their first hiding place in Via Borgognissanti.

THE DIFFICULTIES began immediately, because the landlord, an extremely arrogant and ignorant type, did not want to allow the subletting, and particularly to four people. So they lived there under a temporary concession, until one fine day he announced their eviction within twelve hours, threatening to throw all their things out into the street . . . However this wasn't one of the worst periods, because the house searches quieted down after a few days and, except for a few sporadic cases, there were no real round-ups for several months.

RACHEL: *The landlord . . . was a butcher, he killed animals on the sly, and believed that we could spy on him . . . And so he didn't want his tenant to rent. If not, he says that he would go to police headquarters to say that she had—he didn't know that we were Jewish—but that she had rented, because when you rented, you had to go to police headquarters to report it. Understand?*

I understand. So it wasn't that you were Jews.

No, no, no. It was for this, because he was slaughtering animals . . . And we were afraid and fled.

Anyway, they were evicted, they had to decide what to do, and during the night the N. M. couple developed the plan of going once again to Impruneta, the same day in which their cousins left Florence for a destination unknown. At Impruneta, confiscation measures had been taken for only two or three families who had spent the summer there and had left some things there. And since no one knew the "race" of Prof. N. M.'s family, everything proceeded smoothly without trouble until the Castelvecchio declaration and the consequent orders for the immediate arrest of all Jews, with the subsequent exclusion of mixed couples and their children, if they were Catholic. There were also some lovely days of physical recreation in those two months, because the mostly sunny and dry season permitted, or rather, invited, long walks; in fact the professor and his two children often left the house at 7 A.M. with food for a snack and returned around noon, having stored up a good provision of healthy air. They went to the Falciani Bridge, to Ferrone, to Strada in Chianti, to Mercatale, crossing woods and fields full of attractions. The professor passed the rest of the day in his study because he was preparing the girl for admission to eighth grade and the boy for sixth grade.

The worst was going to Florence, at least two times a week, above all because the professor had to go see his mother, who had been transferred to the Villa of Rovezzano Nursing Home, it being imprudent to keep her at home with the continual air raid alarms. How it hurt to go see her! You could see the joy that lit her face, the effort to talk, the resigned yielding in the face of growing weakness . . . As long as she had stayed at home, she enjoyed the assiduous care of two nurses, one at day and one at night, and the constant concern of her son (who from the day the illness began—August 14, 1942—hadn't left the house except for brief moments, for indispensable errands, or to go to school) and of her daughter-in-law, bound to her by a quite moving filial affection. They had succeeded in keeping the patient as comfortable as possible, above all due to the incessant care taken with her food. The freshest eggs were for her, as were the best filets of fish. What a sad distance, what an emptiness in the great house—despite her absolute silence—the day she left it never to return!

RACHEL: *At this nursing home, we always had our own paid nurse. Some days after Mamma Ada moved there, Aldo went to see her all the time, and the proprietor would tell him either "Come" or "Don't come" because often there were Germans there, understand?*

I also went to see her. Poor thing, she didn't speak anymore, she didn't do anything, she was in her chair alone, her face full of flies. She didn't even have the strength, poor thing, to do anything about them. So I went back home and I said, "Aldo, if we have two cents, it's all because of Mamma Ada. Therefore, Mamma Ada should continue to have her own nurse."

One of the children always wanted to accompany the father, in turn, and as long as the trips could be made by bus, it wasn't too bad, although the buses were so crammed that it was a real torture to stay on them the hour or more of waiting to depart and then the forty-five minutes of the trip. But one fine morning, who showed up? The Brigadier of the Carabinieri with two soldiers who were checking everyone's papers, not permitting anyone to board who wasn't provided with documents proving the necessity of his going to Florence. And so father and daughter set off on foot to Tavarnuzze and from there proceeded by tram, and the trip was so pleasant that they did the same on their return, and many other times, too. Above all, those morning trips, in the middle of winter, almost running, with hands and feet at first frozen and then hotter and hotter, provide one of the nicest memories of that period: what dawns, what beautiful fog! Not even the rain frightened them; one time, they were returning when a tremendous thunderstorm struck, but it didn't in the least discourage the intrepid pedestrians, with all their burden of bags and satchels full of purchases and provisions. Among these it's worth remembering a glass jar full of eggs conserved in liquid lime which replenished the family larder every week.

How you adapted even down there! The apartment was charming, with good exposure, except for the days when the north wind penetrated from every side. But between trunks and suitcases, it was crowded, and the badly made chimney pipe didn't let enough smoke pass through, so that the kitchen filled up with carbonic acid, making the mother and the girl seriously ill. At first the whole family gathered at the table in the kitchen, then, because of the smoke, preferred to take its meals in the children's room, on a minuscule card table, resting bottles, pans, and trays on the ground!

The children did all they could to make themselves useful, the girl in the kitchen and in making the beds, and the boy in setting the table and other jobs. Both of them went from one part of the town square to the other doing the shopping and the errands. What a school in the simple life and in privation these months were! A far cry from proper service, lunch served, and shoes polished by the maid! . . . The Jewish youth of Italy encountered punishment and sufferings, sorrows and privations, hardship and extreme discomfort early on—before and far more than other Italians. The persecution against them started many months before the Germans turned their rabid, inhuman, barbaric outbursts on all Italians, from which no one escaped until the moment of liberation, which arrived later and later, as [the Allies] proceeded slowly from the south to the north of the peninsula. But for the Jews such suffering was law, not abuse, for which those guilty in any case could not be prosecuted; their actions were legal! Oh incredible, to behold the provision, as they called it, for immediate arrest and shipment to concentration camps! What an evening and what a night it was when the professor's family learned of such orders! It was a neighbor, a trustworthy master bricklayer who, returning from Florence, brought the *Nuovo Giornale,* the newspaper, to read, where the measure was published, and when the girl laid eyes on it she let out a desperate cry and everyone devoured with their eyes the few lines that drily reported the order regarding the Jews. This order brought instant fear; it could be presumed that the arrests would begin as soon as the next day. Nevertheless, the professor went back to Florence, leaving a fearful family, to gather provisions and to organize, while there was still time, some of his most pressing affairs.

Then, some extenuation secretly communicated to the authorities momentarily excluded the *discriminati* and those older than seventy years, but quite soon the first exclusion was abolished and the German authorities didn't pay any attention to the second. On the contrary, a charming thing happened: the old people were almost the only ones to remain in their houses, believing themselves to be protected by the law, and so the SS could without difficulty "collect"—as one said—the poor old people, truly harmless, and make them follow the common fate: first prison, then the cattle cars to be sent, well sealed, to Poland . . .

The professor's mother, meanwhile, was rapidly getting worse, despite all the efforts to save her, and one could easily foresee that the end to such suffering was near. A few days before her final decline, the German authorities requisitioned the villa where her nursing home was based, and in twenty-four hours all the patients had to be cleared out. The management, taken by surprise, was unable to find anything but a smaller villa, occupied until then by a German command,

and insufficient for everyone, and so, after various yesses and nos, at the last minute it declared that it wasn't possible to take Mrs. N. M. there. Her son, dismayed, phoned the best-known clinics and nursing homes, but in vain. Desperate, he turned to the Jewish Hospice, where by a miracle he was able to find an empty bed. Taken there by ambulance at 5 P.M., the patient was in agony by 7 P.M., and around 8 P.M., she was breathing her last, attended by her son and by others present, with all the religious comforts. These were a great consolation for the professor, who was, like his mother, profoundly religious, and it seemed to everyone a true divine miracle that in such terrible times, the good deserving lady, beloved by everyone, could have those comforts which were then denied to most people—partly out of the relatives' fear and partly out of real impossibility. Nothing was neglected: the care of the corpse, its washing and laying out, the ritual prayer before, during, and for a month after the burial, the accompaniment to the cemetery and deposition in the grave in the presence of at least ten men.

For months, Jews hadn't dared to go in such numbers to the cemetery, and even for such an occasion, they took care to arrive in small groups, on foot or by tram or bicycle. They even had to resort to a fiction: on the funeral carriage the cross was not removed, as it usually was, and this was authorized by the head rabbi himself, to avoid the Germans' identifying the religious faith—rather the "race"—of the deceased during the journey! How much you had to renounce painfully, at least in appearance, your own faith! It was like returning to the times of the Marranos of Spain . . .

RACHEL: *Poor thing, Mamma Ada, it was a Friday, they brought her, I think at 7:30, at 8 she was dead . . . Then she stayed there, dead, for three days, because there was no gas to carry her to the cemetery. And we took a Catholic funeral carriage because Rabbi Cassuto (poor thing, who was deported and didn't return) had said in a speech that we Jews, he says, unfortunately, we would all die if they had their way. That we shouldn't use a Jewish funeral carriage without a cross, take one with a cross because for us to use that cross is like . . . self-preservation.*

LIONELLA: *For me [Mamma Ada's death] was truly the end. If childhood had already ended in '38, in '42 [when Ada got sick], the tragedy began.*

She was young, no?

Then she seemed old, but she was seventy-two, seventy-one . . . seventy. Not at all old,

right? . . . Soon my age. Seventy. But then she was a very robust woman . . . Very ro-
bust. Mentally, in short. An exception. I always took my example of life from her.
Thank goodness, she lived long enough to set that example.

After a week, the professor and his family went back to pay respects to the
venerated corpse, according to the strict forms of mourning they observed
scrupulously, sitting quietly in their house at Impruneta. Then, bombs hurled
from airplanes right within the cemetery walls (given its adjacency to the gas-
holder and other industrial plants in the Rifredi zone, such a sacrifice was inevitable) and police surveillance persuaded them not to repeat the visits, and so
the son for many years could not have even the comfort of reciting a prayer at his
mother's grave. The situation was so tragic, he was driven to exclaim, "That
saintly woman left just in time!" In fact, as soon as the nursing home was transferred to Poggio Imperiale, the SS came and carried off all the Jews recovering
there, without regard to age or state of health. Among them was a couple of German origin, very well known in Florence, since for a long time the husband had
owned one of the greatest emporia in the city.

RACHEL: *[The Siebzehner] were old, they were no less than the proprietors of a very*
famous store here, it was called the "48." They took them to a new nursing home. But
meanwhile, lo and behold, the Germans who were there, they take them. Husband
and wife. And they never came back.

Mrs. N. M.'s departure was preceded by a few months by that of another distinguished lady, Mrs. Costanza Salmon, who had recovered in the same nursing
home. Destiny had it that a few days after she returned home, hers was one of the
first Jewish homes visited by the SS. They weren't satisfied with making a clean
sweep of everything they found in the apartment that was pretty and valuable,
but robbed the cellar too, slamming all the conserved eggs into the wall and
smashing rich crystal and porcelain services. Even the porter was forbidden to

have any contact with the lady, as was the domestic (Ayran), who was denied access to her own lodgings and mail delivery.

The morning of January 21, a young lady presents herself at the professor's home (Impruneta) and, with an air of surprise and of barely repressed anger, says, "Who are you?"

"The tenants of this apartment."

"I'm the owner and I didn't rent it to you, but to the lawyer, Bettino Errera."

"Fine, but he ceded it to us, his cousins."

"But I had agreed that the lawyer wouldn't be here and that he would only leave some trunks."

"And instead he has given it to us, what does it matter to you? Rest assured that we will keep it in excellent condition. Come in and see."

Once inside, she took out a newspaper and asked, "But you are Israelites?"

"Yes."

"And so you know that we can't rent to Jews; you'll have to leave the apartment free immediately: otherwise I'll be forced to declare your presence, and you are well aware of the consequences."

"All right, we'll go, don't worry."

"Right away."

"You'll leave us time to get our things ready, today is Friday; we'll leave Monday."

And there it was left and, with a kinder air, she said that she was very sorry to have to do it, but if not she ran the risk of being accused of philo-Semitism, and that naturally Monday, when she came to take custody, she would reimburse the rent for the remaining months. And so for the professor's family, another period of wandering and of adventurous and ever more tragic events began. Monday morning the landlady arrived with her husband, both making an effort to be courteous; *naturally* they didn't bring the money, saying that they had forgotten it, but that they would have it delivered as soon as possible. And, having handed over the keys, the family set off on foot to Tavarnuzze, each of them burdened by sacks and bags; the heavy luggage had been sent down early in the morning by cart.

RACHEL: *Our cousins Luisa and her husband had taken a little apartment at Impruneta. But since they left for Rome instead, they said, "Here are the keys, you go and hide yourselves." And we were there for quite some time, for many months. And the*

landlady, poor thing, had seen on walls in the street the photograph of General Graz
...Graziano ... I can't remember the name anymore.

An Italian general. [Graziani, the chief general under the Republic of Salò.]

An Italian general. And it said underneath, "Whoever takes in a Jewish family is an
enemy of the Fatherland." So she, who had rented her very house to Jews, got scared.
And she came to us when, only a few days before, my mother-in-law had died.

Now I'll tell you that it was around ... my mother-in-law died the 14th of Janu-
ary of 1944, she must have come on the 18th. Understand? And Aldo, you know we
Jews, the men, leave their beards be, they don't shave.

All at once, she comes. She says "But I didn't rent my house to you!" I say, "It's true,
you didn't rent it to us." I say, "But they are cousins of mine, and we came to take their
place." "But you are Jews?" "Yes." "I'm very sorry. You have to go. I can't give my house
to Jews because my husband works and he can have problems." She says, "Before com-
ing here I went to church to pray," she says, "to be able to come here and tell you this."
Understand? And so, we had to go.

So, I said to her, "Look," I tell a lie, I say, "my husband has an infection, he's not
well. But the doctors say that everything's getting better, that all's well. In a few, four,
five days, we will leave the house." And we did.

For some time now, several families of officials had been authorized to live in
the villa at Bellosguardo, with the understanding that the second floor would be
left at the disposal of the owners or their relatives.

And so the professor's family thought they had every right to go stay there,
but they found only one room free, the other being full of furniture moved out
of the first floor. On account of which the first night only the professor and the
son could sleep there, while the mother and the girl went to the lodgings in Via
Borgognissanti. The next evening everyone slept in the villa. They had had
many kitchen furnishings and necessities brought over, intending to leave complete autonomy to the family that remained there (the other two had returned
to the city for the moment). There was also a cousin of the professor's,
Valentina Neppi Modona, whose circumstances had brought her back to Florence after many years, and since she had no other relative who could take her
in, the professor welcomed her and left her in that villa, with the consent of the
cousins, even while his family was staying at Impruneta. But they couldn't find
a mattress that had been locked up in a room on the first floor by the other
family. So the professor's wife called the lady downstairs and asked her the favor

of returning the mattress sometime that day. "What? You think you can come stay here?"

"Most certainly, we are *discriminati*, and you have no reason to be concerned."

"Well, do what you will, but I can't give you the mattress."

That was exactly the wind that blew. It was even clearer the next morning, when the senior official who lived at the villa returned alarmed with his wife, saying to Prof. N. M.'s spouse that he had had to tell the Commissariat that the N. M. family was staying there with them and that therefore it would be wise if they left immediately! Since there wasn't any need to make this declaration, everything made them legitimately suspect that it was an expedient for sending that family of Jews away, and staying in blessed peace with all the space in that large villa at their disposal, without spending a cent. And under those circumstances, the desired result was quickly obtained, because, understandably, the first thing the N. M. family did was to get out of the villa. But it was impossible to return to Via Borgognissanti, braving the ire of the sullen landlord. And so, having needlessly carried the electric stove and the pots, the trunks and the suitcases, the mattresses and the pillows from the city to the country . . . once again, more expenses and no income—who could think of giving lessons at this point?—and with the expectation of soon not collecting even the pension, which had been raised, with successive increases, to a grand 400 lire! There should have been a final increase, it's true, of maybe 150 lire, but although it was supposed to be in effect from December 1, as of February it had not yet been paid!

So what to do, where to go? They had many friends in the city, but to whom should they turn at a moment in which it was very dangerous to walk around downtown, to be seen with others, in a period of general fear of having contact with Jews, who were considered to be foreign subjects of an enemy nation? To find yourself with your own house, but rented—however, not really your own anymore, since it was now managed by the organization specially created for the administration of buildings taken from Jews—with a nice rented apartment, now occupied by a Milanese family and an insurance company; with a villa made available by cousins; with a room rented from a family—with four lodgings, in other words, to find yourself without a bed to sleep in that very night, without a room to put your body in! What a cruel destiny, though, of course, less cruel than the one faced by those "collected" by the German SS, now headed toward who knows what atrocious fate.

RACHEL: *We could no longer come to this house [in Via dei Banchi], it was over. And we had someone who came to clean the stairs. The Germans came to look for us.*

And this man here said, "Jews? I don't know any. I know that one old one from the second floor here died, and on the third floor there was another old lady who died." She was my mother-in-law. And so those Germans didn't look for us any more.

So was he lying, or did he really not know?

No, he was lying. The man who cleaned the stairs knew perfectly well who we were.

The Segres lived in Via Masaccio . . . And when the Germans began to pick up the Jews . . . they went to get all the Jews in Via Masaccio, the ones who hadn't escaped. One family, they were mother, father (an engineer), and three daughters.

 When the Germans came to take them, they went in to get that family too, because they came with a truck, understand, and they put all the Jews they could in there. However, there was a store nearby, in Via Masaccio, on the corner of Via Mazzini . . . which sold cigarettes. You couldn't find cigarettes very often, so you had to line up for them and this girl, the youngest Segre, was there to wait for her turn to come, to get the cigarettes . . .

 And so, everyone was astounded, because not only she, but also the others, saw the Germans taking the Jews. And she turns, sees her father, her mother, everyone, and they're putting them in the German truck. And she wants to run to them, and all the people in line grabbed her. They said, "But you at least, come with us, you will be safe." Understand? So she was saved, poor thing.

And the others . . .

The others never returned. And she lives all alone, very fat, poor thing, it hurts me, hurts me. Only a little dog for a friend. Always with her dog.

 That afternoon, anxious and reluctant, the family presented itself at the house of a cousin's secretary to explain the situation. Moved, the young lady's mother offered to keep them for a couple of evenings in the little adjacent apartment belonging to a momentarily absent daughter, as long as it was done discreetly. So the problem was resolved for the moment but they had to plan immediately for the next move. Husband and wife racked their brains to think of whom to turn to, without coming up with any answers. Finally it occurred to Prof. N. M. to go see an old friend of his, the judge Agostino Agostini, Esq., who understood exceptionally well the critical situation the professor's family was in. He offered to telephone a family friend (Balsanti) at Settignano, who in fact arranged for a little room with a humble family of workers, the Messori (Mrs. Beccherini, Via della Pastorella, 39), where the professor and son could find hospitality, but just at night, making do with a sofa-bed that would have been barely sufficient for one person of regular proportions.

And so one fine evening, father and son, with a suitcase and various bundles, raincoats and umbrella, and blanket, go up in the tram and then in the trolley. They introduce themselves to the judge's family friend, who greets them with the utmost cordiality and introduces them to the family whose room they were renting. So began the long period when the professor's family was split into two groups. They reunited only for lunch, and, after spending the afternoon to-gether—always strolling about, or paying some visit, but for the most part spending hours in bars or cafés—they split up again before dark, so that father and son could get back to Settignano before too late on those frozen winter evenings, with a north wind that often blew furiously, with the ever-crowded trams and trolleys. Mother and daughter, on the other hand, braving the ire of the sullen landlord, returned to sleep in Borgognissanti, using the stairs as little as possible, since he often looked out from the door of his own apartment on the second floor as soon as he heard unfamiliar footsteps going up or down.

What months of sacrifice, of worry, in such a harsh season, with the children susceptible to frequent colds, to have to be constantly out in the street, when being out in the street was so dangerous! Without the force of will with which the N. M. couple were endowed, without their admirable endurance and firm faith in divine help, they would not have survived those months. And they did survive them, despite all the adversities that cropped up one by one and the problems that had to be faced every day, above all of an alimentary character. For instance, it would have been a shame to give up that liter of milk that their cousins still had delivered every day, but it was impossible to have it brought directly to an address that had to remain a secret. And so the milk was brought to the city lodgings where a hired man kept it on hand so that the professor could get it each time in a different prearranged location. Then the contents had to be divided in two, one of which was taken by the wife, the other stayed with the professor.

RACHEL: *I once said, "Aldo, I can't take any more of this life," of going to some family or some woman's house. And we were never all four of us together, when we were with these families, because understandably a family couldn't take all four peo-ple, and so two people in one family, two people in another, and then we got together at midday to eat in some far off place, not in the city, you understand . . . It was very difficult. And we were always looking at our watches, because if I was late, my Aldo would get very worried, and the same for me, if he was late . . .*

I said, "Aldo why don't we turn on the gas and die, all of us." And Aldo said to me, "But Rachel, you shouldn't say this. Look, what about your mother, your brother, your sisters, what would they say if we did such an ugly thing? We have to fight to save ourselves."

And I said, "Why? For my family whom I'll never see again, because they're not even in Rhodes? Rhodes was closer, from here," I say, "But now they're in Africa, in Rhodesia." And Aldo said to me, "I'll do everything possible so that you can go see your family."

And so in '49, Aldo, who was already teaching again in the schools, asked the state head of salaries to take some money out of his salary every month, and he gave it to me, he bought me a ticket and I went to Rhodesia. Thus I saw my family. Because Aldo says, "I promised it to you, so go." And so I went.

Certainly in the long run this life would be dangerous and tiring, and it was necessary to find a way to reunite: but how? As soon as he reached Settignano, the professor had looked for lodgings suitable for the whole family, and even under the guidance of a roadcrew foreman, he and his son spent a whole afternoon knocking on doors throughout the countryside between Settignano, Vincigliata, and Fiesole, as far as Cutignano. But it was useless because there was not an attic or a barn that wasn't occupied by evacuees from Florence, Compiobbi, and other neighboring zones. The journey was not useless, however, because on his return the professor saw the name of a noted lawyer friend, Aldo Valori, at the entrance to a villa: inside, the family welcomed him with the utmost cordiality and promised every effort on his behalf. And so even in this period, there were strolls through the sunny countryside; and in the splendid morning, the southwest wind and the warmth of family friends sweetened the spirits of our protagonists, more alarmed every day by the news of what was happening around them.

The troubles continued . . . after about ten days, the family where the father and son were sleeping said that a relative of theirs was coming back and they could no longer accommodate them for the moment; if necessary, they might try . . . in an emergency . . . after a little. It was clear, though, that the real reason was that they feared that their extended stay, if not officially declared, would be noticed. And so renewed searches through trusted friends, and this time a humanitarian colleague of the professor's, Prof. Giulio Giannelli, offered to keep one child at his house for some time and made his sister's lodgings in the city immediately available, without a declaration. And so father and son, with suitcases and bags, moved on again . . . Now they slept in a vast room in a double bed and could use a little parlor and a kitchen, where every morning, the professor boiled milk and cooked an egg for his son, prepared the slices of bread and marmalade, washed the cups and the bowls, then made the bed and swept, while the boy dusted. There at least there was a telephone, which, as long as he was cautious, he was able to use.

Meanwhile there were other complications: the boy got sick with the flu and had to change places with his sister—she went to sleep for a few days with her father and he with his mother. Then the mother too had to stay in bed a few days and then at home, and so the girl, who had returned to her, went out only for errands and for midday meals, meeting her papa and her brother at a predetermined dairy shop. But they couldn't stay there very long either, to be prudent, and, lacking any other solution, there was nothing to do but to go back and beg the hospitality of the good family in Settignano. But even up there, there were unforeseen problems: on the floor above, the son of a tenant was a Republic of Salò Fascist! So even more prudence than usual was indispensable, as was leaving very early in the morning and returning only late at night.

And staying inside wasn't completely safe either because the basement, connected to the ground floor inhabited by the professor—which he only used at night, according to the terms—was rented to the family of an official from police headquarters. The professor therefore had to be careful not to reveal who he was! And the wife would be very pleased to strike up a conversation with the taciturn professor . . .

Nor were things going any easier at the Massini house in Via Borgognissanti, where the landlord had already threatened another eviction, and they urgently needed another arrangement, which they couldn't find. They knocked on this door, they knocked on that. Finally a kind lady who had a store on the banks of the Arno offered to host the mother and daughter for a few days in a dark mezzanine above the shop, where they could set up a bed and use a little kitchen.

RACHEL: *Barberis, she was called . . . She was a knitter . . . I went to her place to beg her to find me a place to sleep . . . And then she started to cry, because she cared a lot about me. And then, suddenly, who was using the telephone? A young man, who was more or less forty years old . . . And then all at once I see that she is telling my story. And I got a little upset, I say to myself, what's happening?*

And so this gentleman calls me and says to me, "Listen, Madam, Mrs. Barberis has told me everything. Look, I'm the son of a milliner with a shop on the Arno. Behind the millinery, there's a mezzanine, which I keep for when I go to the theater in order not to go all the way back to Fiesole, I sleep here . . . And I can give it to you, so that you can sleep there. Only, not all four, which draws too much attention, but two people can come sleep."

And I was quite moved, so I thanked him, and so I left right away and I told Aldo. And that evening we went there. And when we arrived, [his cousin] had already made the bed and had put newspapers on the windows. Because in the evening, the guards pass by there and they didn't want them to see the light, understand, since we were already in the middle of the war. But it was also because if they saw a little light, they could say, "Who's that inside? It's thieves."

This man with the mezzanine didn't want a penny. Nothing, nothing, nothing.

There was nothing to do but accept, while in the meantime, the professor was forced once again, as he had anticipated, to abandon Settignano to take advantage once more of the kindness of his university colleague in Viale Alessandro Volta, although its location was fairly dangerous, given the intensification of enemy aerial attacks around Florence. But even here, on top of everything else, new complications: a nest of Englishmen had been discovered with a family right in the vicinity of his building, and so there were investigations, controls, searches. And one evening coming back home, father and son were stopped at the top of Piazza Savonarola by a Republican patrol, which in the light of their flashlights checked the identity of every passerby on the basis of their identity cards. Luckily everything went smoothly, and only resulted in a terrible scare for the boy, who was already picturing seeing his papa taken and having him disappear forever . . . because the terror of the SS had so insinuated itself into that still childlike and delicate mind that in every uniformed German he saw an agent of the SS and was already more than certain it was so impossible to save oneself that every precaution would be useless.

LIONELLA: *Once he was with Papa during a round-up in Piazza Savanarola. Papa had thrown him in a garden, to hide him in the trees. Luckily, Papa was pretty old, they were looking for young men to draft. They weren't looking for Jews. On the street in general they weren't looking for Jews, they were looking for young men.*

RACHEL: *A German soldier stopped him and asked to see his papers. He didn't have false ones yet, but he wasn't, let's say, Cohen or Levi, so they let him go. Anyway, they were looking for a British prisoner who had escaped, not Jews.*

When Aldo went back to get Leo, he was shaking like a leaf.

Just reasons for this idea weren't lacking, after all. Among the facts that had hit [Leo] hardest was the arrest—in truly dramatic circumstances—of an old cousin, Mrs. Matilde Nissim, so beloved that everyone had called her "Aunt." The protection of the law and the guarantee of police headquarters were worth nothing: at first she was ordered by a squad of Republican Fascists not to leave her home, the pensione where she had lived all by herself for years. She was esteemed and well liked by everyone for her refinement, her natural distinction, the goodness of her heart, her readiness to relieve every suffering, her generosity to relatives and acquaintances. Then she was told by police headquarters that the order she had received was absurd, that she should come and go freely. But one ugly day two agents of the SS showed up and, having made her get in a car with one simple little suitcase, they took her away and, as in all such cases, nothing more was heard from her. They then returned to her room and, as usual, carried off anything that might have a certain value.

RACHEL: *She went to Via Cavour to speak, saying that she was alone, and that she had money in the bank and she had to go collect it, because if not, how could she live. "Oh," they said, "Of course you can go." And then she called us and she said, "But you know, they were so kind."*

The Germans?

No, they were Italians.

Italians, but . . .

It was for . . . the racial matters. And "You too can go to the bank," she said, and so on, poor thing. She went. In fact, the Germans went there, they carried her off, they

emptied her bedroom where she had some nice things, understand, some portraits of
her parents, etc., and they also took the bank teller who was Jewish.
  They say that she died right in prison here. Because first they put them in prison,
understand, and then they put them in trains.

Another upsetting case was that of a childhood friend of the professor, Enrico
Dalla Volta, who continued, as a *discriminato*, his business activity and went to
his office every day. One morning, the SS agents "collected him" and in the afternoon showed up at the pensione, believing his sister, who lived there with their
father, was Enrico's wife. When they discovered she was his sister, they took her
away, and since the old father, Prof. Riccardo Dalla Volta—a very well-known
economist—didn't want to separate from his daughter, they took him too.

RACHEL: *He was a professor, very well-esteemed, a good friend of the prefect of Flo-*
rence. This prefect had said, "Relax, because I won't let them do anything to you, or to
your family." This Enrico had been director of a bank . . . and then, as a Jew he
couldn't. He worked at another job now, I don't know what, but he had his office.
And, sure of the prefect, he went to his office, but he was betrayed . . . They take him,
two Fascists, two SS men get him. But he asked to make a phone call and he called the
pensione where he lived and had his wife hidden there, and so . . . the wife escaped.
Then the Germans heard that he has some people in a pensione, his wife. And they
went to look in all the pensiones. And they arrived at the pensione where Riccardo
Dalla Volta was hidden with his daughter, Margherita . . . Enrico's sister. And so,
these Germans went there and asked for the Dalla Voltas. Margherita, the daughter,
came out. "Ah," they say, "Come with us." She started to yell, and the father who was
in the next room came out too. And, so, they took him too. And that was that, noth-
ing more was heard from them. They died at Auschwitz.

Naturally for many days afterward one saw them carrying away his furnishings and above all books from his rich library. In the same way, books in quantity

were seen leaving the home of an old, very esteemed music critic (Buonaventura), once director of the Conservatory, after which he and his wife—two poor old people who for years battled with grave economic straits—were taken away.

Thus the cases multiplied in that gradual acceleration of the round-ups, no longer en masse, but singly and silently. There was no doubt that the situation was becoming more critical every hour. Many Jews no longer ventured outdoors; they stayed burrowed in precarious and unidentified lodgings.

Meanwhile a new act of infamy was perpetrated against them: their ration cards were not renewed! From the first of February, those of general goods, from the first of March, those of bread and fats, and so to appease their hunger they had to turn to the charity of many good people who were willing to give up their vouchers for meals in a *trattoria* and to procure bread and pasta, even depriving themselves. One could also find bread at compassionate shopkeepers', who set aside goods not bought by other consumers, like the grocer Emo Celli of Via dei Serragli, 95, whose son Walter came to bring us our groceries at our house in Via dei Banchi even after the end of the war.

RACHEL: *In Via dei Serragli there was . . . a shop that sold bread, sugar, cheese, tomato sauce, all the things that a family needs. However, we didn't have ration cards. We could have died of hunger, you understand. So one day I went to buy whatever I could without the cards, and then I went one other time. He understood that I was going without ration cards, I didn't buy anything that was rationed, but I bought other things. He called me into the back of his shop and he said to me, "I understand, Madam. You don't have a ration card. But I can make one for you. I can make a false one, with a false name, and thus, Madam, you can come buy things." Lionella said, "I don't know, Mamma, why everyone is so sweet, maybe it's your smile.". . . I found people who wished me very well.*

Anyway, as we were saying, the professor and his son had to leave the building in Viale Alessandro Volta once more. This time it was a modest family, living beyond the Ponte alle Riffe, to welcome them to their home. They adapted the dining room to a bedroom, with a sofa-bed and a crib, which the boy had to force himself into. The location was one of the city's most dangerous, right along the Faentina railroad tracks, but what fear could the bombings command compared to deportation to Poland? Because by now *discriminazione* meant officially nothing anymore and the risk of being picked up got greater every day, especially having to stay out and about all day to eat meals in public places. It's true that they were always humble trattorias chosen in advance on the outskirts of the city, and for the frugal dinners, cafeterias, very nice and economical—relatively—but often even there documents were requested and unpleasant surprises could be waiting at every moment.

In the period that we are recalling, the professor had mulled over the idea of leaving Florence as soon as possible with his family, and of making them safer, withdrawing to some tranquil little town, far from airplanes and the SS. And he had chosen a pleasant Casentino locality in the Apennines, served by a local rail line that, leaving from Arezzo, penetrated the ———— gorge and reached the plateau after Monterchi, cutting through its vastness to touch Sansepolcro, and from there proceeded to the City of Castello and Fossato di Vico. A lady had made a room available for some time, with access to a parlor and a kitchen, but it hadn't been opportune to leave Florence while the professor's mother was still alive. Now it was possible—but how to show up there with his own name and surname, how to get the ration cards reissued without having to rely any more on charity or to use the black market, which he had always abhorred?

Everyone's advice was the same: get a false identity card. The hesitations of the professor, whose moral uprightness wasn't accustomed to compromise with his conscience, were conquered at last by the spontaneously offered opportunity to perform a good deed of patriotic charity. He could help the "rebels," that is the patriots, by handing over a large sum of money, receiving in exchange a blank card, for himself and his wife, with the stamp of the Municipality of Catanzaro.

RACHEL: *Luckily Aldo ran into the president of the Tribunal who was a good friend of ours. He found Aldo on the street, he says, "What, Neppi, you're still in Florence?" He says, "Yes." He says, "You've got false documents, at least?" He says, "No, I haven't got them yet, I don't know, I don't even know how to get them made." "Listen, I'm telling you, as president of the court of law, go to Such and Such street, on the second floor, I think, or the third floor, you will find some young men, (partisans, they were) and they will give you what you want.". . . Lionella went with her father, and there was a group of anti-Fascists who were making them. They gave us the cards to make identity cards.*

LIONELLA: *Naturally when it was time to collect the false documents, it was decided that it was better that I go, since I was older. And so, if something were going to happen, it was better to save the littler child. In short, it was up to me.*

And there was this committee connected to CLN, National Liberation Committee, partisans, who prepared these documents. In a house right in the center of the city, in Piazza Sant'Elisabetta, where there was this round tower. This committee worked on the top floor. What bad luck! I was savagely afraid of climbing those stairs, you understand, to enter a prison, in short. "But Papa, we have to go up there?" And then, if the Germans come, scram, up! We are all taken up there, there's no other choice, you see? We had to have false documents, it was already very late, we were already at the end of February, it was a crazy thing. I was thirteen. And there were also two Jewish women who worked there, two sisters, very good, named D'Urbino.

And we climbed up, they gave us these documents, blank. And then the descent! I would have loved to have flown down the stairs; but Papa was afraid of the stairs, he says, "We have to go slowly." They never ended! Never! And I was afraid the whole time of hearing the Germans. Later, when I passed Sant'Elisabetta, I felt shivers like then, from the descent down those stairs. Then, please God, we got outside with these blank sheets.

But once he had them, they were the old kind, and backdated, that is, about to expire, so they had to get them renewed. Once they were compiled with a false name and address, a friend offered to have them validated for another three years in a Central Italian Municipality, La Spezia, and so they were entrusted to him.

RACHEL: *At La Spezia, they no longer had any identity cards to make new ones. To renew them, they simply stamped them, and it was the same with ours. They didn't even look at them, because there they had a stack this high to change, so they took them, boom, boom, boom, without even looking at the names.*

But since the cards were slow to return and the family could no longer prolong their stay in the room put at their disposal on the Arno, the professor's family was forced to leave with their own documents, as compromising as that was. The preparations were extremely dramatic and complicated, given that their luggage was scattered in six different places, in each of which it was dangerous to show one's face too often. It was therefore necessary to collect everything a little at a time, without attracting attention to their own home in the city, where they always had their principal nucleus.

RACHEL: *We had to leave for Anghiari. Aldo wasn't bringing in a penny, and so we had to have these bonds. And we found someone who would buy the bonds. But instead of for 100, let's say, for 50. But to us, it was all the same, it was enough to have some money. Because we had no earnings, and no bank to go and get some money.*

And so, Aldo said to me, "You go and ask if they will give you the bonds there in the back. But don't say that you are Jewish." I say, "No, I won't say, certainly."

I didn't send Aldo anywhere because I was always afraid that they would take him. So I go there and I ask for the manager. The manager comes. I say, "Listen, I am Mrs. Neppi Modona, and so on, and I wanted to withdraw the bonds that we have here." He says, "Yes, Madam. But you have to write me a registered letter that you want them." What could I do? I, a Jew, couldn't write a registered letter, because all the letters were opened, understand? So, I said to him, I say, "Look," I say, "I'm a Jew. And I would like these bonds because we have to go, we're going and we have to eat, because my husband doesn't earn anything anymore."

He was very moved by what I said to him. He sat down at the typewriter, he wrote a letter, he had me sign it, because this letter wasn't going by mail, where the Germans could open it. Then he says, "Come back in three days, and you'll have your bonds." And so, I got the bonds, and we sold them, and we left.

And when everything was finally prepared, and there was nothing left to do but send for the things to be picked up from the courier, that same day the professor's wife left just a few minutes before two plain-clothed agents climbed the stairs to ask about the professor himself! You can imagine with what anxiety he was received when, after a few hours, he turned up at that family's house to say goodbye! They were all on him, exclaiming that he should escape, that they could spy him on the street, that he shouldn't show his face in those parts anymore. And so by a thread—but a thread that doesn't break, supported by a destiny that eludes men but is willed by God—he was saved and was able once more to raise from his good heart and his pious soul, a word of thanks to Heaven, which not even the SS had yet succeeded in hindering . . .

The aerial attacks by now represented another serious danger: the alarms followed one upon the other almost every day, and many times during the day, obliging long stays in shelters, or endless marathons when the surveillance had slackened. Once the alarm came right when father and son were near the rail overpass, in the Piazza Vieusseux area, and they stayed in a small but solid refuge for more than an hour. Another time they were at Pino, the crosswalk, right there at the tracks and, with quick steps, proceeded to the Piazza del Duomo, finding safety—trusting in the judgment of the Allies—in the shadow of the dome, literally. Meanwhile the dismal booms, characteristic of the "dropping," were heard heavy and frightening from the Rifredi area, and soon it was learned that the electric locomotive depository and the whole adjacent zone of San Jacopino had been struck. The professor's thoughts ran immediately to a lady, a friend of the family, who was recovering in a nursing home right in that neighborhood. His anxiety grew when, approaching Via della Scala, he saw ambulances and Mobile Public Assistance Unit cars running up and down with the sign "Emergency." So as soon as they'd had their frugal lunch, the whole family rushed to San Jacopino . . . oh, what a terrifying and horrible vision! The whole front of the Villa Flora had collapsed; one could see half-torn rooms from the upper floors, people who were running up and down, prey to desperation, while military ropes were keeping them away from dangerous areas. And all around, rubble and devastation. Certainly the friend was under that rubble!

RACHEL: *We said to ourselves, who lives over there? Over there is the nursing home where our old friend lives, whom I had visited just the day before to say goodbye because we were leaving for Anghiari, where two of her sisters were hiding. And we went there, and that was a bad thing to do because Leo was there who was extremely alarmed. . .*

You all went together?

Yes. And to see the nursing home all bombed . . . you could see everything was destroyed and in ruins, you could see a part of the room where I had been two days before, with the wardrobe and the suitcases on top. Understand?

No. What did this mean?

It means that this lady either saved herself or fell down along with her things in the rubble.

In a breathless hurry, Prof. N. M.'s family went back toward Porta al Prato in search of a telephone, but they were all broken and they had to go all the way to a café on the corner of Via Borgognissanti to find one that worked. The professor calls her closest relatives at a villa nearby and gives one of the sisters the sad news, making it clear that hopes of finding the wretched lady alive were very slim . . . poor lady! A widow for many years, deprived since a couple of years back of her son-in-law, suffering for a long time without hope of recovery, now she left a bachelor son and a daughter with a little boy, both hidden by farmers at the Pian dei Giullari: how to inform them? There was no time to lose; the professor's wife and daughter boarded the tram and went to take the gloomy news up there, witnessing the agonizing scene of the young bride, prey to desperation. The son, meanwhile, having learned what zone was hit, had already rushed to the scene, and stayed to shovel the rubble, without touching food, for hours and hours, until well into the night, when he found intact the body of his beloved mother.

Rachel told me that this scene made a great impression on Leo.

LIONELLA: *Of course, on everyone. Because we went to see an area that had just been bombed, it was smoking, the ruins, dust, roofs that were falling down—in short not a place to take a walk! And then we saw the house torn apart, the son saw his mother under the rubble, definitely dead. He said, "Go tell my sister." So, we took a bus, up above Piazzale Michelangelo where she was hidden . . . And in this villa belonging to Jews was also a hidden Jewish woman, which we didn't know. There was this Jewish woman (a cousin of my friends from Rome), us, four Jews, this little boy who cried, tiny, attached to his mother's neck, "No, no, it's not possible, it's not possible! What are you saying to me?" Then the father of this friend of mine dug out the rubble all night together with the son.*

In short, we weren't obliged to go and make this pilgrimage. We did some crazy things perhaps. We were on the eve of our departure for Anghiari. Three days before. So we barely even saved ourselves with those false documents.

The funeral had to be held almost in secret, early in the morning, without even being able to provide for immediate burial, because of aerial attacks. What pain, what emotional suffering, what discomfort, to feel yourself so tormented by threats from every side, from the ground and the sky, and to have to keep everything inside—to submit to the terrible consequences of war, like everyone else, and not to be able to have the comforts which at least weren't denied to everyone else, however weak and illusory they were.

The air raid of March 11 had interrupted rail traffic and only after several days did the daily departures for Rome resume at the Campo di Marte station. It was therefore necessary to gather the hand-baggage there, a task that was anything but easy, since the checkroom was very small and means of transport in the city were extremely difficult to find, not to mention the exorbitant prices that by now were tacitly acknowledged.

Very early on the morning of the departure, the professor succeeded, with a special concession, in leaving two suitcases at the Campo di Marte station. And around 4 P.M., with a carriage, he transported other suitcases from Borgognissanti and Lungarno with the help of his son, when lo and behold, while he was waiting for his wife and daughter who were supposed to come with another carriage and a bag with provisions, the air alarm sounded. There was a general stampede, but he couldn't move, since he had to watch numerous suitcases, on account of which, in the face of his son's terrible fright, he was forced to stop in a doorway near there, trusting in divine mercy, in which he had profound faith; this protected him always. The alarm lasted a long time and meanwhile his wife and daughter, who had not found another carriage in the piazza, had boarded the tram. Naturally this stopped, and, from Piazza Beccaria, they had to proceed on foot, with the weight of their bundles and bags, full of worry for the two loved ones who were waiting for them. Finally they arrived exhausted, the girl in tears.

Reunited, there was a moment of panic when they entered the station, as soon as the alarm stopped, because there was a great movement of German troops. When they finally found their places inside, the ticket seller says that he's not at all certain that the train would depart, and that in any case who knows when it would . . . Imagine what prospects for the travelers! But things went better than

he had predicted, because around 6:30 P.M.—that is, a half-hour behind schedule—the train arrived, formed of livestock cars with wooden benches, except one
third-class car and one second-class car, this last reserved for the armed forces.
And so, since the N. M. family had second-class tickets, they rushed toward the
third-class wagon, making two, three trips up and down to carry the heavy suitcases, but there was absolutely no room, nor could they accept the invitations of
a few people. So they had to return in pitch darkness to the faraway point from
which they had moved to get themselves into a livestock car equipped with
benches. After hauling up their things in a great hurry, since the railway workers
were rushing them, they situated themselves partly on piled-up suitcases and
partly on the already-full benches; and around 7 P.M., departure!

What thoughts, what conflicted feelings in the hearts of the N. M. couple!
About to abandon themselves to the unknown, they were leaving, who knows for
how long, the city that had been so yearned for during months and months of life
in turmoil, of constant fear, of hideouts, of scraping by, to escape the clutches of
the cursed German SS and its Italian satellites. They aspired, of course, to get
far away from their residence, where the search, the hunt for the resident Jew
was constant, tormenting, but they were going to new hardships, certainly new
wanderings and privations, with two young children who had suffered so much
already. In a winter that was still harsh, they faced a nighttime voyage full of
danger, completely ignorant of the environment they were heading toward.

But at least they were accompanied by courteous strangers, for whom they
could be "Aryans," and it didn't give them misgivings to speak to them . . . And
so, a word with this one, a word with that one, and their souls felt comforted,
and, during the dark journey—luckily on a serene and calm night—the sandwiches were bitten into as were the little omelettes, the children's favorite.

With unhoped-for speed, at 10 P.M. the train stopped at Arezzo, and, in a
chaos of open platforms, of holes and rocks, those who had reached their destination got off—or rather were lowered down—and the suitcases were thrown to
the ground. And so the N. M. family found itself disoriented in the midst of the
tracks of a devastated station, unable, for the moment, to figure out where to go,
where to aim their feet. Then slowly, seeing the direction taken by the more practiced, they headed toward a large room darkened by a fireplace with a dying fire,
full of baggage and soldiers, stretched out on the benches or sitting on their bags.
The prospect of spending the whole night there was not pleasant, but luckily a
few railway workers proposed that they go to their well-heated warehouse
nearby and wait there until dawn to reach the trackman's lodge 2 km away, from
which the Apennine train left. This they did, after loading their luggage on a
cart. And the night passed well enough, conversing with those good people,

dozing, thinking about the past and the future, seated next to a nice constant fire fed by the abundant lumber furnished by all the houses hit by aerial bombs.

The next morning, at 5 A.M., with the little luggage cart, we go to the trackman's lodge, the actual head of the line of the little train that takes us to Anghiari, where we arrive at 9 A.M. Professor N. M. became from today Alfonso Nistri Maddaloni, son of Angelo and Castri Marianna, living in Via XX September, 35, Catanzaro (he was born in Marigliano [Naples] the 20th of November 1892, thus he was fifty-two years old). His wife, seeing electrical wires high above her, got frightened, believing them to be barbed wires for a round-up of children, but then understood her mistake right away.

At the station they saw the trunks they had sent some days earlier and during the day they transported them to the house of Mrs. Rosa Giabbanelli. The small town made a great impression with its location and view, with a magnificent panorama toward Sansepolcro, with tree-lined avenues, and a great street straight to the top of the hospital. Stupendous weather, well-furnished pastry shops. They settled quickly into Mrs. Rosa's house. There was an entrance, from which you entered the dining room, where Mrs. Rosa slept, and from there you passed to a great room, where the family spent the day. There was a three-quarter bed for the parents and the daughter Luisa and a sofa-bed—or rather, a straw mattress—for the son Leonida, a name that many believed to be feminine!

RACHEL: *Leo was called Leonida there at Anghiari, and they said, poor thing, "you know, this little boy, they gave him a feminine name: Leonida."*

. . . And did you choose [the names] . . .

At random? No! For example, Alfonso, Aldo, understand?

Yes. But you made the decision?

Yes, yes, yes, yes, yes, yes, yes, yes. I, Rachel, R, Riccarda, because I had handkerchiefs with Rs, understand? Then Lionella, Luisa. And [Leo], Leonida, because we could often call him Leo by mistake, and so we said it was a nickname for Leonida.

LIONELLA: *My mother came up with the surname of Nistri Maddaloni, but when have you ever heard a surname of this kind? It's crazy! To keep the initials N. M. You could have . . . said even a name with other surnames, no? Norma Melani, I don't know . . . something less peculiar than Nistri Maddaloni, because Nistri is a Tuscan*

False I.D. cards issued in 1944 to
"Alfonso Nistri Maddaloni" and (opposite) "Riccarda Fuciarelli."

name, Maddaloni, well, it's Neapolitan. Where exactly was this born, this Nistri Maddaloni? They had met a family who was from Maddaloni near Naples. But . . . they should have, perhaps, tried to find out what were the surnames of that zone! Thinking back over it, it's craziness.

Then, my brother, they called him Leonida, and my father had to be a Greek professor to call him Leonida. It was already a strange license to give a Southern name to a man who spoke perfect Northern Italian—since my grandfather was Bolognese . . . it was more northern what my Papa spoke. To give him the name Leonida, to keep Leo. Better Leone, Leonuccio, Leonetto, I don't know!

For me, Luisa, in short, let's let it go, a family name, it was fine. And my mother— Riccarda! And my father, Alfonso. In short, they came up with such terrible names! (Laughs) Which then created lots of confusion, because when I heard myself called Luisa, I didn't even respond. The third time, I'd gone deaf, I don't know . . . It was very complicated because as soon as we left home, I had to become Luisa. They should have found a name with Lio, it's easy, Liora, I don't know, no Liora isn't a common name, so maybe it wasn't easy, but for goodness sake . . . (Laughs)

In any case, poor Leonida, which then they said was a woman's name, true? . . . Better Leonardo . . . It's a great name. In short, they had very little imagination, and were very misguided.

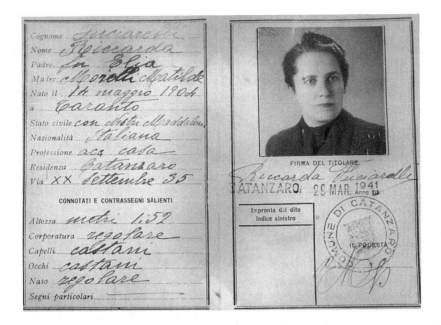

RACHEL: *But Leo always said, "Mamma, you have always taught us that one should never tell a lie, but now we're always telling lies. Lies—the name that isn't my name, we're from Taranto instead of from Florence." Understand?*

And what did you say? How did you explain?

We explained to him, they are lies to save ourselves, that's what we said.

There were two windows, one on the back of the house with a glorious view and one on the side. From the vestibule you entered the kitchenette and the bathroom.

Everything was very clean, but for hot water they had to heat it up a little in the kitchen and put it in the tub. There was a great woodpile, in which the professor hid his *tefillin* and his *tallit katan* until the liberation.

RACHEL: *When we were there, he said his prayers; every morning he wrapped* tefillin *and put on his* tallit, *and then he hid it all, everything under the wood in the bathroom. Every morning he hid everything under the woodpile. In short, it wasn't a very safe thing, I'd say; however, he did it. This gave a sense of heroism, eh? I liked this. This was a very positive side. I heard him pray, I participated.*

The professor's wife immediately went to make the acquaintance of the Spilinger family, who gave her the address of Misia (the maid of Mrs. Costanza Foà) across the street on Via Roma. She went there straight away, finding Mrs. Marietta Guadagni there as well as her niece Bettina Bandinelli with her daughter Fanny. Mrs. Bettina sent food to the professor's family: a pot of broth, boiled potatoes, and bread. And the family members were happy and felt themselves rejuvenated after so many months of fears, troubles, and deprivations. The next day, March 16, the family took a beautiful walk on foot to Ponte alla Piera with Misia and the Spilinger couple. There they found Mrs. Costanza Foà, Mattei, and her mother Adriana, to whom they brought the sad news of Mrs. Luisa Gallichi's death, in the March 11 bombardment of Florence. They left Anghiari at 8 A.M. and returned at 7:30 P.M., in mild, lovely weather.

LIONELLA: *I did not much approve of the great group walks to go see the Jewish friends on the hill. I found this to be a weekly act of madness. We always had to watch our backs, in front, behind. Later, when we were in the partisans' zone, it was a little better. Maybe it was a half-madness.*

The professor lacked ration cards for himself and his family and he had to have them, or else Mrs. Rosa couldn't have boarded the family and wouldn't have understood why. So he went to ask Mrs. Bettina's advice; she informed her cousin Varo, secretary of the Anghiari Fascist Party. With him the professor went to town hall where he recounted to the secretary the complicated fate that had befallen him: having fled from the Naples area to La Spezia, he had his identity card validated shortly before its expiration and he had his legally obtained ration cards with him in Florence. His wife was keeping them in her purse when she went to see a friend recovering at the nursing home in San Jacopino. Right at the moment of the aerial bombardment, she lost her purse with the cards in the stampede! What to do? The secretary told the professor to write all this down so he could get confirmation of the accuracy of the news and the date of the bombardment confirmed by the Fascist Federation of Arezzo. In fact, after about ten days, the confirmation came, and so the family was able to get its ration cards legally—the ones for workers, too, which were more substantial.

On April 10, the professor presented himself at town hall to get his ration cards and sign the register of Anghiari, for a temporary residence.

The father and children took long walks in the surroundings and started to regain their physical health. The professor, who suffered in general from stomach ailments and followed a rigid diet, could eat anything up there—even beans—and every once in a while, while lunching with the children, he enjoyed great slices of chestnut-flour polenta!

LIONELLA: *We were always hungry. Because we were growing children. The food was enough to, well, to survive. We very seldom had full stomachs. I remember stuffing myself on pieces of polenta that were already purple. Mmmm. (Laughs) This polenta—you know what a farinata is? Sweet chestnut flour. It was there one or two days, it became purple, almost. (Laughs)*

April 8, the first day of Passover, the family spends peacefully among friends at Ponte all Piera.

April 9, Sunday, a delicious Easter dinner is eaten with Mrs. Rosa. It was warm out, cloudy.

April 12 at 6:30 A.M., Riccarda notices a little knot in her chest, possibly owing to getting elbowed by Luisa a few nights ago.

Saturday the 15th the whole family had a nice walk to Ponte all Piera, under a cloudy sky.

On the 16th, Riccarda takes a bath and gives one to the children at Mrs. Marietta's house. Then she has Doctor Cristina visit, who advises her to have herself looked at right away by a surgeon in Florence. And so, the next day, April 17, the professor and his wife left for Florence at 6 P.M., entrusting the children to Mrs. Bettina who promised, whatever happened, to consider them her own children.

RACHEL: *And so I went immediately to the doctor in Anghiari, and my landlady, Mrs. Rosa, said to me, "What, you, Madam, are going to the doctor?" I say, "Why not?" I say, "If I need to, I go. It's not like I'm made differently, just because I'm Jewish." (Laughs) And so I went to this doctor, and he looked and said "I advise you to go to your surgeon in Florence. I can't do anything for you."*

And so the landlady immediately—she was old, poor thing—says, "But I can't keep the children. The professor has to stay here." And I said, "Aldo, I'll go alone." But that family that we met there, at Anghiari, whom we hadn't known at all before, but they were marvelously good, we made very good friends, she knew that we were Jewish . . . Well, this lady, Marietta, and Bettina came to tell us, "No, the Professor has to go with you, Madam. You shouldn't go alone to a surgeon for something like this, that you don't know what it is," she says. "We'll take the children to our house. They'll be the grandchildren who came from southern Italy, from Taranto." We had already said that we were from Taranto. See how good they were? And so we went, Aldo and I.

Twice before, when they were still in Florence, Lionella and Leo refused to be separated from their parents.

RACHEL: *We went to the friars at Piazza San Marco and they said they couldn't take us in, that we should go to another place, near the Michelangelo high school. We went there, and there too: nothing. They say, go to the nuns who are there on the road to Fiesole . . . We went. And the Mother Superior says, "Yes, yes, we can take the children. But you two, no." Leo and Lionella started to cry. "What? You're going to leave us here, your lucky charms?" We said, "Darling, calm down, we won't leave you here." The nuns were taking them in to baptize them too. They performed many baptisms.*

When was this?

Before Anghiari. We were trying to organize, you understand, because it was no longer living . . . to stay, Aldo in one house in one week, I in another house. It was a terrible thing. But, for example, there was a Professor Giannelli, professor of ancient history at the university, he was very sweet, very affectionate, . . . he was ready to keep the children at his house. But the children didn't want to.

Because they didn't want to be separated?

Yes, that's it . . . The children, on the other hand, stayed in Anghiari with this family which was marvelous.

They were more willing to be left because . . .

They knew, understand, that I was ill, that I had to go to the surgeon. Then that young girl, Fanny, was there, who was very good, you understand. It was very nice with this family, one ate very well.

LIONELLA: *Another half-madness was when Papa and Mamma went to Florence.*

Were you very afraid for your parents?

I was afraid to be alone in the world. I also recognized that it was crazy to leave, to go to Florence . . . Papa had already gone back once by himself. It was a frightening thing.

They went because Rachel had a . . .

A little knot, yes. In short, it wasn't something, in my opinion, so tragic, to leave two children, two kids alone with a family that they'd known for a month. Look, those nights in that big bed there, I and my brother, in this room that was nicer than our house—these people, they had handmade linen sheets, etc., etc. Poor things, they showered us with kindness, they brought us to the garden to play, there was a delightful girl, so good she refused to read Mussolini's name aloud in school. Which was extremely dangerous.

I thought about being alone, I read books—"The Two Orphans"—so I could cry as much as I wanted. It's a very sad story, famous from the 1800s, a truly heartbreaking thing. And I was there, crying, I was crying over myself and over the two orphans, I felt myself orphaned. And then they called me, "Luisa," and they had to call me three times. (Laughs) In short, it was a hard week, very hard.

RACHEL: *I had to remind myself, when I went to ask permission for a bus ticket, that my name was Nistri Maddaloni. I said it over and over during the journey, on the stairs and then on the street, "Nistri Maddaloni, Nistri Maddaloni!"*

They spend the night at Romito, near Arezzo, in a first-class rail car, and at 5:30 A.M. with a little suitcase they go on foot to lodge #2 to take the Casentino train to Bibbiena. The city appears desolate. They visit San Francesco. They arrive in Bibbiena at 9:30 A.M.

The next day, the 19th, they get up at 6 A.M. Before Pontassieve two alarms force them to get off and disperse in the fields.

At 10:30 A.M. the train arrives in Florence. At noon the N. M.s go to Prof. Comolli's clinic, who takes some liquid from Riccarda with an exploratory injection. The result freed her from every worry, producing a sense of relief and happiness. In the city continual alarms follow one after the other, morning and night, even the next day. Riccarda goes to visit Guido and Evelina De Angelis and Anna Vigevani.

The N. M.s visit the zone hit by the aerial bombardment at Campo di Marte and then go to Professor Siciliano's. Weather quite variable.

The 24th, after the first alarm, the N. M.s go to the station at 10:15 A.M. to get in line, staying on their feet until 4 P.M., with three alarms obliging them to go out, losing time. Departure at 5 P.M. and arrival at Bibbiena at 8:30 P.M., exhausted. Night spent at Bibbiena near the station, each in a different house, to be safer. The day after, the weather was gorgeous, fresh and pure; the couple go up to the town to have one of the renowned cappuccinos. At noon from the Belvedere terrace, they witness the burning and falling of two enemy planes and of one pilot in a parachute beyond Poppi. The people were all worried for the parachutist and inside the N. M.s hoped he would be saved; indeed he was risking his life for the salvation of Italy and the Italians!

RACHEL: *When we arrived at Bibbiena, we found many people who were going to church to pray because the Germans wanted to burn that whole area, because they had found some murdered Germans . . . near Bibbiena.*

Then while we were there in Bibbiena waiting for the bus the whole time, lo and behold we saw an airplane that they were bombing, the Italians, understand . . . and we saw English and American soldiers coming down in parachutes . . . And so everyone prayed, prayed, "poor things, let them not be taken, let them hide, let them succeed." Because we had had enough of these Germans . . . Ah, yes, it was an awful life.

At 1:45 P.M., departure for Arezzo, and from there, at 6 P.M., for Anghiari, where they find their children waiting for them with lots of people. Cold and a storm in sight. Indeed the next day was windy and stormy, and colder. Indescribable the joy and emotion in embracing the children again and they their parents.

On the 3rd, the whole N. M. family takes part in the solemn service in the provostship and listens to the sermon by the Bishop of Arezzo. At 3:30 P.M., Fanny's confirmation was celebrated with a suitable sermon by the Bishop.

On the 5th, the N. M. family made a trip by train to Sansepolcro, visiting the town with its churches and taking a walk to the Capuchins, eating a packed lunch and then a packed tea in the gardens. While they were at the café there was an alarm (1:15 to 2:00 P.M.). Having left Anghiari at 9 A.M., they returned at 6 P.M.

On May 8th, Riccarda begins the injections given her by Misia.

On the 10th there was a great passing of planes in Anghiari and a heavy bombardment nearby. On the 11th, the whole family went to Gattina to stay with the Gotis and rested. Sky overcast.

Sunday the 14th, a serious housecleaning was done during Mrs. Rosa's absence, which she did not appreciate.

The 15th, the Provost came to bless the house.

RACHEL: *We went to church every Sunday . . . The first Sunday that Leo went to church with us, he immediately put on a beret, since one wears a hat in the synagogue, and our landlady came in behind us, she says, "Master, Master, one removes one's hat."*

So it was the first time.

The first time. Then we went every Sunday. And during the Easter period, we did a tour of all seven churches . . . like the Catholics do, because the landlady wanted to show that we were Catholics. We also had false documents . . .

Did the children also learn Catholic prayers?

No, no, no.

So they remained silent.

Yes, yes, yes. I never stood up, I never got on my knees, because our landlady, being very old, didn't kneel or get up . . . so I didn't either . . .

LIONELLA: *Yes, we went to church. Mamma did the sign of the cross, she taught it to us, but I did it wrong. We tried to stay in the back the whole time. Papa—the men generally—stayed in the piazza in front of the church. The church was crowded . . .*

Did you learn some prayers?

No, nothing! They didn't even teach us the Ave Maria! It was truly stupid! It was the first thing they should have done, teach us a prayer, everyone did it, later I read their stories. Nothing! Boys of thirteen years should know a heap of things, no? [Leo] should have done communion, confirmation; they didn't teach us anything.

Later on, I say, "but you were careless." Right? . . . My husband was hidden by a priest. He learned to serve mass; in other words, he was smarter. He fired off the prayers. Much more intelligent, his family. We learned absolutely nothing, only the sign of the cross, which I got wrong, I always did it right to left . . .

Then, the parish priest, I think he was a very intelligent person. There's the tradition in these towns to have a great reception for the priest who brings the holy water. The blessing of the house before Easter; it corresponds to our washing of the pots. And this lady had prepared cookies and vin santo to offer the parish priest. The priest never arrived. So she told me I had to go get him with Leo. Leo knew where the house was, the cathedral in town. So he went. And the priest made him sit there, waiting, about half an hour. And then he crossed the whole town with him, keeping his hand on his shoulder.

This was a very beautiful gesture on the part of the parish priest, don't you think? He did this whole mise-en-scène because, after all, we had only been there a month. To make it clear that he protected us, in short, that if any one had any intention . . . Then we learned that he himself hid other Jews . . . Yes, yes, a wonderful figure.

The professor and Luisa took baths at Mrs. Marietta's house.

May 18, the N. M. family spent a nice day at the Casina del Latte alle Strette, after attending mass in the church of the Carmine together with Mrs. Rosa, Fanny, and the Spilingas.

Midnight on May 25 was the final date for the rebels (partisans!) to surrender, and still be able to enjoy the immunity granted to them by the mercy of the Duce.

Calm days followed, with good weather and cool airy air.

May 29, another lunch at the Strette, where the N. M. family spent a pleasant day, leaving the house at 7:30 A.M. and returning at 8 P.M.

But then Leonida, back home, had a fever of 39.8 C and takes a laxative.

The 30th and the 31st he's still in bed with 37.4 C and swelling on the right part of the throat.

The first of June, still in bed with a temperature. Glorious weather; at 6:15 P.M. they witness the aerial bombing of the outskirts of Sansepolcro.

On the 2nd, Leonida is still in bed with a temperature, and I fear he's got the mumps.

The 3rd, however, his fever is gone. In the evening, tremendous storm with lightning and thunder.

On the 4th, Leonida gets up, but Luisa has a little diarrhea and doesn't eat much.

At noon comes the second aerial bombing, which hits the bridge to Sansepolcro, the railway tracks, and the road, frightening the children terribly. It is announced that the Anglo-Americans entered Rome today, which was evacuated by the Germans and the Fascist Italian Republicans. With the Anglo-Americans are the Italian monarchists and Badoglio's men.

The weather is tremendous the next day, the 5th. All the members of the N. M. family are finally healthy, but they feel very weak. To reanimate themselves a little, they make coffee from beans.

On the 6th, an unexpected event: mail arrives from Aunt Ernesta Neppi Modona and from Leone Ambron. Out of joy they made an autarchic dessert.

On the 7th, Leonida goes out for the first time after his illness. June 8 (Corpus Domini), Riccarda goes to the provostship at 7 A.M. to attend the communion of the young people with Mrs. Rosa and to take part in the mass. The professor and the children also went to mass at 11 A.M., which was sung to the splendid accompaniment of a harmonium and violins.

On the 9th they read that the "enemy" is advancing beyond Viterbo toward Terni and on the 10th that it has reached beyond Montalto di Castro and Pescara.

Sunday the 11th they all go to Ponte alla Piera with Misia, despite the rainy weather, and spend the whole day there. They can hear the roar of the cannon.

On the 12th, Leonida has a swelling on the right side of his neck again. Many German offices and units are installed in town. From this day on, no more newspapers arrive: the last *Nazione* is the 11th/12th issue. No more long-distance mail; everyone remains isolated and deprived of news. Neither the telegraph nor the telephone works anymore.

The 13th, the weather is very windy, pretty, cold.

From 6 to 8 P.M. the town is surrounded by the Fascist militia in search of certain deserters.

Wednesday the 14th of June, dull market. Glorious summer weather; Leonida is still at home with a swelling on his neck.

A rumor circulates that the Anglo-Americans have reached beyond Pescara, Terni, and Orbetello.

On the 15th, enemy planes machine-gun the surroundings of Anghiari, full of German vehicles. Glorious weather.

Dr. Cristina visits Leonida who has lymphatic adenoids on the right side of his throat.

On the 16th, the weather is glorious. Enemy planes bombard the streets near San Leo and surroundings. You can begin to hear the rumble of the cannon very close. Beef and veal are distributed with ration cards at 80 lire a kilo.

From the 17th, you can see a great movement of German vehicles in retreat and in transfer, and from their house, the N.M.s see everything with a superb view, standing on their parlor terrace. Rumor has it that the Allies have occupied the Island of Elba.

Still on the 19th, Leonida is swollen under the right ear and bandaged with ointment.

The whole day, rainy weather and intensified movement of vehicles coming from the village. Almost all the non-food stores remain closed or half-open. Banks, post offices, telegraph office still closed.

From the 20th, everyone carries away carts full of stuff for fear of the Allies, whom they say are advancing beyond Perugia. Variable weather.

From the 21st, no Wednesday market, everything closed, even for coffee. The two pharmacies, the three taverns, and the barbers stay open, and some stores carrying food are open in the morning. In the afternoon a new aerial bombardment of the village. Weather sultry, cloudy, and foggy.

As a precaution, Riccarda prepares a panful of toast and fills a demijohn with drinkable water. Wine has gone up to 20 lire per liter.

From the 22nd, all is dark since the Germans cut the electricity lines.

On the 25th, the Germans blow up the factories of Sansepolcro and the railroad to Arezzo with mines.

The 26th of June, the whole family gets up at 5:45 A.M. on account of the planes.

A notice posted in town announces that the towns of Giove, Montauto, and Anghiari will be burned if the recent rebel killing of Germans is repeated. In the evening, many flee from here to the country, alarmed. We go to bed half-dressed. Meanwhile, the enemy airplanes continue to fly over the zone, bombing and machine-gunning it, and anti-aircraft artillery fires from below, frightening Leonida terribly. Everyone stays closed up in their houses, shops closed, town deserted. We no longer know anything about the world or the war.

The following day, June 27, we rise at 5:30 A.M. on account of the anti-aircraft explosions. Every day, as much meat as you want!

RACHEL: *When there was no more kosher meat, when they wouldn't allow it, Mamma Ada went to the rabbi, David Cassuto, Nathan's father. She said, "What do we do, how do we feed the children?" And the rabbi said, "Our religion permits it for the health of the children." Meat that isn't kosher. They had their own plates and forks. After the war we boiled the forks, to make them clean, and we used them for fruit.*

Did you ever eat meat that wasn't kosher?

I did too, toward the end.

You also ate meat that wasn't kosher?

LIONELLA: *Yes, during the war. Papa, no . . . Never. Poor thing, they gave it to him then in the last weeks of his life when he was in the hospital . . .*

And he didn't know?

No, he didn't know.

Around 5 P.M., an enemy plane is hit by anti-aircraft fire and we watch the fall of a parachutist toward Tavernelle, among the sunny clouds. Continual aerial attacks in the surroundings all day long.

From today on, you must furnish your own wood in order to bake bread in the town oven. The rumbling of the cannons can be heard continually.

Wednesday, June 28, no weekly market! We hear talk of clashes between Germans and rebels and of hangings of the latter in nearby towns. Sky cloudy, oppressive.

The following day, though, one could finally enjoy a day with truly gorgeous constant summer weather.

Lots of times enemy planes are attacked by anti-aircraft artillery. The whole family continues to stay home, particularly the professor, and lacks all news of the world! It's getting to be an exhausting life!

July first, awake as usual at 5:45 A.M. with the anti-aircraft fire. Season still beautiful, hot but airy. Because Riccarda doesn't feel well, Luisa is forced to make her first dried pea soup, which comes out wonderfully.

On the 4th, the usual anti-aircraft "alarm clock" at 5:45 A.M., after a sweltering night interrupted often by anti-aircraft fire. Moreover there are continual explosions from the laying of mines in Via Nuova near La Quercia. It rains a little and cools off a lot. The professor goes out after ten days of confinement to get his hair cut with Leonida who also gets his cut. What depressing squalor! German proclamations on the walls announce fires and death if the evasions continue.

The 5th of July, with variable and cloudy weather, the professor's family celebrates Leonida's birthday with a sweet flour and zabaglione cake, pasta and beans, and milk-fed veal steaks, according to his wishes.

The following days, the usual anti-aircraft alarm clock.

Sunday the 9th of July, they hear the rumble of the cannon nearby. Swelter, clouds. At 9 P.M., the water is cut off, and it's gone for the whole next day also and we have to resort to the only fountain under the loggias and to household reserves.

Great explosions and cannon rolls continue. The whole town is deserted; all is quiet through the streets. They say the enemy is at the Ville di Monterchio, but we don't know anything for sure. From around 5 P.M., there's an enormous fire of warehouses and stores in Sansepolcro.

The children are still getting the water at the fountain.

The next day, the smoke keeps rising from the fire in Sansepolcro. Cold wind. We go to have tea at Mrs. Marietta's . . .

The professor's family begins its fourth to last flask of oil.

RACHEL: *There wasn't any oil. I went to a grocer's who also sold oil. And I said to him, "Please, could you give me a bottle of oil?" And he said, "Yes, yes, Madam, I can give you a bottle." I went and I knew the price they were asking, the black market price. But he says to me, instead of 10, he says 5. I say, "Excuse me," I say, "I heard you wrong . . ." "No, no," he says, "Madam, you heard perfectly well. What do you want? That I ask a high price and then after the war, what will you say? 'That scoundrel! That oil that cost 5, he charged me 10!'"*

Luisa vomits and has a temperature of 37 C. Pretty, temperate. Riccarda has a stomach ache and takes a laxative; in the evening Agnese, who came every once in a while to help, cleans. The professor and Luisa take care of the cooking.

In the night, heavy enemy artillery fire.

The evening of the 14th, great storm. Continual passage of enemy planes. They say the Anglo-Americans are at Sasso and at Città di Castello.

Grain is distributed; the ration of bread and pasta for the month.

They say the enemy has taken Città di Castello. Leonida makes his parents despair on account of bread that's a little moldy . . .

The family begins another bottle of oil.

On the 18th they finish the pasta with a minestrone. Riccarda toasts a tiny residue of black coffee from South Africa.

The Germans down various trees with cannonfire at the top of a hill near the Via del Ponte alla Pieve.

The night of the 19th, Leonida complains of stomach pains with diarrhea and his father has to accompany him twice to the toilet by candlelight.

Terrible cannon shots are heard, coming and going, very nearby; many fall around the train station.

On the 20th, Leonida is very bad and makes his parents despair.

The shelling continues nearby. Rumor has it that yesterday Florence was taken by the Anglo-Americans.

On the 21st, there is a continual duel by opposing artillery. The German artillery is positioned around the station and near Gattina.

That night there's no sleeping from the terrible artillery fire; storm and a rapid cooling off. All the members of the professor's family are digesting poorly. Water is boiled. The bread gets moldy after weeks and much of it is thrown away. All the members of the family are morally and physically worn out by the prolonged anguish—no news, no light, no water, closed up in the house, lacking necessities more and more.

Sunday the 23rd of July it cools down and the wind blows. The activity of the opposing artilleries almost never ceases. Around 2:30 P.M., two shots fall, one near La Croce in the country, and the other right in Via Roma, near Checca's butcher shop; no one is hurt. Luisa and Riccarda were at the fountain and rushed home. Enormous din; Leonida is completely terrified. We no longer know what to do or how to withstand this state of things.

In the evening, six or seven prominent men are taken by the Germans and led to the German command. We always sleep half-dressed . . .

July 27th is a beautiful and very hot day.

Luisa continues to be wonderful and full of courage in lining up at the butcher's and for water and going to the garden, even amid the rumble of the cannons.

RACHEL: *It was the end of May, I think, when we saw the SS for the first time at Anghiari. You can imagine our fright! We were here and facing us there was a house with the SS on the other side of the street.*

In Anghiari?

In Anghiari.

And so Aldo couldn't ever go out.

He did not go out. I absolutely didn't want him to go out. Here too when things began all of a sudden I didn't want Aldo to go out because the Germans could pick him up and put him to work.

I let Aldo go out as little as possible in Florence and in Anghiari. The children were marvelous, they went themselves to do our shopping, they went themselves to buy our vegetables, everything, understand?

LIONELLA: *I always did the shopping, eh? Always, during the war.*

Why?

I don't know. Because Mamma didn't compete with me for the privilege! (Laughs)

Your father wasn't supposed to go out, or not?

Well, for the men, it was always better that they didn't walk around a lot. We were at Consuma in '43, immediately after Mussolini fell. Then in September, after the 8th . . . we were hidden at Impruneta. At Impruneta I did the shopping. To the piazza to buy milk, bread, then to the greengrocer's, those who had the gardens, where one had to buy beet root, zucchini, the vegetables. It was entertaining. However, it was always my job. Then at Anghiari, too, the same thing. Later, when there was no water, I stood at the fountain with the pots. I had to fill them, then Papa came to carry them up. But I stood in line . . . A line for water. It came to that too.

At night the terrible din from continual duels of opposing artilleries continues. Since yesterday a second tap has been opened at the fountain. All day long, intense bombardment. Every day all kinds of meat and vegetables, and pears.

Boiling heat.

Another German cannon is installed in Palazzo Martini.

Riccarda is very nervous.

Around 2:30 P.M., a tremendous shot falls near our house and the glass over the door shatters. We take refuge along with the streetsweeper under our house and we stay until 4:15 P.M. What fright! We even spend the night at the streetsweeper Lisino's under tremendous shellings. The town is half-lit by a great fire in a villa at La Croce. Leonida sleeps on the floor with all the other members of that family; the professor, his wife, and Luisa stay a little on Lisino's bed, but most of the time they sit in the kitchen, from 8:30 P.M. to 5 A.M. A hard day, never to be forgotten!

RACHEL: *The Allies bombed Anghiari and the Germans were leaving and so we went to this streetsweeper's to spend the night, because it was a house that was safe, understand?*

Because it was underground.

Underground. And so we heard the steps of the Germans as they were leaving. We watched when the Germans were leaving Rome. They all passed by on foot, and then in the back you saw cows, horses, which they had taken from the farms.

Which they stole.

They stole and then they killed them to eat.

I understand.

Yes, yes, we saw the overthrow (laughs), how happy we were! Ah, yes. And then, for example, when we saw the shelling? We had a high terrace in this house and we saw the German cannon that shelled the Allies. And then came the Allied response, and we said, "A little bit more!" (Laughs) Because we wanted them to destroy this cannon.

And did they?

Yes, yes.

Tremendous shots explode next to the house around 2 P.M. and then at 5:30 P.M. All the glass in the entranceway shatters; shards make holes in the cushions and the door. We flee to the town ovens and then to the trattoria, Il Cantinone, where we eat our own dinner, on empty stomachs, and we sleep sitting on benches and leaning on tables, amid tremendous rumbles, until 5:30 A.M.

Around 10 A.M., Riccarda sees two Indians, whose presence had been signaled to us shortly before by Mrs. Spilinga. They are sent ahead by the enemies to remove the mines and then withdraw; there's not a single German in town!

July 30, 1944, a Sunday, the professor's family goes back home; the professor and Leonida return to Il Cantinone for an hour. Agnese is also there with typhus, and sleeping there has created a great scare of the contagion, above all in Leonida. The professor and Leonida are exhausted. We break our fast of the 9th of Av (*Tishah B'Av*) before evening: the professor at 3 P.M. and Riccarda at 7 P.M., except for a marsala.

The weather is nice.

At 10 A.M. the water that the rebels had cut off so that the Germans couldn't use it comes back on.

At noon, the cannon shots begin again and the whole family takes refuge once more at the town ovens. Tremendous hits arrive a few steps from the house, and so at 3:15 P.M., they decide all of a sudden to go toward Monterchi with a few necessities and three loaves of bread. Just outside of town they meet English soldiers who pick them up in a jeep and leave them at the top of the Sorci farm. The English soldiers who are camped there put some land with straw and a tent, one table, and four stools at their disposal.

RACHEL: *I wanted to leave. I was fed up with this life. As long as we could we were hidden there . . . But one day when we were still there, from far away we saw some Englishmen talking in an office where the Fascists used to be. The Germans were no longer there—they had already fled Anghiari—but they kept on firing cannons. And all at once, boom, a cannon, right in the window, we were at the table drinking a bit of real coffee to celebrate the arrival of the Allies. And so Aldo and I said, we can't stay here any longer. We said, let's go toward the Allied lines. And under the trees, we saw three English soldiers. And I went to embrace them, to kiss them, I say, "It's for our liberty,"* . . . *all at once, here comes a jeep, it was the first time I'd seen one, a jeep, how do you say it?*

Jeep, yes.

With two English officers inside. And they stopped to see these soldiers talking with us.

Aldo spoke English, remember? And so, I asked them, "English?" Of course! And so, these officers said, "Come on up and we'll take you to where we're camped." And so they took us to a farm and put us in a room where fruit was put to dry. They gave us some straw and we slept there and ate there.

There is a command brigade [at the encampment] and the 43rd Artillery Regiment, with many Indians.

July 31st was a day of enormous interest and great moral relief! After so long, we read English newspapers of the 8th Army and, thus, we know nothing less than King George of England's visit to Italy, and many other pieces of news. We speak with many non-commissioned officers, very kind soldiers, who give us cigarettes, soap, and chocolate; there is also a Cypriot, to whom Riccarda speaks in Greek, and with the others we make ourselves understood well enough in English.

Florence is surrounded on three sides by the Allies against the Germans, who defend themselves on the surrounding hills. At 9 A.M. the news is read in English over the radio. In the farmhouse are evacuees from Sicily and Arezzo and two rebel fighters.

The professor's family (but by now it continues . . . as it has already happened many times even before now) eats tinned meat and hard biscuits and bread as long as it lasts, managing as best we can, washing ourselves from a bucket. The first night an Englishman gave us four very warm blankets.

Even there the enemy shells whistle, falling not far off, toward Sovara.

Continual airplane passings! And it's already August first!

Living this new and precarious life among the English and reading such unforeseen news is like being drunk! Among the news, the attempt on Hitler's life.

Glorious weather. We always eat cold food, except for a cafforzo [a coffee substitute made of orzo] made for us by the farmer's brother-in-law. That night, continual duel of anti-aircraft artillery. They tell us that Anghiari is still being hit by the enemy. We can't walk around on account of the shooting and we are always sitting on our stools or standing. We witness the preparations for the unit's departure; it's going farther north after nightfall, leaving us very alone. The command had put trusted soldiers in front of the door to guard us from the Indian ladies' men. There's no finding anything to eat, only four eggs for 30 lire!

We ask a soldier going to Rome on leave to take a letter for the Erreras with a note inside for Riccarda's relatives in Rhodesia, begging him to forward it through the Amgot [Allied Military Government]. What emotion to think of Mamma Rebecca's joy! After so many years! It's like a dream!

August 2 there is a continual and gradual passage of Indians and Englishmen. We make a short tour of the fields. Some meat is bought and cooked by a farmer who also gives us plates and silverware.

We read a book of English short stories left by the English. I interpret for a medical assistant who comes to see a farmer wounded while he was going with the Germans to take oxen to Pieve San Stefano.

Great battle activity and intense traffic. Sleepless night, often on our feet: we never undress, except to take off our shoes, on account of the constant passing of planes machine-gunning the Germans and their anti-aircraft defenses. Also, shooting from large-caliber cannons.

An officer's club is installed in the farmhouse and an Italian lieutenant sleeps there, with an attendant and an English artillery captain.

On the morning of August 3rd, the professor decides to venture to Anghiari (45 minutes) with Luisa amid the whistling of the cannon; they throw themselves to the ground many times in order not to be hit.

I've heard, and I read also, in your father's book, that you were always courageous.

LIONELLA: *Eh, well, there was no other choice, but to be courageous. It was the only thing.*

But they also say that Leo wasn't.

He was frightened, he was very frightened. Yes. He lived in this continual state of fear. Which probably affected his health after, in short, his nervous system, everything . . . Fear of the airplanes, which he heard from far away, with his very keen hearing; he perceived them before the sirens. Like radar. Right after he started to yell, "The airplanes, the airplanes!" the siren sounded. And then there were incursions, airplanes passed by, and he threw himself into his father's arms, sobbing.

RACHEL: *Afterwards, Leo, when we were hidden at Anghiari, he had marvelous hearing, they still hadn't rung the alarm and he already heard the airplanes and he said "They're coming, they're coming, they're coming, they're coming, they're coming . . ." We said, "Who?" And then the alarm would go. And he would say, "They're killing us, they're killing us, they're killing us."*

He was afraid, very afraid. In fact, on account of this great fear that he had, he later got infantile diabetes . . . from all of the frights.

So he had this disease already during the war or . . .

No, no, no. . .

Afterward. But it was the fear . . .

The fear, understand?

LIONELLA: *We noticed the diabetes at eighteen years. He . . . never told me that it was the war.*

In town we encounter a disastrous situation; all the streets are strewn with rubble and wreckage, and Mrs. Rosa's house, where we were living, was hit the previous evening at the far corner. Incendiary bombs and splinters had broken the marble table on the terrace as well as the flooring. Other glass articles had been broken and the window decorations had been moved. Everything full of dust and debris of every kind. We take the necessities: five kilos of flour, cookies, etcetera, and we flee at 8:30 A.M. amid the deafening English mortar bombardment and the landing of German hits.

In the street a very dense dust raised up. There were new signs with many instructions and there was a great passage of armed trucks and Anglo-Indian police. We arrive at the Sorci farm exhausted and with throats burning with thirst, but a hot grain coffee and a rest set us right again. We spend a boring afternoon. For dinner a wonderful broth with rice and boiled meat.

On August 4th, we continue to hear clearly the echo of the battle and the machine-gunning from the San Sepolcro and Monte Dolio area. They say that the Ponte alla Piera has been taken, and we have no news of our friends from there.

After many days we brush our teeth, with toothpaste presented to us by an Englishman. They say that San Sepolcro has been taken by the Alpine troops.

The water is dirty and bad and must be boiled. The farmers present us with plums, roasted corn cobs, and bread, and thus we have a magnificent lunch!

Starting from 3 P.M. the weather changes and it rains a lot that evening. Frequent passings of enemy planes. Anti-aircraft attacks.

Luisa starts studying with me again.[27] Leonida on the other hand doesn't want to, he is bad, he makes me angry, and I have to strike him.

LIONELLA: *My brother refused to do anything . . . He was afraid and he said it was useless to study, since he would die . . .*

Yes, yes, he refused everything; he was very sad. I always tried to make him play, I always invented very complicated games. My Mamma says, "No, you study." And so on . . . How come Mamma kept me from playing with my brother? How come Mamma kept me from chatting, from talking? If she saw us together, she always said, "Ah, talking, chatting, that girl, that girl . . ." Continually dividing us.

RACHEL: *Leo didn't study, didn't want to study . . . And then all at once came the desire to study.*

Yes . . . Do we know why he didn't want to study?

You know, he was very down morally, he had understood and he knew already what was happening . . .

On the 6th, they continue to bombard Anghiari with cannonfire and so we are forced to remain longer at the Sorci farm, terribly weary and sore as a result of sleeping on the straw. Luckily we were able to cook at a farmer's house and have plates and bread.

I finish reading the "Conte Kostia." Riccarda is very worried and vexed. The lieutenant paints us a very dismal picture of the future. In the 8th Army's little paper with Churchill's speech to the municipalities we read of the rosy military situation on every front.

We succeed in having some eggs.

On the 7th we spend another long day at the Sorci farm, conversing often with the Italian lieutenant. The German cannon shots keep landing in the surroundings and the police aren't letting anyone enter Anghiari because of the danger.

Variable weather. We eat a tinned antipasto of Luisa's.

On the 8th of August there was glorious weather. We went to Mulinaccio in Sovara to get two eggs. Leonida makes us despair with his pessimism and disobedience.

I learn to draw water from the well. We make bread with that of a farmer's wife. It's the first August 8th in mourning (Mamma Ada's birthday) . . .

Day and night peaceful, except for anti-aircraft fire . . .

On August 10th at 6:20 A.M., in oppressive and rainy weather, we go, over-burdened, to Anghiari along Via Maestra, and we arrive at 8 A.M. We find every-thing quiet and cleaned, but the house is full of debris. We call a woman in to do a special cleaning. Mrs. Rosa and Mrs. Marietta come to greet us. Mrs. Rosa is sleeping at a relative's house. Two of the Sorcis' dogs follow us the whole way! One refuses to leave me and plants himself in front of the door to the house and doesn't even want to go back when the farmers call him specially.

After so long, we eat at our table with a tablecloth! But we still lack water and light. We are tired and dazed. Our acquaintances are still at Ponte alla Piera. There are very few Englishmen in town. And at night we are finally in our beds, but still half-dressed and we get up three times on account of the cannonfire which is still nearby.

With a voucher from the municipality, we collect flour, grain, and salt. The town is full of posters in English and Italian, with all the regulations for civil life and the Allied laws of war.

We meet and greet the Viterbos freely! (They are Jews from Florence, not known before, and not relatives of my future son-in-law.)

RACHEL: *Aldo was a professor of the Viterbo girl . . . But when Aldo sees them, he has to pretend he doesn't know them. Not even Good day, not even Good evening, he comes home and says to me, "You know, the Viterbos are here," and so on. We looked at each other, like this, as if we knew each other, but then, once the war was over, we met.*

At noon the German cannonfire starts to fall again in town and we go to Il Cantinone to eat our lunch, staying there all day and for supper. Afterward we go to Mrs. Marietta's where we sleep in the cellar with the Guastallas and Mr. Anni-bale. How badly we sleep! On a mattress on top of crates, hard and flea-ridden.

On the 12th, the weather is glorious. At 6:30 A.M. we leave the cellar and go home to wash up completely, or as best we can. At 3:30 cannon shots very close by force us to run to Il Cantinone for an hour.

That evening at 8:30, we are once more in Mrs. Marietta's cellar and we sleep better with a sheet, but too much on a slant, and we slide continually.

I continue to give lessons to Luisa (by now Lionella once more!) in whatever situation we find ourselves and even during the shellings.

On the 13th, at 6:30 A.M., we returned home, in still beautiful weather. But around 4 P.M. some shellings kept us at Il Cantinone for an hour.

Around evening we are talking with the Viterbos and learn that their son was killed in these environs in an ambush. His wife and daughter are left behind.

RACHEL: *This is a story: This Viterbo family was Florentine, and they had a son and a daughter. The son was killed near Anghiari . . . There were three of them. One Viterbo, and the other two brothers. They were hidden in the countryside. When they were coming back from visiting their relatives, they met some Fascists and some Germans. And three young men could be, let's say, sent to war. They could have been deserters, etc. When the Germans learned that they were Jewish, they took all the money they had and their watches, and they said, "Now go, go all of you. Only don't go by this street, go on that other street." Where there was a cannon, boom, boom, boom, and they killed all three. Understand?*

And having killed these three, they left them there for many days . . . I don't know who, a priest, took them and put them in the cemetery and later gave them back to the community of Florence, and in the cemetery there's the tomb of these three. And this Viterbo family, what did they do? They immediately left where they were living because they could be searched for, and they came to Anghiari.

German patrols are still arriving in Santa Fiora and rounding up men. Finally on the 14th we spend the day and night in calm, but we continue to sleep at Mrs. Marietta's. Still beautiful and very hot.

Fascist women's heads are shaved.

On the 15th the heat is still enormous, with beautiful weather. And we go back to sleeping at home! The children in Mrs. Rosa's bed, I in the armchair until 12:30 A.M., then on our bed; no one undresses.

On the 17th, for the second time, we send our relatives in southern Rhodesia a letter via the Amgot, with an English medical soldier.

For the whole night we hear distant shellings and around 3:30 A.M., some very close, obliging us to run to Il Cantinone until 5:30 A.M.

Then Riccarda (Rachel) returns home to bed, and I to the armchair, where I had been until midnight, and then in bed.

On the 18th we sleep at Mrs. Marietta's again.

At 11:30 A.M. I have a terrifying sight, in front of our little terrace: after a tremendous mine explosion, the house across the street, where the carabinieri live, is *ripped apart* and the walls fall down amid enormous dust and a mountain of debris. I explain in time to my family what happened, so they won't be afraid. For us, no danger.

RACHEL: *The war was about to end, the Germans were no longer in Anghiari. But before leaving, these cursed Germans mined the house, the palazzo where they had been. It was a beautiful villa . . . And then there was also a little prison that they had put inside there for the people. And while we were eating, we had a little terrace, with this window. All at once, Aldo said, "Children, Rachel, don't be afraid." Because he had seen, understand, that the whole villa was about to go down.*

And there was a lady there whom we always saw pass by our house . . . And this lady, poor thing, was there to celebrate her name day . . . They were all gathered there and they all died. And near this one, there were also two, three boys, who were very German, very Fascist, and they had put them in prison. They also died that way. In this villa.

Nothing remains of the barracks but heaped-up debris.

The 19th is beautiful, with a storm. We watch the removal of the corpses from Villa Bartolini next to the carabinieri. We stay at home for fear of other mines nearby. At night we return to Mrs. Marietta's cellar, where a lady from Arezzo also sleeps with her girl Leonella. So there were twelve of us. We brought a mattress of Mrs. Rosa's and wool blankets, but there's no defense against the fleas.

The 20th, too, a Sunday, is splendid. Great movement of armed trucks toward Caprese. The removal of corpses from Palazzo Bartolini continues, which Leo (no longer Leonida) and I go to watch. But to be prudent, we continue to use the cards with the false names until our return to Florence.

Great cannon duel, machine guns and armed trucks, toward Motnia, Monte Dolio, and on the mountains of Pieve Santo Stefano.

Leo writes a story, to our great delight!

The 21st is still very hot and beautiful. Leo starts a novel on this period. The shellings continue.

It's like a dream to us that Leo is taking up his writing again after so many months of inactivity! . . .

On August 25th, I begin this "Tale of Life Lived" with our experiences from 1938 on, and I continue them later, from the point I had reached, on the basis of pocket diaries, only during the summer of 1977, after having finished correcting the proofs of the second edition of my book on "Etruscan and Roman Cortona in History and Art," in the "Studies of the Colombaria" series.

And I wanted to know, did Aldo keep notes all the time, every day?

RACHEL: *Every day, yes.*

What happened, etc.

Yes, yes, yes, yes.

Wasn't it dangerous to keep these notes?

During the war. But he wrote, they were so small, understand, no one would look at these little things. Then in the evening he made them larger, like this, or if not, then after, with the war over, he took all his little books, he wrote everything, understand?

And do you still have these little. . .

Yes, but I can't read them. They are written all in pencil, and the pencil is all faded. I have that suitcase that's near that trunk. It's full of these little books.

And in his notes, did he put all the names of those who helped, etc.?

Yes, yes.

Because wasn't there a fear that the notes would be . . .

No, he could put an M to remind himself, he didn't put the whole entire name.

So there was a little fear . . .

Certainly.

of putting others in danger.

Of course, yes, yes, yes, yes.

But there was also the desire to remember.

To remember, eh . . . I'll show you all the little books.

The 26th is still beautiful. During the day the artillery is always active.

Finally we decide, with permission from Leo, who is terrified, to go back home to sleep, and for the first time I put on my nightshirt, though keeping on my underwear and socks. The children still sleep in Mrs. Rosa's bed, since Mrs. Rosa is still at the Testas'.

A magnificent poster is hung of the new "Italian Confederation of Work," which invites workers to adhere to the principal of "freedom of thought, religion, and politics and minority representation."

On August 27th (glorious weather), by order of the new Mayor, the shops have to open on a regular schedule.

At night around 11 P.M., a German plane passes at a low altitude and machine-guns the area.

From 5:30 until 7 P.M. we go visit the Guastallas at Mrs. Marietta's.

The 28th is beautiful, hot. I put myself down at town hall for a return to Florence, but it will take time, as we will see!

From tonight we all sleep in our rooms again, but always half-dressed. Mrs. Rosa returns home.

The 1st of September there is still an enormous heat. We finish arranging the house, putting glass and paintings back in place.

They water down the streets. Permission to circulate, which was only 1 km, from today is extended to 10 km, except toward the north, which is brought to 3 km.

Saturday, September 2nd, it's still oppressively hot. We have spoken to two young men who came from Florence, who give us our first direct news: Via Guicciardini and Via Por Santa Maria were razed to the ground by mines, and Via dei Bardi was also heavily damaged—as an alternative to blowing up the Ponte Vecchio. All the other bridges had been blown up, however, some of which are replaced by military bridges built by the Allies. The cannonfire still reaches the city, since the Germans are still in Fiesole . . .

On the 4th, it's still nice out, but much cooler. I begin Latin with Leo.

On the 8th it rains in torrents. A little muggy.

By means of an evacuee going to Rome, I send the Minister an application to reenter my position in the high schools, requesting a transfer from Rome to Florence, with preference for the Michelangelo.

RACHEL: *Then, after the war, when we were in Anghiari, Aldo wrote the Minister, saying all these things that had happened, so he couldn't return anymore to Rome, he no longer had a house there, while in Florence we had a house, etc., etc. And so they assigned him immediately. Because he was a persecuted Jew, they did it right away. Because they saw that as a Jew, he had suffered much, he left Rome, he went to Florence, and in Florence we had our house, and they sent him right away to Florence.*

On the day of the 9th, I read, for the first time, an issue (89), dated 2 September 1944, of the newspaper, *Corriere della Sera*, of which Arrigo Jacchia is the editor-in-chief.

The account of the Council of Ministers continues, on the reform of the laws, with quotations of the law that abrogates racism: only now am I becoming thus informed!

Windy, beautiful, cool days follow.

Finally I take a good hot bath, in a full tub, at Mrs. Marietta's! We walk toward Campo della Fiera with the Bolaffis, and I meet an English motorcycle messenger, with whom Lucia has made friends, so much so that every day she waits for him and takes him to her room in Mrs. Marietta's house. He promises to marry her, extols his properties in England.

We open the second-to-last flask of oil.

On the 15th of September, Mr. Viterbo brings me an issue of the Roman newspaper *Unità*, the organ of the Communist Party, where the reopening of the Temple is announced, for Rosh Hashanah (the Jewish New Year) next Monday.

On the 16th Rachel and Leo take baths. Leo reads us the beginning of his story, "I Forgive," very well written, very promising.

With Sunday, the 17th of September, we return to standard time.

We dine with traditional New Year foods. Only pomegranates and dates are missing.

On the 18th, for our New Year, the day is gorgeous.

I go to bring New Year's greetings to a captain, a Jewish English doctor, Kraus, and I ask him if there's a gathering of Jewish soldiers, but he knows nothing of it.

I present a written request to the local Governor to return to Florence.

On the 23rd, in the Arezzo newspaper, we read the text of Badoglio's speech to the officers, and we learn of the decree for the expulsion of the Fascists.

Sunday the 24th, we attend a solemn ceremony for the victims of the mine in Villa Bartolomei, in the provostship, and the religious concert in honor of the A.M.G. The Mayor, Rosariva, delivers a nice speech. Muggy.

Tuesday, September 26, the day before the fast of Kippur; lunch is eaten at 10:30 A.M. and dinner at 4:15, all cooked by Rachel, without any help.

Menu: Soup of tagliatelle in broth, spinach with giblets, chicken roast in the oven with potatoes, cooked apples, real coffee. And the next day we had a very good fast, all four of us (Leo for the first time).

Menu of the dinner: broth, stewed pigeon with zucchini, potatoes, cooked fruit.

On the 28th, Mrs. Ferrucci brings us a *Nazione of the People of Florence*, where we read the scholastic regulations of the Commissariat for Education, Prof. Alessandro Setti, a friend and colleague of mine.

It pours and cools off.

On the 29th, first it rains, but around 9 A.M. it clears up and I go to Sansepolcro to press Governor Golding for permission to return to Florence. He receives me at 1 P.M. and tells me that a truck will come tomorrow morning to get us.

I arrive home and announce the departure. Rachel is beside herself, between pleasure and displeasure; Lionella jumps up and hugs me from joy; Leo is indifferent.

I work hard all evening until 11 P.M. on the preparations. Mrs. Rosa is unbearable, with her pedantry and her open windows, despite the icy wind. The provisions are assembled, all by candlelight. Goodbyes and emotion all around.

Saturday, September 30th, wake-up at 5:30 A.M. Rachel is trembling. Grand farewells from everyone. At 10 A.M. we leave, everyone at the fountain. A crate is overturned and many beans and much wheat and barley are lost. At 10:30 we leave with the Servi family of Florence, coming from Sansepolcro. We descend to the Fortress of Arezzo, to the Refugee Center, where we would have to wait who knows how many days, out in the open. I obtain permission to stay in the city, and after much walking around, we find two rooms with difficulty, just before curfew, on Corso Italia. Finally Leo and Lionella each sleep in a single bed, in a room just for them!

After so many months, we use our real last name with our real identity cards!!

We see many trucks with the star of David, the Jewish double triangle. At the refugee center they give us a nice loaf of bread, the English kind, which we had never eaten, very good, and cans of Argentinian beef, exquisite. Rachel has a bad headache.

Varied weather, cold, windy. We meet a Palestinian motorcyclist and Rachel speaks to him in Hebrew: it's a moment of great emotion!

October 2nd is the first day of Sukkot!

On the 3rd, after a five-hour wait, I speak with Captain Fielding's secretary, who denies permission for Florence. Emotional meetings with various Palestinians.

On the morning of the 4th, I return to insist with Lieutenant Ariel, but in vain.

The same result with the Major. Lunch at Buca di S. Francesco.

In the afternoon I speak with a Jewish major, a Russian, who gives me some hope.

We visit Lisino's relative, who offers us coffee, and we meet the Vigevanis.

In the afternoon, tea with cakes and hot roulôt, exquisite, at the non-commissioned officer's canteen of a Jewish unit, with an interesting German-English-Hebrew-French conversation. After dinner two Palestinian Jews come over, with many little gifts, useful and appreciated. Beautiful, hot weather.

After a great moral depression, Rachel is reanimated, and we enjoy these days greatly.

Aldo said in his book that when you were about to return to Florence, you weren't very sure or happy about coming back.

RACHEL: *I? . . . No, no, I was happy to come back, of course.*

You weren't depressed?

Maybe a little depressed, on account of the landlady in Anghiari, whom I could no longer stand. It was there that I was depressed, and I even wanted to leave, because of this old lady. I had always been very grateful that she kept us, but it was very difficult to live with her . . . Very difficult . . .

For example, we couldn't clean the floor very well, because we would ruin the pavement, you understand, spoil it. For example, to light the fire, it was necessary to put a long thing like this to the coal. But she didn't let me do it, because she said I would ruin this thing, which she wanted to leave to her granddaughter. Like that, everything was like that. I couldn't clean tomatoes near her sink because it wasn't marble, it was stone, and she said that the acid from the tomatoes could . . . You understand, all these kinds of things.

We stayed two weeks in Arezzo, we couldn't yet go to Florence because there was still danger in Florence. There were still Germans in the middle of . . . Fiesole . . . And they were bombing Florence, understand? And Aldo went all the time to the head of the Allies, who said, "No, not yet," "No, not yet," "No, not yet," but meanwhile, we were spending money, for the room, and for food. And the first time that we spent the sum of 25 lire, which was typical, it seemed to us very much! Because we had all these expenses now, how were we supposed to stay? We couldn't go to the bank to get money.

LIONELLA: *After the months of segregation [Mamma] wanted to return to her house . . . In order to quiet her, we were forced, almost, to leave Anghiari, ending in the chaos of Arezzo for two weeks, truly in poverty, living off the help of the Jewish Brigade and with the risk of ending up in a refugee camp. [Letter, March 1994]*

We read in *La Nazione* of the solemn inauguration of the Temple of Florence.

I read in a newspaper that teachers, middle and elementary, are being recalled to service by the Superintendent of Florence, Prof. Setti.

We continue to go to the partisan's canteen, only the children and I; Rachel prefers to eat cold food at home.

Wednesday, October 10th, more tremendous downpours.

With a statement by the Superintendent of Studies, I receive from the Amgot permission for Florence. Unspeakable joy, for all of us! We all go to the partisan canteen, the Vigevanis also.

Electric light returns; it seems like a dream!

On the 11th the weather is variable. We wait for the army vehicle to depart.

I have obtained for Mrs. Vigevani permission to go to Florence with a statement by the Superintendent.

After so many months, Rachel listens to a radio that works!

Thursday, October 12th, exhausting wait for the truck all morning, but it doesn't arrive . . .

Friday, October 13th, a motorcyclist notifies us at 6:15 that in a half-hour a truck is coming to get us! What ineffable joy! It comes at 7 A.M., after an anxious wait for them to open the road transport to get the baggage. At 7:45 A.M. we leave for Florence, passing Figline, San Giovanni, San Donato in Collina, Bagno a Ripoli, and at 10 A.M. we're on Via dei Banchi!!!

But we find everything occupied, and so we go to Bellosguardo, which is empty; we unload our things there. Rachel is left with Lionella and Leo and I go to the Palestinian garage in Borgognissanti (across from where we were hidden) with many signs in Hebrew. I see Mr. Mafini again. Then I go to take care of my ration cards. Lunch in Piazza Cavour. I see Ferdinando again at his house and then I run into Bettino in front of his house, where the Palestinian Club is now in place of the Office of Race—the Palestinian Jewish flag is even on the little terrace!! On Via Cavour—what emotion!

RACHEL: *And who gave light, water? Palestinian soldiers, Jews. Because most of them were lawyers, engineers, and it was they who gave us water, light, everything . . . And they who brought us to Florence, too.*

Near Bettino's house, there was the Office of Race.

Right in the house! When we left, there was a German flag on the balcony! And then, when we returned, there was our flag, the Palestinian flag, understand? And so immediately, I went up and introduced myself as a relative of Bettino's . . . Ooh, they made me welcome, they gave me tea, cookies, all these things (laughs).

From today the blackout is removed!

What an unforgettable day, Saturday, October 14! At 9 A.M., we go to Temple in Via delle Oche after having seen the disastrous destruction of all the houses near the Ponte Vecchio. It's stirring to see the ruin where Mrs. Barberis once lived. It's hard to identify the exact site.

I go to *sefer* and perform the *hagomel* and recite the *Kaddish*. I see Valentina of Ferrara once more, Mario Cassuto, Giuseppino, De Rossi, *hazzanim*, couriers, etc.

Sunday, October 15th. Leo enters the Palestinian school on Via Farini with a 9–12 schedule and refreshments (milk, cookies, and chocolate).

At Temple I open the strongbox which I find miraculously intact!! Incredible joy!! We all assemble for Leo's first departure from the Palestinian school.

Monday, October 16th, for the first time I put back on my large *tallit*, saying the morning prayer at home! I run into the Siebzehner (children).

I tour the school with Lionella to sign her up for preparatory classes, but I am advised not to.

RACHEL: *Everyone said no. From Bellosguardo it was difficult to get to the city—the bridges were all destroyed. [Letter, March 11, 1994]*

And so Lionella couldn't go to school that year because the bridges were all topsy-turvy, and for a young girl to walk under the rubble like that was impossible. And so she was enrolled in a teaching school. But this was only for a year, because when she returned home, she took the exam to enter the scientific high school.

I argue with the Nutis, father and mother, for the rooms in Via dei Banchi, which ends cordially after a semicomic session, she in bed and the daughter shouting from behind a door.

Rachel is very nervous and of the worst humor, to the great surprise and sadness of the three of us.

Lionella goes to the Palestinian school. The lights go every other minute.

The Banca Commerciale Italiana informs me that the German SS has broken open our strong box, but there were few savings books.

On the 18th, Lionella takes her first mathematics lesson with Miss Frankental. I go to Bellosguardo with Raffaello and give him flour to get bread from a baker. At 6:45 Mrs. Becattini comes to say that her mother, Mrs. Rosa, is very ill from typhoid fever and in the hospital. How astounded I am!

Rachel is terribly nervous and makes me despair, worrying about the house and the furniture. What a shame!

LIONELLA: *Certainly [Mamma] did not share my and my father's enthusiasm for being "liberated" and for having survived, moments to which I still often turn, denying myself the right to complain about anything:* I AM STILL ALIVE—*Mamma didn't feel this like we did . . .*

Having arrived in Florence, we had to settle in at Bellosguardo, without light, without running water, without heat. It certainly was not pleasant—but while Papa and I took everything with renewed strength, Mamma cried over every missing comfort, every lack of news from Africa, over the ruins after the bombing of the house in Via Masaccio, over our very serious economic difficulties, over the prolonged occupation of "her house" on Via dei Banchi—hard months for me . . .

And Leo, much more fragile and a slave to his mother's mood, suffered the effects right away . . . and I couldn't be any help to him because in those months a chasm opened between us on account of behavioral differences that were too large. [Letter, March 1994]

Thursday, October 19th, rainy and humid. Rachel has returned to good humor and we come to a friendly agreement with Mr. Campi and Dr. Nuti for the house and my study. We find the two closed rooms in a terrible state, plus damages in the dining room and in Mamma's room . . .

RACHEL: *No, they didn't want to leave. These Nuti weren't Florentines, understand. Those others who stayed in the living room were from an insurance company near the Piazza della Repubblica. And since it was large, the Allies requisitioned it. And so they couldn't go back, understand.*

But then when we returned to our house, I—as always I did everything myself—I entered and I said, "Look, until now, you have stayed here without paying me a cent. Now I wish for you either to leave, or to pay me something. Because I have to bring in the workers to fix everything that you have damaged in the house."

They said to me, "Excuse us. We are not leaving here until the Allies leave us our office."

"This I understand. But I want you in the meantime to pay me something for this period."

"But you wouldn't ask the Allies to pay."

I say, "No, I would not have asked the Allies. Because they have given us our freedom. They have saved us as Jews." I answer just like that. I say, "Look, you have to give it to me, but I don't want your money in hand. You will put it in the bank for me, so that then I'll have a sum to call the workers who will clean the house for me." They had reduced the living room to an awful state. They had ruined everything, understand.

"Ah, Madam, we'll get a lawyer. We'll see what the lawyer says."

"Ah," I say, "you get yourself a lawyer, and I'll get myself a lawyer." And so I immediately telephoned Bettino Errera, Luisa's husband, who was a lawyer. "Ah, of course, you're right Rachel, wait." And so, brriinng, he telephones right away. So they

call me, "What, Madam, you have already called a lawyer?" "Eh," I said, "didn't you
tell me that you were calling a lawyer? So I called mine . . ."

And so they gave me 2,000 lire a month, in the bank. And so when they went away,
I had 50,000 lire. That's how it went.

Monday, October 23rd, we all go to Bellosguardo, settling in as best we can.

I pass through Via Masaccio to see our building, which is in a disastrous state. At the Cassa di Risparmio, I report the removal of our savings books from the Banca Commerciale Italiana. I present an application for Lionella's middle school certificate exams. I accompany Mrs. Beccattini to the garage. Always on foot, you understand—I'm wearing out myself and my shoes!

That evening we ate under an oil lamp in the billiard room, one dish in one pan, cooked by peasants, and at 7 P.M. to bed, all without light and without coal!

Wednesday the 25th we brought all our things from the Sestini house to the attic of Via dei Banchi, and I reassemble my study in the dining room.

RACHEL: *Sestini is someone who runs a moving company . . . We knew him well because he moved us from Rome to Florence and then . . . when we came to this house, Sestini brought our stuff here. And then when we had to run away from Florence, and it upset us to leave this house with all these things, Aldo went to Sestini, and he said, "Listen, I would like to ask you a favor. We are leaving our apartment. Could you save my books for me, which are the tools of my trade?" And he said to him, "Professor, not only will I try to save your books, but the whole house, all the furniture." He was wonderful, Sestini. Wonderful.*

On October 26th, it pours violently. I go see the Crisciones to talk about what was missing in the Ambron Villa. I sit down for the first time at my desk in the dining room—what an effect it has on me! I meet Giorgio Dalla Volta.

Friday, October 27th, I sign Leo up for the seventh grade in the Machiavelli school in Piazza Pitti.

The jewelry box is withdrawn intact from Mrs. Mealli. The box of books is emptied by Ferdinando . . .

Rachel had been responsible, back in the early days of the German occupation, before they went to Anghiari, for depositing their goods for safekeeping.

RACHEL: *I said, "Aldo," I said, "What do we do with these jewels we have in a box at the bank? Let's get them, and I'll give them to this friend, and then to another friend whom I had met earlier." I say, "But you don't know them. How can I do it, Aldo, give all this stuff" that isn't mine, it's his mother's, understand? Aldo replied, "If you know her, and you trust her . . . do it." And so I took a little box, I put everything in it, and I took it to her . . . Because this lady was so good to me, when we didn't have the ration cards to buy bread, she gave me a package with bread, with some things to eat, covered in the wrapping paper from her shop. I went out as if I had bought something from her. She was very good . . . Mrs. Mealli. Anyway, when we returned, she offered me tea, so great was her joy to see me. Because I had said to her, "Take this box. If we return, give it back to me, if we don't come back, it will be yours." And she was very happy to give it back to me, understand?*

November 1st, Rachel and the children go to see "The Dictator" (Mussolini and Hitler) at the cinema.

Before dinner, a terrible scene on account of Leo's naughtiness, which upset us all. Sobs and bad headaches for Rachel.

Flooding of the Arno damages the English bridge, the ex-Santa Trinità, and one can cross only at the Ponte Vecchio, where there's a fantastic clutter and terrible mud, pools of water and rain.

Horrible weather, continual downpours. Leo stays out of school because of the bad weather and last evening's scenes. The Paliotti come to see us to talk about our building in Via Masaccio where some tenants were living.

I continue to empty the boxes of books, as I do the next day.

Saturday, November 4th, rest in the villa. I test Lionella for the exams.

On November 6th, Lionella begins the exams for her middle school certificate.

Leo makes a terrible scene because Rachel said he had a shabby shirt; Rachel and I are very worried about him.

RACHEL: *Meanwhile, Leo had taken the fifth grade certificate exam and had entered middle school . . . And Aldo went to the principal right away to say, Please, don't tell Leo to move to the seventh grade, but only to the sixth, because Aldo didn't want Leo to tire himself. He was very good . . .*

And so it went like that, he did magnificently well, and after the exam, he had to take the gymnastics exam, too . . . And so the first thing they tell him to do, is they had a rope like this, and they said to climb it. But he couldn't climb it. And so, the gymnastics professor who was a Fascist, from the militia, said, "This boy has failed." So, after the academic year during which Leo had done poorly at gymnastics, we went to see the results which were all posted. And we saw Leo Neppi Modona—Good. The principal saw us looking for "Leo Neppi Modona." "Ah," he says, "you are Professor Neppi Modona. Please come into my offices." He says, "I wanted to show you the results of your son's exams." Excellent, excellent, excellent, excellent, excellent. He says, "Now you'll ask me, why the result is Good and not Excellent." And he told us that the gymnastics professor wanted to fail him, but the other professors rebelled. Because they said, "What?! We have to fail a boy who has all Excellents because of gymnastics? He has to be held back?" And so, to solve everything, they put Good.

Leo is wicked, he makes us despair more and more every day. Lionella begins her exams at 2:30 P.M. with drawing.

The Arno can still only be crossed at the Ponte Vecchio with an enormous crowd.

Lionella proceeds with her exams. It rains, terrible humidity. Funeral of Enzo Bonaventura's mother. Lionella comes home at 12:30 P.M., triumphant after her exams.

I confer with Eugenio Artom and I join the Italian Liberal Party. After several months, a postcard from Leone arrives from Rome! November 10th is beautiful and cold. Lionella receives a "good," one of only six out of fifty-one; no one receives an "excellent" for the certificate. She goes back to the Palestinian school.

Sestini takes back the forty book crates, empty.

I get twenty kilos of potatoes from the Delasem [Jewish relief organization] and I haul the sack on my shoulders from Via Farini to Via Banchi, helped in part by two of the children's string bags.

LIONELLA: *Ah, after the war, we had little to eat, I think it was a little less disgusting than what we had during the war, a little less of a mess of things. In short, it wasn't anything special. We stuffed ourselves on legumes imported from America, little cans of green peas, yellow peas, very nice: one evening green peas, the next, yellow peas. How nice! And full of weevils. The peas made long summer trips in ships, you see. Then they sat in the grape storehouses. Then they were distributed, then they arrived at our house, then they stayed there because one couldn't use all these things at once. We boiled them and we made this cream. Before you could eat this soup, you had to bring it to a boil and take out all these weevils. They weren't very clean. They weren't very kosher. (Laughs) We took these all out, and then we ate it. Delicious, eh?*

Every day the same?

Every day, no, because luckily at Bellosguardo there was a little beet root, local greens. And then packages began to arrive from relatives in Africa and America with sugar and coffee.

Saturday, November 11th, recital of the Palestinian school at the small reception room of the Verdi Theater, with our children participating. Great, moving success. Too bad we didn't have light!

Icy day, beautiful, as was Sunday the 12th. Sunday I go on foot to the cemetery. Very sad afternoon on account of a curse Leo pronounced against his parents: Lionella and Rachel cry, and great melancholy on my part. Only after seven hours does he ask our forgiveness, showing selfish feelings and little affection.

Monday, November 13th, at 8:30 A.M. I take Leo to school in Piazza Pitti, for the first time, to the Machiavelli school, but he is assigned to the afternoon session, section "D" (hours 1:30–4:30).

I go with Lionella to pick up her middle school certificate, and register her for the first year of teacher's school in Via Santo Spirito.

That evening, tremendous rain, under which Rachel, Lionella, and I return home, while Leo, home from school, waits alone in the villa.

For some time after our return, every week, a subsidy is given to the evacuees, the victims of persecution, etc., with precedence to the Jews and the carriage drivers, at the E.C.A. (Community Assistence Organization) in Via degli Orti Oricellari.

I speak with Leo's teacher and exempt Leo from writing on Saturday.

Rachel withdraws her package of jewels from the Masieri and we return together under the downpour and through the mud on the Ponte Vecchio.

Wednesday, November 29th, I confer with the Principal of the Michelangelo and get a schedule and list of books. Rachel and Lionella come to the city in the afternoon. Fantastic crowd at the crossing of the Santa Trinità bridge, reopened to traffic. I buy the first books for Lionella (music, singing, and drawing). I bathe at the establishment in Via Cavour. I collect my card and pay for the year 1944 at the Liberal Party Headquarters. It's raining, humid.

Friday, December 1st, I collect various ration cards at the Santa Maria Novella parish. The Superintendent authorizes me to begin lessons from next Monday at the Michelangelo school, my school!! Yes!!

I go to *arvit* in Via delle Oche.

The weather is stupendous. I return to lunch at the villa, where we eat delicious food on the terrace. In the afternoon, I accompany Leo to school and exempt him from writing on Saturday with Miss Ferrara in mathematics . . .

Monday, December 4th, first day of lessons at the Michelangelo! What joy! Section C is assigned to me, all female and pleasant. The lesson is now forty-five minutes, though I'll still be paid for an hour.

The 7th is the eleven-month anniversary of Mamma's death. With Rachel and the children we go to the service in Via delle Oche, where we light two candles with Leone's candelabras.

On December 9th, Prof. Minto shows me the work on the offices of the Institute of Etruscan Studies in Santissima Annunziata (Via Gino Capponi).

Rachel goes to speak with Leo's Principal on account of the children who pick on him as a Jew.

LIONELLA: *My brother lost this year of study. He started seventh grade across the river. An extremely working-class area. They didn't give this little boy a bit of sexual education! He found himself, therefore, by now he was almost thirteen, a young man who didn't know anything. With boys from the San Frediano area who were completely knowing.*

One day they took him, they put him against the wall. "Pee! Pee!" They were making fun of him because he was circumcised. So, they are traumas for which he found himself unprepared on account of my parents' ineptitude.

These are all criticisms that I did not make then—I couldn't have this under-standing. I make them after. But, come on, they were older, I was fourteen years old, I couldn't give him the sex education that even I had not had. Mamma said, "Look, you'll have blood, menstruation, here's the little belt of red cotton . . . Attach this here." This was in my room, then when it came, I was thirteen, it was on the sly, just like a birthday present. (Laughs) So, it's true, it wasn't easy, am I right?

And my brother must have been terribly shocked by this . . . I think it was more this shock that . . . He had no ties to his companions, in fact, and as soon as I discov-ered someone who remembered him, he remembered him precisely as a shocked, iso-lated boy, traumatized by his professors, that he didn't know how to hold a pen, he turned over the India ink—the professor was crazy to have all the written assignments in India ink. And so he sent him to handwriting lessons, for goodness' sake. And this for him was terrible, no? To take handwriting lessons! And then after, he had to change classes, because we came to live here in the city. They didn't let him stay there at the Machiavelli, where he may have found his niche by then.

December 10th, cold and pretty weather.

With Rachel and the children we choose toys to sell at home.

In Via delle Oche, moving service with Belgrado for the first day of Chanukah, with the singing of *Ha-tikvah*. The Chanukah is lit with a candle of ours left over from Mamma's anniversary.

The 14th is beautiful. I sell books and sheet music for 400 lire.

Meeting at Michelangelo of the new professors to get to know the programs.

Leo, waking up, makes a scene about the French books to be bought and makes us despair. With Rachel, I set the prices for the sale of the toys . . .

Friday, December 15th, I sit in on the first exams of Greek and Roman history at the university with Giannelli and Norsa, what joy! What moral rehabilitation!

On December 17th, in the afternoon, profitable and interesting sale of toys and other things to several pleasant private citizens.

RACHEL: *We also needed money. Because Aldo didn't have a brother who could help, he didn't have anyone. And so we said, "We'll sell what we have." For example, one thing I cried about, when I saw it leave the house, was a beautiful mirror of*

Murano glass, very beautiful, large, almost half of this table, with a frame like this, also from Murano, beautiful, *and we sold it for 7,000 lire. Which now would be 7,000,000, let's say. Then the piano, then a chaise lounge, a small armchair, all my son—my children's toys. We needed money.*

But who bought these things?

People.

LIONELLA: *In this atmosphere it was decided, to help our parents, that we would sell our toys, but it was a disappointment. I thought that parents and children would show up, to whom I could entrust my treasures, happy that others would enjoy them. Instead they were taken as a group by a storekeeper—at that point I would not have wanted to get rid of it all! On the other hand, I was less attached to them than to other objects, from my earliest childhood, which bit by bit were always eliminated by Mamma in various moves. [Letter, March 1994]*

Unpredictable weather.

Monday, December 18th, from today postal service is extended to the rest of Italy toward the south. It rains. I go to school on my bicycle with an umbrella.

From December 19th, electric light returns to Bellosguardo! On the return from Florence, I find an enormous clutter at the Santa Trinità bridge.

We sell the grand Venetian mirror and the four paintings of the seasons . . .

Again on the 24th a great icy wind blows; the sale of the toys continues. Leo has a cold and stays home with Lionella, and that evening has a temperature of 38 C.

Wednesday, December 27th, is icy but gorgeous.

In the afternoon I go with Leo to see Mrs. Lurini, who gives him a good philo-sophical-moral lesson on serenity. She offers me black coffee.

Isola comes to see us with Giuliana.

I carry Leo on my bicycle for the first time from 2 to 7 P.M., going with vases of flowers to thank the Tagliaferri family at the cure, then Prof. Momigliano, then the lawyer Agostini and Mrs. Giannelli, then the lawyer Federigo Maracchi for the sale of our building. Beautiful return trip by moonlight.

Friday, December 29th, after *arvit* I speak briefly at 4:30 P.M. in Via delle Oche on Job. Leo and a great crowd were present, in the light of the *menorah* and on *echal*.

In the morning the weather is beautiful, very cold, the afternoon is windy.

Saturday, December 30th, is beautiful. Outside at 7 A.M. it's one degree.

First lesson of Uzzielli to Leo to become *bar mitzvah*.

1 9 4 5

The continuation can be found in the normal pocket diaries! I note here only that we have returned to live regularly in the apartment in Via dei Banchi, leaving Bellosguardo definitively on September 24th, a Monday, with an incredible haul on Paulo's cart, but half of the apartment remains for a while with the Riunione Adriatica di Sicurtà.

Beyond that, I extract some of the more interesting and important news items:

March 28: At 6 P.M., first *seder* at the Villa in Bellosguardo with Bettino and Luigi Gallichi. Immense happiness, exquisite dinner, serenity after so much suffering!

March 29, First day of *pesach*, ceremony at the central Temple, renovated and reconsecrated, crowded with Allied soldiers.

April 21, Bologna is retaken by the Allies with an outflanking.

April 29, we learn that among other Fascist leaders, Mussolini, Farinacci, and Turati have been executed. Northern Italy is all but liberated!

April 30, a day off to celebrate. We eat baked yeast cakes to celebrate the death of Fascism.

The first letter direct from Israel and Lucia arrives, sent March 2.

May 7, the armistice for the ending of the war in Europe is signed. Bettino has returned from Rome and tells us that Leone is renamed Director General of the National Institute of Insurance.

Saturday, June 16, Leo is *bar mitzvah* in Via delle Oche. Celebration at Bellosguardo.

On June 30th, the first letter arrives from Gino in Bogotà and the first message via the C.R.I. from Vico in Switzerland.

RACHEL: *And I, when I was in the street, I looked for some soldiers from Salisbury, Rhodesians. And I found one, who had written here, "Rhodesian," understand? And so I immediately stopped him with my English (laughs) and I asked him if he could write a letter to my family. One was there, he said, "Yes, yes, yes," and he didn't do anything. Another, on the other hand, did it. He wrote to my family . . . that I was fine, that I was in Florence, etc. And so immediately my brother sent him a telegram,*

"Very happy, letter follows," he wrote. It was all in this soldier's hands because we couldn't write, or anything. Because the war still wasn't over. And so this soldier brought me the letter and when my mother and my brother sent some packages of food, he brought them to me.

August 17, a Friday, at 11 A.M. moving meeting with Cecil Roth at the Hotel Excelsior. Together with him, the military captain Pimental, and Lionella, a visit to Via delle Oche.

August 18th, Saturday, I see Roth again at the central Temple, where I go with Lionella. At 7 P.M., a speech by Roth in the garden of Via Farini, introduced by me. Affectionate meeting with Rachel.

August 20, transfer to our house of the last group of things from Miss Giacone, Mamma's nurse, where it had been deposited.

August 28, Luisa arrives from Rome, met at the station by me, the children, and Bettino, and comes with us to Bellosguardo.

September 7, day before Rosh Hashanah, we dine under the *berceau* with Luisa, Bettino, and Giuseppino, with dishes prepared by Rachel. It's like a dream! . . .

On the 19th, I sign Leo up for the eighth grade and the Boy Scouts.

On September 30, the turn of the *sefarin* in Via delle Oche, where everyone goes, exultant. Our house is almost ready, on account of Rachel who hasn't rested a minute for seven days.

Friday, the 28th, we had a great festive dinner in our dining room all in order on account of Rachel.

October 13th, glorious day, everyone to lunch at Bellosguardo with Bettino and Luisa. Leo had stayed up there since our departure for the city house . . .

RACHEL: *From Bellosguardo we came home. Leo stayed there the last and finally . . .*

Why, why did he stay up there?

Because the house still wasn't completely settled.

So, there wasn't enough room, or . . .

Yes, but it was necessary to prepare the beds, because we had given them to Sestini.

On October 22nd, everyone to lunch at Bellosguardo and Leo comes back to sleep at home definitively. And so on the 23rd, with the return of Leo and his things after two years, happy, we are returned to our house!

PART FOUR

Readings

False Names

L ANGUAGE IS THE KEY to a culture; a single word can deliver a shock of understanding. What English speaker can ignore, for example, the interaction of gender politics and the Italian language? You can't say "baby" in modern Italian without specifying the sex; the word for abortion is the same as the word for miscarriage; if there are thirty women and one man in a room, the group is grammatically male. Cultures might not be determined by language, but they are certainly informed by them, which is why the word "Ms." is essential, not decorative, to the feminist movement in America.

In Italian, there is a word, *la dopoguerra*, which means the post-war period, literally, the after-war. It was a period of political and economic chaos, a slow, hungry, ragged return to normality. People began to find out which of their friends and family had died, what property they had lost forever, what they could expect from their "liberators," and what they could not. For the Neppi Modonas, it was a period of both relief and disappointment; they were now free and equal, but they had to sell their children's toys for lack of money; they were back home again, but for two years they had to share that home with the strangers who had commandeered it. The racial laws were gone, but somehow their disappearance didn't put right the lives they had disrupted. Memo Bemporad remembered his father saying: "We'll carry the consequences of the racial laws with us to our tombs . . . The injustice we suffered will perpetuate itself and nothing will be able to stop it."[28]

Some wrongs were righted, however; the upside-down language of Fascist culture began to turn right side up. Take the word *pietisti*, for example, pietists or pityists, depending on how you translate it. Fascists used this label to mean those who sympathized with or helped the Jews. It was a word that threatened non-Jews and kept them from helping when they could. The landlady at Impruneta knew it was wrong to kick out the Neppi Modonas—she stopped at church that morning to pray for guidance— but she was afraid to help, afraid to be labeled a *pietista* and suffer the consequences. The word, of course, is positive in derivation and in actual meaning. Who wouldn't want to be someone who was helping, someone pious, someone who pitied others? And yet, who, under the racial laws and especially once the Germans occupied, would want to be considered one of the *pietisti*? No one.

Then there was the word *discriminato*, discriminated, the word applied to those Jews exempt from some of the racial laws. Not discriminated *against* but selected, set apart from those discriminated against. The word *ariano*, Aryan, had taken on an equally bizarre meaning when applied to Fascist Italy: a swarthy Southern Catholic was Aryan whereas a blond and blue-eyed Milanese Jew was not. Aldo referred in amazement to the "pure (!) Aryan (?) Italian race (!)."

And yet even he could not resist these strange false words. He applied to be discriminated, and surely, once or twice, called some Catholic neighbor an Aryan without ironical parentheses or quotation marks. From our first "mamma" we are taught to absorb language and adapt to its changes; it is against our natures to resist new words, even if at first they seem ridiculous.

Fascist words certainly pushed ridiculous to the limit: one could, for example, *become* Aryan, which would seem to be biologically impossible. Children of mixed marriages who had been baptized by a certain time were officially Aryan, so a friendly priest might predate your baptismal certificate. But trying to be Aryan or discriminated had a price, and the price was allowing these false words into your vocabulary. Aren't you then making a mockery of true words, even The Word, baptism, true faith, God? Or are you justified in speaking the government's language to save yourself, even if that means accepting baptism as a way to political rather than spiritual salvation?

The hero of Luigi Preti's novel *A Jew in Fascism* is the son of a nonreligious Jew and a Catholic. He never stepped in a synagogue. But when he was about to marry a Catholic, he refused, out of principle, to be baptized. With the advent of the racial laws, he is faced with the decision once again. A friend tries to convince him to let the Church turn him into an Aryan:

> "You know, don't you, that the so-called mixed people, even the circumcised ones, can procure a valid certificate of baptism? There are obliging priests who release the certificate with a date previous to the 30th of September, as the law requests for the declaration of Aryanness."

"It's fraud."

"It's legitimate defense. It serves to get around an unjust law, which banishes faultless citizens."

"It's not the predating that bothers me. It's the device of baptism that disgusts me."[29]

Preti's hero refused to accept the idea that the word *baptism* had lost its true meaning, while his friend has decided that, given the circumstances, *baptism* merely means "legitimate defense." Should cynicism be matched with cynicism, should baptism be used blasphemously to evade the law, since the Fascists set it up that way? Or should their callous sacrilege be shunned, even at personal risk? Should one resist, refuse to accept false definitions, whatever the circumstances? Or are Fascists perhaps not merely distorting the meaning of baptism (and Catholicism and Judaism) but *changing* it; perhaps the political realities have changed those words for good—and the sooner one realizes it the better.

Under Fascism and especially under the racial laws, nothing meant what it once did. The idea of an Italian Aryan race, already laughable, was rendered more absurd by the possibility of being Aryanized. All one had to do was prove that one's father was not Jewish, but Aryan, and one did that by claiming that one was born as a result of one's mother's adultery. Presto, different "race." Not many people availed themselves of this insulting option, but there it was, the grotesque child of twisted Fascist logic and Jewish desperation.

Making Jews into a race, making Italians Aryan, the Fascists took meaning away, rendered words not nebulous as they were before, but empty. If I make a law that says all Americans, except those with freckles, are geniuses, what does "genius" mean? Nothing. In struggling with the Fascist laws, Jews found the same thing happening with their most personal words, their own names. The writer Moravia said that, "Because of the absurdity (always present under dictatorships), my mother decided to take the necessary steps to change our *Jewish* name into another *Aryan*, that of my maternal grandmother, to be precise. To my objections, my mother, with good sense, said that one name is worth as much as another. Finally, discriminated, but still suspect, I was prohibited from writing in newspapers under my own name. So I chose the transparent pseudonym of *Pseudo* . . . In those years, for reasons all connected to Fascism, my identity became more uncertain every day, more problematic, more ephemeral."[30]

Even before the racial laws, the Fascists were forcing people to change their names. According to Rachel, by the time Leo was born, in 1932, children weren't supposed to be named after animals. But Rachel and Aldo wanted to name their son after the grandfather, Leone Neppi Modona, and *leone* means lion. So instead they named him Leo, which means lion in Latin. Rachel loves the story of how they fooled the Fascist officials. Yet they didn't get to name him Leone; in fact they ended up naming him not after Leone, but after *leone*, that is, not after the man but after the beast. And the point—both theirs and Mussolini's—got lost.

Eleven years later, Leo's name had to be changed again. "But why do we have to tell all these lies, Mamma? I thought we weren't supposed to lie," said Leo, when instructed to tell people his name was Leonida Nistri Maddaloni. But now "lie" did not mean what it once did; it meant "survive." It was a commandment, not a sin. It took Aldo a long time to realize that; he was so honest, so law-abiding. At first he spoke the Fascist language, accepting *discriminato* as his new name; and before the Germans came, his most egregious crime against the Fascist code was publishing under someone else's name. Even that might have pleased the Fascists, since it helped "prove" that Jewish intellectuals could be silenced without damaging Italian intellectual life. But when the Germans took over Italy in September 1943, propped Mussolini back up, and started threatening the Jews in a way many had never imagined, he had to tell lies, real direct lies: "I'm Alfonso Nistri Maddaloni, from the town of Catanzaro."

Once the Neppi Modonas get their false names, he refers to them that way in his diary—calls his wife Riccarda, his children Luisa and Leonida. This was not a safety precaution; he mentions other names and even addresses, and he didn't even begin to construct the diary from his notes until most of the danger had passed and the war was just a matter of waiting for the Allies. He could have called them by their real names. It was as if in some way during this time they had changed into their false selves, they were not who they were before the war. I suppose they weren't. But then, who were they? Rachel says that at home in Anghiari they called each other by their real names. And Lionella says that though they frequently went to mass, they never learned so much as the Lord's Prayer to make their "Catholicism" more believable. Too many people knew the truth, she said; everybody knew. They were too much who they were before, and not enough. Was their essence shifting or was it just their names? Is this who they were or were they who they had been before?

"Each one asked himself deep down question on top of question," wrote Aldo in his journal, "and felt a kind of uneasiness inside, an agony never felt; it seemed like an awakening from a lethargy. But then was it all a trick, bad faith to call us Italians, an ongoing fiction since birth—parents, relatives, everyone complicit? But no, no, *this* is the fiction, a fictitious construction."

By this time, they had their false names, Leo had stopped writing, and Aldo had begun to turn his notebooks into a proper memoir. He called his family by their false names, and in fact, it seemed as if everything was false, that all the names were false. In his journal, Aldo refers to the "enemy" in quotation marks, so we know that it means the Allies. Aldo is aware of the space between the word and its meaning, aware of how the newspapers now said the opposite of what all but Fascist hardliners felt, how everyone spoke and wrote and read in code.

The newspapers, by now two-sided sheets, were controlled by the false government—the Republic of Salò—and lauded the activities of false friends—the Germans. "There were fourteen dead, said the newspapers, but goodness knows how many there really had been, you had to multiply what the papers said by ten if it was bad . . . divide it by ten if it was good."[31] Papers had to be read inside out: the "enemy" wasn't the Allies, it was the Germans, and the sooner the Americans could bring their troops up the peninsula to "occupy" (liberate) the northern cities, the better. Because what the papers never said was that the longer the war went on, the longer Italians ate hard, moldy bread (if they could get it), feared they would be impressed into the German army or shot for desertion, listened to bombs exploding, or died in the rubble. The longer the war went on, the longer the Jews risked round-ups and a fate unknowable, unthinkable, unbelievable even after the war when the propaganda, the rumors, the false names subsided and the truth emerged.

False names were, of course, far more extensive and far more necessary in countries where people's neighbors were routinely massacred close enough for the odor to be detected. Hannah Arendt describes the language surrounding the death camps:

> All correspondence referring to the matter was subject to rigid "language rules," and, except in the reports from the *Einsatzgruppen*, it is rare to find documents in which such bald words as "extermination," "liquidation," or "killing" occur. The prescribed code names for killing were "final solution," "evacuation" (*Aussiedlung*), and "special treatment" (*Sonderbehandlung*); deportation—unless it involved Jews directed to Theresienstadt, the "old people's ghetto" for privileged Jews, in which case it was called "change of residence"—received the name of "resettlement" (*Umsiedlung*) and "labor in the East" (*Arbeitseinsatz im Osten*), the point of these latter names being that Jews were indeed often temporarily resettled in ghettos and that a certain percentage of them were temporarily used for labor.[32]

"Romanzo di Vita Vissuta" is what Aldo named his journal—A Tale of Life Lived. Like our word "tale," *romanzo* means a story, which can be real or invented, but it has whispers of fiction about it, just as "tall" and "fairy" hover about our word "tale." Aldo himself uses *romanzo* to mean fiction. "É realtà o romanzo?" he asks when he sees his cousin for the first time after the liberation: is it reality or fiction? So "Romanzo di Vita Vissuta" implies fiction while asserting real life, life lived. It wasn't real, but he lived through it.

Liberation meant a return to reality, a righting of those upside-down words. The Allies could be called friends in public, and *pietisti* became something it was good to have been. But "liberation" itself hints that there were problems in changing the words back, because "liberation" does not begin to describe what the Allies did to and for the Italians. It encompasses neither bombing nor plunder nor patronage. Today Lionella still writes of being "liberated" like that, in quotation marks.

So liberation was also a linguistically confusing time. Fascists could now be criticized, but who were the *Fascisti*? Somehow, there weren't any after the war; everyone was a *partigiano*. Was a Fascist someone who belonged to the party, worked for the party? Or was it someone who, once Fascism fell, joined up with Mussolini at the Republic of Salò (and was therefore called *repubblichino*—little republican)? And what if they didn't want to fight the Allies, but were somehow forced? And what if they wanted to fight, but only because they were ashamed that Italy had turned traitor to Germany? Who were the real *Fascisti*?

During the *dopoguerra, ebreo* was a good thing to be politically; it could even bring you special privileges. Rachel said Aldo got to teach in Florence at his old high school when he returned simply because he was Jewish. Jewish teachers got seven years of seniority for the years they hadn't worked; even Lionella did, when she became a teacher, though she was only fourteen when the war ended. So the word "Jew" did something of an about-face, at least in the official arena. Even stranger for Aldo must have been words like "patriot" and "Fatherland." And how could he say "German" the same way, or even "Italian"? How could anyone?

Whoever wins the war gets to decide what the words mean, and finally the war was over and the decisions were being made. There was a point when the fate of all those words was in doubt. The Neppi Modonas must have imagined the possibility that "Jew" would forever mean "marked for death," in the event that Germany won the war. "Professor" would, for Aldo, be a bitter nod to an unrecoverable past. "Sabbath" would be a day to hide, for the observant, and a day to forget for others. "Hitler" might mean the dictator of Europe. Mussolini's Republic of Salò would be the puppet government of a beaten country. Or it could be a sick two-year joke. No one knew. Words lurched precariously in the unsteady grasp of history, and with them, lives.

No one suffered from this linguistic insecurity more than Leo, whose trust in people and what they said was probably never restored. To his terror that his parents would die was added the very real possibility that they weren't telling him the truth. After all, he was told little or nothing, every new move, every new bed was a surprise. He saw that lying was indeed the new rule. He was told: Your name is Leonida Nistri Maddaloni. You come from Catanzaro. You must tell strangers that your name is Leonida and you come from Catanzaro.

Gaia Servadio, in her book *Un'infanzia diversa (A Different Childhood)*, describes the scene as it happened to her.

> Speaking *sottovoce* Papa and Mama had told me that we were in danger. "It's very important. Listen carefully, children. Pay attention: now your name is Prinzi. It's not Servadio anymore. When you go to school, when someone asks you what your name is, your last name from now on is Prinzi . . . If someone asks you where you come from, we're refugees from Trieste where the bombardments have destroyed everything, our house, our papers. We no longer have anything in Trieste."
>
> "Not in Padua?"
>
> "In Trieste."
>
> Then there was the test. Papa, kneeling, looked at me intensely: "What's your name?"
>
> "Gaia Servadio."
>
> "No!"
>
> I hadn't understood.[33]

Leo and Lionella understood. Gaia was only five. Leo was by that point eleven, Lionella just thirteen. Understanding only made it stranger, though. He thought we weren't supposed to lie.

Just after that he stopped writing, according to all accounts because he had lost hope, because he thought it was no use, that they would all die. But he also faced a difficult problem as a writer: How do you write the true story of your life if you're living a lie? What joy is there in changing your name when you're not called by the real one anyhow? Would Andrea take on the name Leonida? Or would he acquire a false false name? Fiction and nonfiction, true and false, Leo, Leone, Leonida, these words started to blur. How *could* he write?

Leo started to write again at a certain point in Anghiari when liberation was at hand. But it was different. Rachel said she had the story somewhere, though she couldn't find it, but she described it.

> There's still another writing of Leo's, but very difficult. But he was already a boy who knew about Dante, about . . .
>
> So it's not so charming.
>
> *No, no, no.*

A little more adult . . .

Stranger, understand.

I understand.

And this [Barbarians in the 20th Century] *is how I knew that I knew everything then about his life. This really and truly is a diary, the other was instead a story.*

Everyone was relieved when Leo started to write again. But the old Leo had not returned. The new one knew about Dante (or, perhaps more to the point, he knew about hell) and stopped writing about himself and his life and started writing Fiction. Leo started to write again, Jews were equals again, the Neppi Modonas were home again. But Mamma Ada was dead, six million Jews were dead, the Jewish community of Rhodes was annihilated. The words had settled perhaps, but could they ever be what they were? They were like broken bones, set crooked in wartime haste—they were healed, but they weren't quite right. Elie Wiesel wrote, "Would it ever again be possible to speak of justice, of truth, of divine charity, after the murder of one million Jewish children?"[34]

During the *dopoguerra*, the word *discriminato* took on an even stranger definition. It meant someone who was brought to trial as a Fascist after the war and found innocent.

The Strength to Go On

WHEN THE Neppi Modonas came back from Anghiari, Leo went to school in a tough neighborhood, San Frediano. He had no choice because the family was living at Bellosguardo which is *oltr'Arno*, that is, across the river from most of Florence. The bridges were almost all destroyed by bombs; at one time only the Ponte Vecchio was passable—and that only if you were willing to crowd in and clamber over the rubble of the surrounding streets. And so he had to go to school *oltr'Arno* too, where, according to Lionella, the kids were tough and knowing and tortured him for his naiveté, good manners, good grades, and clumsiness. He suffered school in a state of torment, knocking over his ink bottle, tripping over his shoes, trying harder and getting clumsier with every bark from his teachers and jeer from his classmates.

Perhaps it wasn't San Frediano, perhaps it would have been the same anywhere. Leo was twelve, a confusing age, when suddenly your body seems to separate from you, mock you, embarrass you in public. And your parents seem farther away and distorted, as if seen through a glass, and certain things they say echo loudly in your head and other things you can't hear at all, though you can see their lips moving. Leo's parents weren't the kind to prepare him for the changes in his body and the torture of his peers: his father's letters home from the front during World War I are so genteel they make war sound like a pleasant social gathering; and his mother makes a face when people on TV open their mouths when they kiss. She likes closed-lipped kisses, or *bacini* (little kisses), as Aldo called them.

And too, Leo had just suffered in a way that few of the other boys had suffered: six years of official persecution for being Jewish, a year of hiding, running, fearing that his parents would be snatched from him, legally, on the street. He was stunned, dazed, and his body responded to his brain a split second later than the bodies of other boys responded to theirs, which gave them the right to torment him.

Maybe if he'd been going to public school for the past six years, he would have fitted in by age twelve, or maybe he was simply the kind of boy who would inevitably be the butt of his classmates' humor. Being Jewish didn't help: it was just another thing to mock. One day, says Lionella, they forced him to urinate against a wall so they could tease him for being circumcised. In fact, she has told me that story three times, once in an interview and twice in letters. Lionella does not repeat herself lightly.

I asked Lionella how she knew about this episode—it was hard for me to imagine him describing it to his family. She wrote that she was at home that day when he arrived, "shaken and sobbing." He wasn't trying to play brave, so he had no choice but to explain; the story must have come out in hiccup-splattered fragments. Lionella wrote, "It was also difficult to persuade him to return to school the next day."

His parents were asking a lot of him when they asked him to do that, but academic perseverance overruled almost all circumstance (even war, if you remember Lionella's studying in the midst of a shelling), and their children both persevered. Leo was a good student, too good to earn the respect of his peers. And he was an equally good and devoted son. For a class assignment soon after the war, Leo wrote, "In all the turmoil of the war, in the great confusion of this our miserable world, we have fully realized how our papas and our mammas didn't leave us in the midst of dangers but protected us with the utmost desire to die themselves if someone had to die—but not us: and down there in the horrible German death camps so many mammas died holding their little ones . . . but often, we children remain indifferent to the great gift that God has given us."

At twelve years old to call the world miserable, at twelve not to be able to take your parents for granted, at twelve to be grateful not to have been abandoned. It is a twelve I cannot imagine. Awkwardness, self-consciousness, innocence I can imagine, but this I cannot. At twelve, I thought I was gorgeous and hideous, that everyone and no one was watching me, that I would be famous; at twelve I was reading *Pride and Prejudice* in a Milan train station and coyly fending off the advances of three Italian teenagers. The world was *magical*.

At the end of the war, Lionella was full of energy, liberated and alive. Leo was stunned and felt only relief: his parents never abandoned him. What made him consider that possibility—not the very real possibility that his parents would be snatched up by the SS, but the nightmare that they would *choose* to leave him? Was it that time at the convent in Florence when the nuns said they would take

the children but not the parents? Or when Professor Giannelli and his wife offered to keep the children as their own? Or when Rachel and Aldo left them with
neighbors in Anghiari and traveled to Florence for a doctor's appointment? Was
Leo relieved that they came back—not that they made it, but that they chose to
come back?

Maybe it was simply the sense he must have had throughout the war that he
didn't quite know what was going on at all, what decisions his parents were making. The truth was something he gathered, or overheard, or figured out afterward. His parents thought telling children the truth would frighten them, so they
gave them only concrete directions without much explanation: You must walk
ten paces behind your father when you go through the city. If someone stops
him, wait until he comes back for you. If they take him, run away. You have
50,000 lire in this locket around your neck. Take it and run away.

On *Santa Barbara*, saintly and blond Eden Capwell is in the hospital, paralyzed.
She begs her doctor for the truth, which turns out to be, "You may never walk
again." Rachel, watching from her favorite rocking chair, is outraged. "Cretin!"
she hisses at the doctor. "One shouldn't say such things to sick people."

Leo, a sickly boy, must have had many of his own illnesses hushed up. And
others' of course. When Rachel and the children returned home by train because
Mamma Ada was dying, cousins met them at the station and whisked the children away. Clattering toward their cousins' house on the tram, they passed their
own home and, twisting around, they could watch their parents disappearing
into what was now a frightening mystery.

The one scene in Leo's diary in which he seems to be consciously writing
tragedy has nothing whatever to do with religious persecution or the "barbarians
in the twentieth century." It involves a mother, a son, a death, and a deceit. Remember when Fritz Modigliano dies?

"Why are you crying, Mamma?"

"Nothing, Berto."

"And Papa?"

"Papa? Papa is far away . . ."

The last operation on his stomach did not succeed and the next day Berto had
no father.

"And Papa?"

"Papa? Papa is in America."

"And we're not going?"

The response was a kiss on his blond curls; Berto thought about the big tear of
the day before and didn't understand.

Leo is sympathetic to the mother; she tries to hide her grief for her son's sake, and it clearly takes strength to do that. But we feel sorriest for Berto, who is not allowed to feel the importance of this moment; he is there but he is not allowed to participate. His ignorance, his innocence, is painful. When Leo's book begins, it is with the collusive secrecy of his parents, speaking in French, sending the kids away, lying, and with Erminia the cook lying too. Leo must have lived the years of the racial laws with a pervasive sense that his parents were keeping things from him, that he was there but not participating. At any moment, while his parents might be deciding to hide or to flee, he would be in limbo: enough of an adult to be aware that something was going on but too much a child to know *what*. How sickening to think that as you are studying your Latin verbs or getting water at the fountain or carefully stacking stones until they tumble, your parents might be plotting to leave, plotting to put you in the care of a neighbor. They might tell you they were going to be gone for a week, but what did that mean? This was a world where death could be called "America." They might tell you anything, to avoid the tears, the explanations, the pain.

Rachel and Aldo might not have been more secretive than most parents in that situation; the times might simply have been so frightening that Leo had imagined the awfulest, the most awfulest thing that could happen, a step beyond the worst possibility. The worst possibility was that you could be dutifully walking ten paces behind your father when an SS patrol stopped him and shoved him into a truck, and you would be left alone in the world. That your parents might *choose* to leave you alone in the world was the only imaginable thing that was worse. That is the fear that caught Leo's imagination.

Only it wasn't "Leo" of course, at the time. He was called by his false name, Leonida, the name Lionella says "only a Greek professor" could come up with. Leonidas was a Spartan king who led his army in the battle of Thermopylae during the first Persian war, in 480 B.C.E. The Spartans were guarding a pass between the mountains and the sea on the eastern shore of mainland Greece, trying to prevent the Persians from coming southeast. They might have kept them back, except that Leonidas was betrayed; one of his men showed the Persians a path through the mountains. The Persians surprised the Spartans and decimated them.

That was the name Leo carried with him through the war and that was the nightmare: utter betrayal. But it never came to that, and Leo, called Leo again, is grateful. Slowly, though his vision of the world remains bleak, his fears become more mundane. School and friends and girls. When they moved to Via dei Banchi, he changed schools again, readjusted. He even made some friends, according to Lionella.

And then he had to change classes, because we came to live here in the city . . . it was behind the Galileo high school in Piazza San Lorenzo, at the market. Very close to home, so he went alone. He had a professor from the Jewish school, a marvelous woman. Who tried in every way to meet him half-way. There was also another Jewish girl in class, so it was a more positive year. And he made good friends with some boys . . . One went to a scientific high school, he was really his best friend. And Leo went to his house all the time to play . . .

There an enormous passion was born, of Leo's for his friend's sister. But a truly beautiful love. He spent hours listening to her play her scales, he also gave her dolls. So Mamma flew into a rage, "She's Catholic! They're extremely Catholic." So the two mothers decided that the thing couldn't go on. Meanwhile my brother was nineteen, seventeen, eighteen years old, they are the very moments of passion, no? And I saw him suffer so much, so, so much, because the family then officially engaged this love of Leo's to another friend of her brother's, whom Leo knew. And I suffered, I found him on the ground, he beat his head against the wall. A frightening thing.

Leo was writing again after the war—he stopped only for that one year of terror—poems, treatises, stories, and later academic papers and essays. He wrote a short story called "Dream Life" that captured those "very moments of passion."

In "Dream Life," Giustino, "aged fifteen more or less," meets a girl named Gisella in his dreams. He has never seen her before. Soon she is there every night and they fall in love, in the dreams. "You should sleep all the time," she says, "so that you'll never leave me." He's reluctant, tells her one can't sleep all the time, one has to study, to work. But then, in one dream, they have a wreck on a motor scooter and she is taken to the hospital, where he stays by her bed. When it is time for him to wake in the morning, she grabs him and begs him not to leave. He pushes her to get away, but then, awake and penitent, tells his mother that he must return to her, return to sleep. Gisella instructs him to take sleeping pills, so she doesn't have to wait for him all day. So he does, and then more and more. Giustino finally asks Gisella whether, if he takes enough sleeping pills to die, he will meet her after death. "Of course, take a lot of them, come join me." On the day of the funeral, there is another procession. The two sets of parents meet on the steps of the church.

"Ours was called Gisella, she was sixteen."

"Ours was called Giustino. He was seventeen. Our Giustino dreamt all the time of a girl named Gisella."

"Our Gisella dreamt all the time of a boy named Giustino."

In the papers appeared the opinion of an illustrious psychiatrist:

"It happens sometimes that two people who have never seen each other meet in a dream and that their actions coincide unconsciously, without anything being pre-arranged between them, in reality."

At age eighteen, Leo was diagnosed a diabetic, a sickness Rachel attributes to the accumulated stress of the war. "You want to know many things about my Leo," she writes, "my Leo was always an excellent son—the war destroyed him with all the frights he had." Lionella thinks the stress that overwhelmed her brother's fragile body may instead have been thwarted love. "According to me, it might be a mistaken theory of mine, but it was that. That created such a shock, yes. Because it was right after . . . all this. In short, it was this sexual development conducted extremely poorly from age thirteen to then . . . One never knows, right? One never knows. Then he broke with all his friends."

A few years later, Leo had another inappropriate romance. This time she was a southerner, no degree, no money. Lionella wrote, "At the age of twenty-two he had a great love for a Jewish girl from Naples, cut short secretly by my mother (who interfered with the girl's family) on account of the 'difference in social class.'" Once again the mothers decided it was not such a good thing. And Aldo?

Papa was closed in his study . . .

He didn't enter into . . .

Yes, he suffered a little like me. But he understood Mamma very well, he knew better than I that there was no way, my mother had decided . . . She was apprehensive.

Rachel approved of the woman Leo eventually married. Marie-Louise Rotsaert was cultured and educated, though she was not Jewish. But she wasn't Catholic either. "He met Marie-Louise in a hostel in Nice—they started talking in French—she being Belgian speaks French very well, she also speaks English, German, and Flemish—with her father she wrote in Flemish," wrote Rachel. French was dear to Rachel's heart since her days at the *Ecole Alliance Israelite* in Rhodes. Leo and Marie-Louise married in 1959. Rachel wrote:

For ten years all went well for Leo and Marie-Louise—she said that she was agnostic but for Leo she observed all our holidays and on the doors of their home there was even a *mezzuzah*. They were with us in Florence for four years and in Cagliari for six years everything was perfect.

Lionella saw their relationship a little differently. She would not have used the word "perfect."

> I think that the spiritual gap between him and his wife was unbridgeable—she is a rational positivist atheist. She met Leo in a moment of grave crisis, after the rupture with the girl from Naples. She convinced him to be her first man (as for him she was the first woman) and Leo felt morally bound to marry her, to take care of her since, according to her, she was a poor motherless orphan, with an evil stepmother and brother forced to teach in Africa (Belgian Congo).

Ten years after they married, six years after they had both taken positions at the University of Cagliari in Sardinia, their marriage fell apart. Rachel wrote to tell me why she thought that happened:

> My Leo was very friendly—he invited a high school teacher to lunch and thus made Marie-Louise lose her head. She went to live with him—but briefly—he was a dishonest person—he was married with two daughters. Then he came to Florence and got engaged to an acquaintance of Lionella's, a professor, and she told her that she was about to get married and told her the name—Lionella immediately told her what a dishonest type this professor was. She, poor thing, started to cry, and to hug Lionella . . . Marie-Louise always tells me Leo was an exceptional, good, intelligent person.

Marie-Louise calls Rachel from time to time. There was no divorce. Lionella says, "He considered Marie-Louise, with her often hysterical attitudes, to have a nervous condition. He didn't want to divorce for years—when finally he met a girl (who stayed with him until the end) perhaps worthy to be married, it was M. Louise's turn not to want to renounce her rights as a wife (and an heir)." To Lionella, it seems unfair that the woman who left her brother inherited his money, and she has little patience when Rachel mentions Marie-Louise's name.

Perhaps Marie-Louise regrets leaving Leo; certainly she has written lovingly of him since his death and still uses his name. Perhaps she did not realize that ending their relationship could be so crushing, so irredeemable—for some other man it might not have been. For Leo it was unbearable. While she was still with him, but planning to leave, he was betrayed, duped, forced to be present, ignorant, foolish while his future was being decided. She turned him into a protected child again, into the unsuspecting Leonidas, and then, as in the nightmare, she abandoned him "in the midst of dangers."

Once again, writing must have helped.

Anguish

All night
he suffers from anguish.
The rivers shake
from cliff to cliff,
the water falls
killing ants,
while the cat chases them,
but already the cat is pursued
by the ferocious dog,
and while the woman spins
tranquil in front of her home
her son, running,
falls in the ravine
and sadly dies.
The man knows
everything of the past
and of the future he sees
that which can happen,
and though not flying
as the bird does,
he flies with his mind back and forth
and is consumed with rage
and worry.
But if instead of thinking of himself
and the fate of his family,
he sees himself inserted deep
in the whirlwind of things
he knows that there is no truce
and every day he prepares
his strengths for battle
not for pleasure
but for the purpose
unknown to him
that the Lord prepares for him.

Leo continued to live a public life marked by hope and faith in others. He was politically cynical and yet politically active, believing that there was essential good in people, a good that could be discerned even in the darkest of times.

Certainly he had, as a child of the war, experienced some of that goodness, and he still believed in the possibility that people could change.

For twenty-three years—until he died at age fifty-five—Leo taught French language and literature at the University of Cagliari on the island of Sardinia. He devoted himself not just to his teaching but to his adopted town—which, compared to Florence, was culturally desolate. A needy place, a hurting place, with the hard beaten strength of a survivor.

from "Beloved Island"

Beloved island
Endured island
Island that suffers,
And that lives in my blood.
Leaving Tuscany
fertile with green
and with fecund ideas
already I see you appear.
I go toward you
as toward a bride
who offers me in a cup
of hardened earth
her golden tears . . .

Sardinia, like Sicily, is Italy's answer to the southern United States, considered by mainlanders and especially northerners to be backward and intellectually barren. But Sicily is a tourist spot, full of historical landmarks from the ancient world right up to World War II; it is like the Confederate South—the butt of innumerable jokes, but romanticized and respected for its fierce history and powerful families. Sardinia is more like southern Appalachia, forgotten and foreign to almost all Italians. For twenty-three years, Leo devoted himself to Sardinia with a passion, researching and inspiring others to research her history, publishing in her local papers and magazines, helping stir her to cultural life. In 1977, in perhaps his greatest gesture of love and hope, he opened his private library to public borrowing. There was no new building to house the books; he simply opened his home in Pirri to the public. Pirri is a city contiguous to Cagliari, in (as he writes) "a zone dominated by (or abandoned to) a great cultural indolence and lack of bookstores . . . a place where the people read little or poorly or not at all." He couldn't get public funds to help protect this gift to the public (though he noted that private museums, castles, and parks do) and he blamed lack of funds for a building project on "political ill-will." Yet, despite political ill-will, despite illiteracy, despite public indifference, he was able to imagine a "future we hope near, when there will be in Pirri secure and convenient places for reading even rare or antique texts and periodicals."

His books, about eight thousand of them when he wrote about his library a few years before he died, weigh heavily in French literature and history, French and English literary criticism. Giampietro Vieusseux, one of Leo's academic passions, gets his own section. There's European history, country by country and as a whole, and a section each on America, Asia, Africa, and Maghreb (the region of northwestern Africa from which hail many immigrants to Italy). Each province of Italy gets its own section, and so does Corsica. There's Italian literature, with a separate section on Dante. Greek and Latin history is followed in the category list by general Italian history, medieval history, the Renaissance, modern history, history of the Risorgimento, contemporary history, and finally, Fascism and Nazism. There's music, art, poetry, and economics.

There's no Judaica, no religion, no Israel, no Middle East. Why? Did he simply think there would be no audience for them in Sardinia? Were they too personal to put on public display? I don't think so. This library was in his home, and Leo, devoted to his project, his vision of a literate Sardinia, would not have withheld any book from a potential reader. Indeed he seems to have catalogued the depths of his bookshelves, offering up his manuals and magazines, children's books and romance novels—though they could hardly have been exhaustive collections or, indeed, what he hoped his neighbors would be borrowing.

No, I don't think he withheld his books on Judaism. I think he didn't have them—or rather, he didn't have them in Sardinia. In the attic in Florence there is quite a collection, uneven but large, and I believe it is Leo's. In his early twenties, Leo was turning out a small magazine, typed and dittoed, called *Il Hamim*, which is a Sephardic Jewish stew. *Il Hamim* was a "monthly for Jewish youth." The February/March issue of 1955 (Adar Nissan 5715) includes an essay on some letters of Kafka's, a poem, a rambling Notice Board, a list of new books out, items of interest, and museum exhibits. And it had this small notice on the second-to-last page: "Numerous books have been given in the last month by Dr. Marco Treves of New York for our Library. There are 235 books to date and 350 pamphlets."

The books stayed at Via dei Banchi, 5, when Leo left for Sardinia. He was leaving behind something of his Judaism—the part that belonged to his parents and his beautiful, cultured birth city, the part that belonged to ritual and rules and maybe even the part that belonged to words.

The Neppi Modonas were strict about ritual; Rachel still is. And though Aldo loved God deeply, he did not try to teach a love of God to his children. He taught the ritual. Lionella accepted this, her spiritual and moral education having been firmly established by her grandmother, Mamma Ada. But Leo, she says, did not. "Leo was a profound believer," she writes, "but certainly not convinced religiously, having been raised in an arid application of the *mitzvot*."

> It is quite true that my father was very religious, attached to the traditions, so profoundly believing that in all things and for all things, he confided in the guidance of the Lord. However he often imposed observance on his children, avoiding any explanatory dialogue—One does it like this, and that's that, you'll understand later—Leo was a very precocious little boy and accepted things gracelessly—so for him they became impositions. As I told you, Leo didn't spend as much time with Grandma as I did.

Though Aldo was intensely involved in the Jewish community after the war, Rachel was not. She rarely went to synagogue, according to Lionella. As for Aldo, Lionella says that, after the war, he "didn't find much time to dedicate himself to my brother who besides everything found himself at age twelve on the outside of Hebrew school and of every formative activity. Putting 'lay' studies in front of everything, my parents pushed him away from Judaism." Leo was out of step with the rest of Florence's educated children, and the Neppi Modonas rushed to get him back in. He did have a few Jewish friends, but Rachel set very high standards of Judaism and Jewish ritual and, writes Lionella, "little by little she distanced him from them, looking for new friends for him, keeping him far from Jewish life."

After his first traumatic love affair, he got closer again, perhaps in rebellion against his mother. He started to go to Jewish retreats and he started to edit *Il Hamim*. He did not embrace all things Jewish; he had an aversion to dogma that might well have come from living through a strict childhood and the Fascist regime. There was a core of belief in him—belief in human decency and human possibility, belief in God and reason, belief in learning and hope. But he was suspicious of the practical daily aspects of his religion; he cared deeply for the theory, to which the practice never lived up. That's why Israel upset him.

Leo "placed himself among the accusers of Israel," wrote Lionella. In her next letter, she explained what that meant. "Leo accepted the idea of the Jewish state but almost immediately placed himself among the defenders of the poor Arabs driven out by the Zionists, etc., etc." He must have felt his objections and his disappointment strongly, for according to Lionella it was a disagreement they could never overcome.

I entered, in marrying, a family that worked hard for Israel from here—these ideals were also at the base of our marriage, obviously much disapproved by Leo. But I have always known how to maintain my convictions, though I suffered greatly (and I believe my brother did too) for the (even physical) distance that we imposed on ourselves in order not to fight.

When Lionella's daughter, Ada, decided to move to Israel, Leo disapproved, though the move made his sister happy. Leo's beliefs, profoundly Jewish though they were, led him to show no special interest in Judaism or the Jewish people; his Jewish beliefs, odd as it may sound, made him identify not with Jews but with all of humanity. He saw himself not in the struggling Israelis, but in the poverty-stricken, illiterate Sardinians.

"The most salient features of his literary work and of his conception of the world and of existence appear, on the one hand, in his civic commitment, and on the other in his tendency to universalize his own experience as a Jew who had known persecution during his adolescence," wrote Gabriella Lampronti, in memoriam. In 1959, in his mid-twenties, he started a monthly entitled *Jews of Europe*. "The persecution of the Jews," wrote Lampronti, "was for him a symbol of every persecution and racial discrimination, which can only be overcome by a victim's positive commitment to change the heart and the mentality of his perse-cutor." In *Jews of Europe*, even more than in *Il Hamim*, being Jewish is the place from which he looks out over the world, but his gaze rests on more than Jews and Jewish issues. It embraces everyone.

The fifty-first issue of *Jews of Europe* (Oct.–Dec. 1965) is forty-three pages long. The cover is glossy and typeset, in black and green. "For peace, for life, for the world" are the first words on the page, and then "Jews of Europe: Monthly re-view of old and new books and periodicals regarding Judaism." The inside is sta-pled pages of typing paper and the contents for that month include a poem from the 1760s dedicated to the Jews of Livorno, an essay on three books about con-centration camps, and a 1938 essay in memory of Dante Lattes, "a dreamer of the ghetto." Books reviewed include *Braunbuch*, a denunciation of Nazi criminals who were still holding top positions in the German government, and *The Jews*, French anti-Semitic propaganda by Roger Peyrefitte. Leo reviewed *The Jews*, as well as a periodical for children called *A.B.C.* But his voice comes through clear-est in his opening essay, "The Necessity of Continuing to Fight."

First Leo gives evidence of a strengthening neo-Nazi movement in France and Belgium. He describes the twisted arguments of Holocaust deniers and expresses his wish that German Jews had not accepted guilt money from the government and in doing so opened themselves to the accusation that they invented the crimes for profit. On and on, he says, the Holocaust is being minimized.

But why? It's clear. To begin again tomorrow with the backing of the ingenuous and ignorant population a campaign of hate and blood. We could conclude with a banal and trite question: why is all this tolerated? But the answer is not so ordinary. The solution is in a total change in European society. Because as long as civilization is conceived as a knife-fight for a place in the sun, it's clear that no one will stop searching for expedients to gain that place in the sun. And if to get the place in the sun one must cry, 'death to the Jews,' (because this pleases people, to know that the devil exists and will be exterminated), if the mediocrities who want to rise have no other system than earning the place of their neighbor, asserting that that man brings bad luck to others, or exclaiming that the Fatherland is great and that it is necessary to defend it (from whom? Always from the Jews. To whom today are added especially in France many many men of color who, at the moment of choosing between their new independent country and their adopted fatherland, preferred to live in France. The racists rub their hands because those one recognizes easily, there will be no need of a yellow star, it will be enough to yell, 'after the negro!'). If it is necessary, these mediocrities will do all of this, and they will have once again the sceptre of destruction in their hands. And in one point only will they be right: that they will be doing nothing but manifesting externally and explicitly that injustice that already reigned before them, in which they were born. Yes, every dictator is nothing but the son of injustice, every criminal government is nothing but the fruit of capitalistic society. Meanwhile the solution to every problem is in a society based exclusively on love for one's neighbor and on the progress of collective social well-being.

A few days before he died, Leo wrote a letter for the periodical *Shalom*. He said, "A Chinese proverb says: Pray for them and they will pray for you, but to pray for them doesn't mean just reading prayers and sermons, but studying and deepening the truth." Praying, for Leo, meant not just sitting in a synagogue reciting Hebrew, but also—and perhaps more and more as he got older—reading and listening, learning more about the world and his neighbors. Lionella says he loved to express his opinions in writing, and I think that's how he prayed as well, in anguish and in hope.

Leo and Aldo could not understand one another, would always start to argue, loved but could not reach one another. Perhaps they were too much alike. The two of them suffered great disappointment and betrayal, Aldo in his public life and Leo in his private. And yet they remained gentle and idealistic, when they could have been bitter. Leo kept his belief in People even after people betrayed him. Such a broad view of the world, such faith in the face of cruelty. For Aldo this came from God, and the religious community in which he lived. For Leo, not religion, but God, and I think literature too. Words were his solace, his writings were his prayers, and his library became his great spiritual offering. God and literature. Both can redeem humanity, both can link men, unite them in something greater than themselves. Both thrive in community but can be the comfort of the lonely man. Both reassure a sick man in the face of death, in the face of life.

To Florence

Florence, three times
I have seen you afflicted,
destroyed,
humiliated,
offended.
The first time
it was the fault
of the terrible war:
bombs from on high,
mines from below,
and rough plunders
of things and of people
work of the barbaric
Germans
in your noble,
graceful houses,
like the slap
of a brutal man
on a defenseless young virgin.
The second time
by unknown hands
all your streets were soiled
with black swastikas,
and that was the signal
that induced us
to begin the fight
with this paper.
The third time
it was the flood.
Whose fault?
We don't know
if it was the ministers'

or the technicians' fault.
But over such a disaster
this time descended
the rainbow,
and it was that chain
of hands from every nation
that formed
by itself, without command,
to save
books
and works of art.
Yes, young people
don't want war,
they want love,
but also love
for that which is beautiful
and doesn't have to die.
This rainbow
has consoled us
and has given us the strength
to go on,
despite Strauss,
despite Munich,
despite Hesse,
despite the mud
and whoever doesn't remove it.

A Pillar of Community

May such a holocaust bring closer the era of human brotherhood
foretold by the prophets of Israel for all peoples.

Inscription beneath the names of the 248 Florentine Jews who died in the
Holocaust, on a plaque on the synagogue grounds in Florence.

FIFTEEN SEPARATE STREETS lead to the Duomo, Florence's central
church; if you're lost or simply not paying attention, you can get there without even meaning to. You have to mean to get to the synagogue. Indeed, you
might check your map a few times hastily on the way because you seem to be
leaving all monumental architecture behind you and entering a neighborhood of
houses and small shops. Even when you turn onto the modest Via Farini, it's hard
to see the synagogue; the trees and the gate around it almost completely obscure
it. You're in the right place, though: there on the street outside the gate is the police van with two *carabinieri* impeccably dressed inside it. Every major synagogue
in Italy has such a van; the one in Rome has three.

By "major," I mean post-emancipation big-city synagogues. Not the ones carefully camouflaged to avoid attracting attention, as in the Venetian ghetto,
cramped houses exactly like their neighbors, their religious purpose identifiable
only by the number of windows: five, for the five books of the Torah. In Siena,
too, you have to know street name and number and look carefully at the name-
plates on the building to find the synagogue. Small unobtrusive synagogues still
exist in Rome, like the one the Neppi Modonas attended on Via Balbo; and in

Florence there was one, in Via delle Oche, before the community closed it down
in 1966. The great flood of that year had filled the larger synagogue in Via Farini
with seven feet of water and the community had to sell the little *scola* in Via delle
Oche in order to pay for the repairs. War repairs had already depleted its coffers.

Scole or "schools" was the name for those little pre-emancipation synagogues;
in ghetto times they were not so much houses of celebration as houses of study.
Worshippers were keeping their heads down, in their books. Why make trouble?
But when Florence's ghetto was opened in 1848, the city's Jews immediately
started making plans for a synagogue, a grand synagogue. It was thirty years before they got the money to finance an appropriately grandiose design, when the
former president of the community left his estate to build "a monumental temple
worthy of Florence."

Today it is the police van you notice first. Then, to see the temple without
squinting through the trees, you must go through a little guardhouse. A student
takes his head out of his books, searches your bags, stores your camera in a cub-
byhole next to his desk, sells you a ticket, and shows you through to the courtyard. There you can finally see it, and it is indeed magnificent: domed, turreted,
spired, Moorish in its rounded shape—rounded, but not stooped, not in the
least humble. Like a Byzantine church, like the Hagia Sophia after which it was
modeled.

Inside, the sanctuary is so spacious and light that the walls covered by
arabesque and the floor of inlaid marble look grand instead of gaudy. The
women's gallery is railed in intricately carved bronze and the windows are stained
glass. All over, gold inlay, rich mosaics—no surface is left undecorated. What
wealth, what exuberance, what pride, what a sense of security allowed this community to go from little *scole* at the tops of undistinguished buildings to this
domed temple, this monument. It calls out to be noticed.

Or it once called out. The stand of trees, the guardhouse, the van of policemen cutting it off from the city of Florence came later, when the community
learned not to feel so secure.

Aldo returned to Via dei Banchi in 1945 ready to face the world "with renewed
strength," says Lionella. They were safe; they had survived, and now it was time
to set to work. For Aldo, that meant, in part, retrieving his profession. Competi-
tions for university posts had been held in 1940 when Aldo and his fellow Jews
were unable to attend. He had to sue to have another competition held; it turned
into a legal tangle that would last over ten years, after which he finally received a
seat in a university. While he fought that battle, he taught at the Liceo Classico
Michelangelo in Florence, where he had gone to school as a boy. And in the sum-
mers, he resumed his popular courses at the University for Foreigners in Perugia.

Meanwhile, his research flourished; he turned out books and articles in a rush of words, as if he were letting out his breath after holding it almost to bursting.

Aldo taught Greek and Roman antiquity, but he specialized in Etruscan studies—archeology, anthropology, and art history. The Etruscans had become quite glamorous under Mussolini because the Fascists enjoyed the idea of an original master race of Italians, and the Etruscans were supposed to be it. No matter that their chief qualities were (1) the fact that no one knows quite where they came from (Aldo offers four separate theories in his *Guide to Etruscan Antiquities*), (2) the fact that they mingled with the Umbrians, the people of central Italy, and (3) the fact that they were subsumed into the Roman empire. A mixed race, in short, of uncertain origin. No wonder that in his record of the racial laws, Aldo mocks the idea of a "pure (!) Aryan (?) Italian race (!)."

After the war, he continued to focus on Etruscan studies, though they were no longer quite so *di moda*. I wonder whether the Etruscans appealed to him even more after the Holocaust. The Holocaust was, after all, a determined attempt to exterminate an ancient people, language, religion, way of life. If it had succeeded, centuries later, some gentle academic would have been trying to reconstruct Hebrew, figure out what a *mezzuzah* was, posit a belief system that might have determined the Jewish fate. Even though it didn't succeed, the Holocaust did impress upon all Jews, including those who, like Aldo, had once lived without a thought of anti-Semitism, that they were a vulnerable minority. It put them on their guard too against less violent roads to extinction, like assimilation. The Etruscans weren't killed *in massa*; they were merely swallowed up by another culture, besieged militarily in some cases, but mostly scattered, appropriated, indoctrinated, intermarried. Aldo's job was to bring the Etruscans back to life, to separate their culture from that of Rome. Through the strength of his imagination and his interest, he defended a vulnerable people from the power of the majority.

In the prologue to *The Garden of the Finzi-Contini*, Giorgio Bassani describes why he decided to write about the Ferrarese Jews who were swallowed up in the Holocaust. He was spurred on by a visit, in 1957, to an Etruscan burial place outside of Rome. One of his companions was a nine-year-old girl, who, when quizzed by her father, said she knew that the Etruscans came at the beginning of her history book, near the Egyptians and the Jews. Then she asked,

"Papa . . . why is it that ancient tombs are not as sad as new ones?". . .

"That's obvious," he answered. "People who have just died are closer to us, and so we are fonder of them. The Etruscans, after all, have been dead for a long time . . . so long it's as if they had never lived, as if they had *always* been dead."

Another, longer pause. At the end of it . . . , it was Giannina's turn to impart the lesson. "But now, if you say that," she ventured softly, "you remind me that Etruscans were also alive once, and so I'm fond of them, like everyone else."

And so, said Bassani, "it was she, the youngest, who somehow guided us."[35]

Aldo was determined, like Giannina, to defend the integrity of the Etruscans; however long dead, they still deserved that. And like Bassani, whose thoughts sped back from that necropolis to the Jewish cemetery of Ferrara, Aldo might well have made the connection between the Etruscans and the Jews, between two ancient peoples, two peoples from the beginning of the history books, one disappeared and one just stumbled back, dazed, from the brink of disappearance. Bassani imagined how the Etruscans who survived the Roman conquest must have felt visiting this burial ground on an evening stroll.

> The world changed, of course—they must have said to themselves—it was no longer what it had once been, when Etruria, with its confederation of free, aristocratic city-states, had dominated almost the whole Italian peninsula. New civilizations, more crude and popular, but also stronger and more inured, now reigned. But what did it matter? . . . The future might cause all the upheavals it liked in the world. But still, there, in the brief enclosure sacred to the familiar dead, in the heart of those tombs where, along with the dead, they arranged to carry down everything that made life beautiful and desirable, in that defended, sheltered corner of the world: there at least . . . nothing would ever change.[36]

Aldo was in a sense a caretaker of that cemetery, of those tombs. He tended the graves of the Etruscans, translated their inscriptions, interpreted their contents. He helped shelter an ancient people against the crude new civilizations that reigned. The legacy of the dead would live on, despite "all the upheavals" of life.

When Ada, Aldo's mother, died in January of 1944, she had to be brought to the cemetery in Via Casciolle in a hearse with the cross left on. Only Aldo and a friend accompanied his mother's corpse; it was not the grand procession that, before the occupation, would have made its way to the outskirts of the city. There were other mourners who risked attending Ada's burial, but they had to arrive separately, on foot and on bicycle, sneaking in like boys stealing apples. A procession to a Jewish cemetery behind a crossless hearse would fairly call out for the attentions of the SS. It had been four months since the German occupation: they knew better than that.

Fifty years later, I took a bus to the outskirts and then, on foot, followed the street signs with the tourist symbol for cemetery: three crosses within a simple tombstone line. When I got there the cemetery was closed up, high stone walls broken only by a solid iron gate—not iron bars but iron sheeting. A tall, white-haired man was reading the sign on the gate. "Is it open?" I asked.

"I can't figure it out. 'Closed for the sabbath and Jewish holidays.' So when's it open?"

"All the other days I guess. What time is it?"

"Eleven twenty." The sign said it closed at noon.

We stood there in shared puzzlement until I noticed a bell on the wall beside the gate. I gestured toward it and he shrugged and I rang—or rather, I pressed; no sound could be heard.

A little door next to the gate opened and a young woman stuck her head out, expressionless. "Yes?"

"I—I was looking for the tomb of a relative of mine."

"Name?"

"Ada Neppi Modona."

"Come in." Relieved, I slipped through the door and waited while she turned to my companion. "And you?" He had kept his distance behind me when I stepped forward to ring the bell and had not moved when the woman appeared. He said, "Can one visit the cemetery?"

"If you leave your name," she said; one hand was resting on the door handle and she brought the other across the opening to the jamb. "It's private." And then, as explanation or rebuke (for the fact itself was obvious): "It's Jewish."

"Oh," he said. His curiosity was not strong enough to make him go where he was not wanted. He turned to me and gave a little bow. "Goodbye, Signorina."

"Goodbye."

The caretaker shut the door.

Aldo had told Rachel upon their engagement that "before everything, before the mother, before the wife, came the Fatherland." Rachel said that after World War II she must have come first, since the other two were gone. Now his mother was dead and his country had betrayed him. They had been two of the longest-standing guideposts of his life. For fifty years, they had required from him duty, love, and pride; for fifty years, fulfilling those requirements made up the core of who he was. But both had left him a legacy. Italy and her racial laws taught him to follow none but his own beliefs and ideas, to allow no intermediary author-ity—such as King or government—to determine where his duty lay. His mother taught him from an early age (and by example all her life) where it did lie: with his family, with the Jewish community, and with God.

The first thing he did upon his return was to go to his synagogue and thank God for His help. Lionella says that after the war, his greatest interest was the life in his Community (where *everyone* esteemed and loved him) and the study of Jewish history and culture. He was a true *tzaddik*—every morning he put on the *tefillin* and he contented himself for days with milk, vegetables, and fish if he didn't have a kosher kitchen. His Zionism was long-standing—in 1928 he went to Erez Israel from Rhodes—He had grown up in the same school as my father-in-law, Carlo Alberto Viterbo, for years the head of Italian Zionism. His best friends, the thinker and scholar of Judaism Alfonso Pacifici, the famous psychologist Enzo Bonaventura, and various others moved to Israel in the 30s . . . I believe that if Mamma's Zionism had not always been very tepid, he would have followed their example. In Rhodes, one didn't look much to Eretz Israel as the land of the future: the young people all emigrated to America and Africa.

Aldo, in fact, never went to Israel again. But no one ever doubted his religious commitment. He was an observant Jew, rising every morning to wrap *tefillin*, using the sabbath as a day of rest and study, contributing to the intellectual and spiritual debate in his synagogue. Lionella remembers every Passover the ritual of boiling the pots to purify them; it was her father who boiled them, and he took great pleasure in it. He kept kosher carefully until his dying days in a hospital, where they fed him non-kosher meat without his knowledge.

And yet, he was not fanatical about the rules nor did he force others to be. When living and observing were in irreconcilable conflict, living won out. During the period of the racial laws, with kosher meat increasingly unavailable, he bought separate forks and plates and let his children eat non-kosher meat. Rachel ate it too, once or twice. And when he was old and Rachel was getting older, and they didn't have servants to deal with the dishes, he told Rachel she should organize the kitchen in whichever way was easier for her—they could use the same plates for milk and meat, they would just not eat the two at the same time. "It's tradition," he said. "It's not religion."

Aldo knew the difference, and though he treasured both, it was his religiousness that glowed from him with a special energy. An academic colleague named Guglielmo Maetzke described Aldo's faith as "that religiousness that one knows and feels profoundly, even though he made neither show nor propaganda of it, and which had given him strength during the most difficult moments and always guided him in understanding and judging men and things . . ." Lionella described him as "so profoundly believing that in all things and for all things, he trusted in the guidance of the Lord." Vittoria Lucchini, who worked on a non-academic project with him, testified to that. She wrote in memoriam: "More than once in his writings I had intuited a reserved and profound religiousness; of one circumstance favorable to our plans, he wrote, 'doesn't this coincidence reenter into the mysterious divine plan in which you and I firmly believe?'"

"Profound" is the word that no one seems to be able to escape; for all the trappings and traditions that he cherished, Aldo's beliefs were not stored in his *mezzuzah* or his *tefillin* or even in his Torah. They ran right through him and rested at his core.

In 1986, a year after his father's death, Leo reviewed a book by Nantas Salvalaggio called *I Resign from My Father*.

> Reading this book teaches us that religion isn't simply confined to church pews and rules out of books, it's in the air and perfumes everything. So it was for me as well. I too don't adopt all of my father's rules, but I know that he is there around me and that he will not be dismissed . . . My father had received a rigorous upbringing in the circle of a highly Jewish family, and carried in himself an immense dose of culture (languages, sport, music, Judaism, etc.) which he didn't always need in practice, but which made him cautious to judge and condemn . . . Nantas' father . . . died at 45 years, a few months after the Liberation, and he said to the priest: "What a shame to go away, now that one could talk at last." My father died at age 89; if he had known that the Pope was going to embrace the Rabbi in the synagogue of Rome, he would have said, "What a shame that I can't be there."

Aldo would have wanted to see the Pope embrace the Rabbi in the synagogue of Rome because he worked from the end of World War II to the end of his life for greater understanding between Jews and Christians. After the war he turned to family, career, community, and God—but these had always been part of his life. His one new direction, his one distinct response to the Holocaust was a commitment to interreligious dialogue. In 1950, he was one of five founders of the Amicizia Ebraico-Cristiana, or Jewish-Christian Friendship.

When Aldo died thirty-five years later, a member of the AEC, Elio Nissim, wrote from England: "That which I have always admired immensely in him was his vision of peace and tolerance for which he was able to reconcile his perfect religious observation with the principles of friendship and understanding among Jews and Christians."

From 1951, the AEC published a bulletin, and on the inside cover of this bulletin, still a thriving quarterly today, are listed the eleven statutes of the organization. The last six are administrative. We can, I think, read the first five as Aldo's answer to the Holocaust.

> 1. "Jewish-Christian Friendship" is a free gathering of people of religious spirit (whatever be the way in which this feeling of theirs is manifested) who desire love

and collaboration among Christians and Jews, and in fact among men, with the aim of creating a truly human society, from which every form of incomprehension and hate is forever excluded.

2. All the associates, without renouncing a single part of their beliefs or agreeing to doctrinal confusions or compromises, intend to understand one another, love one another, and also collaborate spiritually in the defense of ideal values and common morals.

3. The Association will study the causes of anti-Semitism and of every other form of religious intolerance and will propose remedies for them, intervening every time there is an opportunity to do so.

4. The Association sets itself philanthropic and cultural goals, not denominational or political ones.

5. The Association intends to reach its goals using meetings, readings, conferences, discussions, distributions of pamphlets, seeking always to obtain new support and making sure to diffuse its own program widely by means of the press, the radio, and every other form of propaganda.

This is the religious, learned man's reaction to hatred and violence. He still believes in the power, not just of human compassion and sentiment, but of human reason. He believes that reading pamphlets, listening to lectures, engaging in discussion will change men's minds and ultimately result in a human society free from hatred and incomprehension. Aldo still believed, despite his sufferings, that people could learn to understand and tolerate one another. It's a courageous assumption in a post-Holocaust world. But perhaps it almost makes sense after living through the period of the racial laws in Italy—where a country learned remarkably quickly *not* to tolerate its Jews. If you can learn intolerance, why not tolerance as well?

The room was packed, so that we had to squeeze past the people standing in the doorway. We got there late because Rachel didn't want to go and I had to say twice, "well, that's no problem, I'll go alone," before she agreed. So we squeezed in, she taking a chair in the very back that someone brought in for her, I perching on the edge of an already occupied window seat. The president of the Florentine chapter of the Association of Italian Jewish Women (ADEI) quieted the crowd of Jews and non-Jews, saying that the men and women who had lived through the round-ups of 1943, which this evening commemorated, had "a drama to recount."

Then the rabbi got up to speak. He said that he teaches his children "the *shema* and what the Nazis were capable of doing to our brothers. Just as they should say the *shema* three times a day so should they remember the Holocaust and what the Germans did to our brothers." His voice started to raise and roughen. He said he taught his children that they shouldn't—none of us should—learn to speak "their horrible language" or (and here he was shaking) "set foot in that country." A murmur went through the crowd; I couldn't tell whether it was a murmur of approval or disapproval, bored familiarity or shock.

Next came a moment of silence in memoriam for the Jews who were killed. Everyone stood; shuffles and murmurs ceased. I bowed my head but glanced surreptitiously around the room, looking for familiar faces. Rachel was doing the same, I noticed, only without pretending she wasn't. The crowd was female, with a few men sprinkled about; there were very few faces younger than fifty.

When we sat and settled, the main speaker was introduced. She was a Christian witness to an attempt by a convent to protect a group of Jewish women and children—and witness also to the round-up that followed someone's tip to the SS. It was a simple account, read from longhand notes on a stationery pad and some photocopied pages; she constantly squared the edges of her papers, hands never gesturing, always fiddling, carrying out a wholly separate operation from her voice. She spoke quietly—sometimes too quietly for me: my window seat provided lots of street noise and no view of the lips forming the words I was hearing; it was like trying to listen to a foreign radio station with static. Every once in a while, speaking of the children or of the dignity of their mothers, her voice broke. The audience was silent until she began again.

There was conversation, debate even, when she finished, but a woman on crutches quieted the room by laboring to her feet. She said she wanted to proclaim her solidarity with the Jews. The fact that she was a cripple, she said, had always made her sympathetic to Jewish people, "the only people of the ancient world to survive, and with dignity." She tossed her head about emphatically as she spoke, as if making up for the fact that she couldn't gesture with her hands; it made her look a little crazy, a mental patient on a soapbox. "Inside of me," she said, "whenever I hear or read anything about the Holocaust, I feel that I am Jewish." She said, crying now, that she believed no one had ever asked forgiveness; "I, as a non-Jew, ask forgiveness from the Jewish people."

It was then that Rachel finally got me to leave, though the meeting wasn't over. I was tired of whispering "Just a few more minutes" when she asked me if I wanted to go. Besides there were no more scheduled speakers, and the Jews themselves seemed, if not reluctant, then at least not eager to tell their stories; perhaps they felt they were nothing special, that everyone in that room had suffered more or less the same troubles and was grateful for more or less the same help from outsiders.

Certainly, Rachel wasn't interested in telling her story, and she was barely interested in hearing the others; only the woman who had asked forgiveness made an impression on her. On the way up the stairs to her apartment, I asked her to clear up some of my questions, since I had been able to hear only some of what was being said. Could she tell me exactly who each of those women was? But she was vague on the particulars, even about the woman on crutches, she wasn't sure what she had said about a nurse that she had had or a Jew that she had known. She shrugged and we lapsed into silence and focused on the stairs; she was holding the rail on one side and me on the other, moving steadily, one step per step.

Then she started shaking her head. "That rabbi, that rabbi," she said.

"What do you mean?"

"What stupid things he said, what idiotic things. Yes, there were bad Germans, but there were also good Germans."

"Yes, I agree."

"There were German Jews too . . ."

"Do you think other people agreed with him?"

"Of course not . . . And this is what he's teaching his daughters, when they're going out in skirts up to here!" She drew a hand across her upper thigh.

A part of or apart from? Jews or citizens of the world? In the utopian vision of the Amicizia Ebraico-Cristiana, in Aldo's vision, both are possible. The second point in its statute declares that "All the associates, without renouncing a single part of their beliefs or agreeing to doctrinal confusions or compromises, intend to understand one another, love one another, and also collaborate spiritually in the defense of ideal values and common morals." It sounds so easy, to be firmly and uncompromisingly who you are while understanding and loving others. To belong to both the community of fellow believers and the community of the world.

But it's not easy. The Florentine community has struck a balance only in contrasts: on the one side there's the rabbi telling his congregants they should recite a daily mantra of bitterness and hate, and on the other there's Manuela Sadun Paggi, a secretary for the AEC who started working against violence eleven years ago by fighting anti-Semitism and then decided she shouldn't shut herself off from the rest of the world. She told me that the Jewish community was too wedded to its own history and suffering. "They just learn about the Holocaust and their own history and they're so attached to Israel they can't see the suffering of the Palestinians."

I went to her home to join the AEC a couple of weeks after the ADEI meeting. We were standing in a study cluttered with magazines and pamphlets, stacks of books, scraps of paper. When I told her I had been to the meeting, she let out a cry—"oh, no, oh *no.*" She was mortified that I had heard the rabbi's outburst; how could he do that, in front of all those non-Jews as well? But she was also bothered by the non-Jewish crippled woman who declared herself a friend and supporter of the Jews. "If you love one group," she said, "you can easily hate another."

When I left, Paggi wished me good work (*buon lavoro,* an expression that doesn't exist in English) and hoped that I would continue to be a good Jew and a good citizen of the world. She wrote later what she—and the AEC—feels is the way to do both. "Serious dialogue," she said, "which involves the whole human being, is the only road to travel for everyone, so that life will improve, for oneself and for others."

Dialogue is a word that comes up again and again in AEC bulletins. Dialogue is the answer Aldo found. What frightened him most about the persecution he had suffered was not the Allied bombings or the SS trucks, but the fact that talking stopped. Colleagues, acquaintances, even people he had thought of as friends would avoid him on the street. At vacation spots, where Catholics and Jews had once mingled unthinkingly, there was silence and suspicion. When on a train heading out of Florence, he felt his soul comforted simply because he could make small talk with strangers who didn't know he was Jewish. Professional dialogue was cut off too—two manuscripts already accepted for publication were returned to him; all the academic organizations he had joined kicked him out and wouldn't even send him their newsletters. Only the University for Foreigners at Perugia kept him on its mailing list, an act so rare that Aldo praised it in his diary, and Rachel, after all those years, mentioned it to me twice.

Primo Levi experienced the same sense of isolation, got the same silent treatment from his colleagues, and understood clearly that more than any other single thing, this silence supported his persecution.

> I understood at that point that this strange haste of "Aryan" Italians in dealing with Jews was not accidental. Whether intuition or calculation, it served a purpose: with a Jew, at a time of the Defense of the Race, one could be polite, one could even help him, and even boast (cautiously) about having helped him, but it was not advisable to have human relations with him, nor to compromise oneself too deeply, so as not to be forced later to offer understanding or compassion.[37]

Dialogue during that time could have saved Aldo and Levi emotional anguish, but it could have saved lives as well. If more people in German-occupied Europe had talked about what they had seen and heard, if more people had listened, surely fewer would have stayed in their homes and awaited their fates— or gathered in the town square to be deported. If neighbors had continued to have "human relations" with neighbors, they would have turned fewer of them over to the SS. If the Pope had spoken out rather than just instructing priests in private to do what they could; if the BBC had issued daily radio reports of what the British Foreign Office suspected; if, in the Oval Office, American Jewish organizations had more forcefully pressed their point . . .

The ifs must have gotten to Aldo, along with the renewed joy he must have felt about being able to talk about things—who he was, what he thought, what he believed. If only people could talk to, listen to, hear one another, then it wouldn't happen again.

The AEC did as it said it was going to do, and still does. It sponsors lectures, debates, and conferences; it prints epistolary exchanges, editorials, and reviews of sharply differing books, contributed by rabbis and priests, psychiatrists and sociologists, politicians and statesmen. The bulletin is fat with their theories, analyses, speculation, prayers, visions of the future. The AEC has promoted dialogue, though perhaps only among people who were willing to talk—who *were* talking—in the first place. It has not, I think, reached people as a whole; it has reached a small, select group of people. Yes, some of them are Jews and some are Christians, yes, they come from many different countries, but they are all intellectual, socially minded Europeans.

The AEC has suffered the fate of many well-meaning organizations: it has become a club. Lionella says of it, "Little by little, I got fed up with a dialogue that seems more a pose, a sense of pietism, a research, yes, of how much can be united, but only superficially."

Still, dialogue and unity, however superficial, are rare in even the smallest of communities. In Florence there is a split in the 1,200-member Jewish community over the question of intermarriage; over, in other words, the very question of what community means and who belongs. Paggi said that throughout Italy, there is a kind of "psychological terrorism against mixed marriages." Later she wrote me, "Thirty years ago it was easy to make one's children Jewish, at birth; today the Rabbis are opposed to mixed marriage and refuse to make children Jewish if their mothers are not." She included a copy of a letter on the subject "written by a group of young Jews who have intermarried; among the signatures appear non-Jews as well."

To the Head Rabbi of the Jewish Community of Florence
To the President of the Jewish Community of Florence

A small community such as the Jewish one lives as a minority in the midst of a society that overwhelms it numerically. This is a situation in which the defense of one's own identity inevitably becomes more difficult. Judaism has always survived this condition, handing down from generation to generation its own style and philosophy of life. It is therefore a task that we cannot avoid, on pain of the disappearance of our tradition.

Today an unfavorable situation from the demographic point of view and a progressive distancing from our traditions has made this task more and more difficult. In this framework, among the many problems that our little community finds itself confronting, we believe one ought to pay particular attention to the fact that it is becoming statistically more and more difficult to construct nuclear families composed of spouses who both come from Jewish families. Because family life is one of the central points of education in Jewish life, the difficulty of making entirely Jewish families makes it more difficult to keep our tradition going. On the other hand to ignore the issue means simply wanting to ignore a reality without having the strength to confront it. This is not an attitude consonant with a tradition such as the Jewish one, which has succeeded in maintaining its own identity for two millennia of diaspora.

It's for this reason that we believe it's important to confront with clarity, and without hypocrisy, a problem that assails the community as a whole and is not only a "personal" problem for the individuals involved . . .

Without denying the difficulties inherent in what is commonly defined as "mixed marriage," it would be important to succeed in reversing the readiness to assign guilt that has often circulated in our environment, and to affirm instead that, if a member of the community is in trouble, he or she should be supported and not made to feel guilty.

Often the couples in this situation find themselves unprepared to confront the inevitable problems that different origins bring.

— Why add to such difficulties with attitudes of closed-ness rather than make clear in advance the situation so as not to end up arguing later and at the expense of the children?

— The birth of children is certainly one of the most important moments in the life of a man and a woman: why should they not be able to live to the utmost the joy of these moments on account of not having confronted these problems in advance with clarity and serenity?

It's not easy to answer these questions, but we believe that a serious effort to change an attitude that has borne only negative results, pushing Jews away from "Jewish things," can at least be attempted.

And finally because, as we have already said, the birth of children becomes one of the most complex moments, and since often parents can have trouble with the arduous task of bringing up their children, we believe that it's important to help, within the limits that a community can, many of us to recapture the capacity and the pride of keeping alive this our millennial tradition.

In view of this we believe that it would be possible to organize a series of specific meetings on themes that involve family life, the raising of children, relationship with children, etc.

The definition of a program and the organization of these meetings would help many people decide to participate in community activity . . .

We are available for any other initiative of merit, and we send a cordial shalom.

Being a Jew and a citizen of the world at the same time is as impossible to some Jewish communities as being an Italian and a Jew was to the Fascists under the racial laws. Turned by love and marriage into citizens of the world, these people could not in the eyes of their community be "good Jews" as well. They want dual citizenship; they feel, and they want to be allowed to live, a double loyalty. Like Italian Jews from 1938 to 1945, they are suspected of not truly belonging to, of not really loving their community, and of not wanting their children to belong to that community. They are suspected, even worse, of letting an enemy infiltrate the community, of putting it in peril.

What they are asking for, more than anything else, is dialogue. They want their position in the community not ignored for fear of unpleasantness or embarrassment, but discussed in the open. Then and only then will the community as a whole understand that they too care about being Jewish, want to raise their children as Jews, need help as Jewish parents. They want what Aldo wanted in 1938 when his neighbors started crossing the street instead of having to face him: recognition of a common identity, of community.

Secure communities do not define themselves by their barriers or make elaborate rules about who belongs and who does not. If the Jewish community of Florence did not feel threatened by the outside world, even now, fifty years after the Holocaust, the intermarried members would not have had to plead for recognition. They are the Florentine Jews with the closest links to the outside world on whom suspicion first rests. But the members at the margins aren't the only ones who bear the burden of the community's anxiety; it is a burden they all share.

Florentine Jews have to pass through their own guardhouses to get to the synagogues; they have to wait at the gate of their own cemetery. They cannot glance up from across the street of either to enjoy the splendor they have created. A huddle, a crouch, a hiding place is good defense, perhaps, but it's an uncomfortable way to live.

Before October 9, 1982, the synagogue in Rome was protected by day by a single security guard hired by the Jewish community. That date marked the holiday of *Shemini Atzereth*, when all the children are brought to the synagogue to be blessed. Arab terrorists were waiting for them when they came out. With machine guns and bombs, they killed one child and injured thirty-seven other people.

Today, three police vans are on a twenty-four-hour watch around the synagogue. One of the policemen pointed out the entrance to me and my boyfriend; it was around the corner from the grand portal the architect had intended as the entrance. We entered the first door and were told we had to wait, and so we did, next to a glass-enclosed guard's roost in the small space between two electronic doors. They were like the doors of a bank, constructed so that no one could come and go in a hurry; the second wouldn't open unless the first was closed. Ten minutes later, the guard returned, checked our bags, and buzzed us into the synagogue.

This is not how a house of worship should be. But the Roman Jews have no choice but to close themselves off from the world physically, to crouch down and protect their lives and the lives of their children.

They can still open themselves to the world spiritually. Inside the synagogue, inside the protective shell, there is still a willingness to communicate. When I was there, a synagogue volunteer was talking to a group of schoolchildren, answering questions about Judaism. Was there music during the services? Not during the services, but sometimes at weddings. Is the rabbi like a priest? A rabbi is a teacher, he is no closer to God than you or I, but he has studied the word of God. And then, in a small advertising coup, she mentioned offhand to her Catholic listeners: "Going to synagogue is not obligatory for us. If we want to go, we go."

As Aldo would say, it's tradition, it's not religion. Not going to synagogue won't break the bond between a Jew and his God; it's not a religion with lines you can't cross—there is no Jewish excommunication. Aldo knew that if his children ate non-kosher meat, or if he and Rachel stopped using two sets of dishes, he would still be Jewish. He knew that wasn't where his religion lay. A shift in ritual, an opening up, wouldn't dissolve what was in his heart. He could relax his grip on his kitchen, and his Judaism wouldn't break. His son could marry a non-Jew and he would still be Jewish. The only thing that had to be protected fiercely was his own faith.

> The Lord will scatter you among the peoples, and only a scant few of you shall be left among the nations to which the Lord will drive you. There you will serve man-made gods of wood and stone, that cannot see or hear or eat or smell. But if you search there for the Lord your God, you will find Him, if only you seek Him with your heart and soul—when you are in distress because all these things have befallen you and, in the end, return to the Lord your God and obey Him. For the Lord your God is a compassionate God: He will not fail you nor will He let you perish; He will not forget the covenant which He made an oath with your fathers. (Deut. 4: 27–31)

Survival

AN OBEDIENT CHILD, Lionella had one persistent vice: reading. She was capable of ignoring her schoolwork, her chores, her bedtime, and her parents in order to read, and so, though she was raised in a literate household, she was scolded. This illicit reading was Leo's trump card when he argued with his sister. To her taunts, he could retort, "And you, who don't hear Mamma when she calls you to her because you're reading stories?" He was right. Lionella herself reminisces about the days when she got in trouble for reading so much. She would hide behind the billiard table to read, and her mother would inevitably find her and say, "What, you're reading? It is possible? You have to study!" So she would place a novel inside her textbooks or wait, if she had to, until she was supposed to be sleeping and shine a flashlight under her covers onto the beloved pages.

Rachel has a photograph of the family in the garden in Galluzzo. Sunlit vines cover a trellis behind the enormous wicker chairs and a little table on which rests a ball of yarn. Rachel is sitting and knitting, with Leo standing to her left holding more yarn; it's not clear if he's helping or preparing to use the ball in ways it was not intended to be used. To Rachel's right sits Ada, her head inclined toward Lionella, who leans against her right shoulder; together they are reading the newspaper. It's around 1940; the children are barred from school for being Jews, a crime for which their father has lost his livelihood.

The very existence of the photograph strikes me as odd; I expected there to be a blank in the family album where the years 1938–1945 should have been. Amateur photographs signal normalcy, happy childhoods recorded. Novels strike me the same way, as accoutrements to calm and leisurely living, not to tense, precarious survival.

Lionella, Mamma Ada, Rachel, and Leo in Galluzzo, circa 1940.

For Lionella, novels were like a security blanket, materially functional, yes, but psychologically vital. At thirteen, she was in hiding in Florence waiting for her parents to figure out how to flee the city. Trips beyond the apartment where she hid with her mother were strictly regulated; even in the apartment, she had to keep completely quiet. So she lay belly-down in bed reading books from a traveling library. "I read all of *Anna Karenina*," she said. "Above all, *War and Peace* was my companion for those tragic hours." "Andrei was my Prince Charming"—and she sat, along with Prince Andrei Bolkonsky's sister Marie and his beloved Natasha, at his death bed, hoping against hope.

Tolstoy allowed Lionella to weep for the sufferings of fictional characters rather than for her own. He also gave her the pleasure of pure escape from her own suffering. "I read the book for hours and hours as an evasion of the surrounding world." Tolstoy created a world so complete, so real, that Lionella could certainly have lost herself in it, as in a long and complicated fairy tale. And yet, Andrei's world was not entirely removed from hers.

The Russian wars created for me a parallel with the war that was happening. As the French were sent back from Moscow, the German army would also be turned back . . . When everyone applauded the departure of the Italian soldiers for the Russian front, I remember that I thought of the ice and the snow they would find and I did not think they would be victorious even if they waved lots of flags.

Eventually, in *War and Peace*, the invaders are driven out; calamity occurs, but it also comes to an end. Lionella's suffering was easy to connect to that of the Muscovites under Napoleon's attack: they had in common the foreign and previously admired invader (indeed, Hitler liked to compare himself to Napoleon), the difficulty of finding food, the terrible emotional discomfort of not knowing what to do. When the French approach Moscow in *War and Peace*, the Muscovites experience a kind of paralysis that must have seemed familiar to Lionella.

> At the advent of danger, there are always two voices that speak with equal force in the human heart: one very reasonably invites a man to consider the nature of the peril and the means of escaping it; the other, with a still greater show of reason, argues that it is too depressing and painful to think of the danger since it is not in man's power to foresee everything and avert the general march of events, and it is better therefore to shut one's eyes to the disagreeable until it actually comes, and to think instead of what is pleasant.[38]

In Florence, the round-ups had begun. The rabbi who had warned them all to get false documents and flee had been captured by the Nazis. The city was perilous, their hiding places precarious, and still they walked the streets under their own names. Lionella had learned in 1939 that one did not have to wait around until the disagreeable came—her friend Giulio left that year for Israel. Giulio's father told Aldo (with Lionella, as usual, eavesdropping): "At least one member of my family will survive." She knew waiting wasn't the only option; Tolstoy only made her realize that she knew.

"What was my attitude to the war?" asks Lionella. "Maybe tragically mature—I was grown up inside from the age of five (Ethiopia, Spain, etc.), hating it. I always read a lot and also books on history and many many wars of the past—and I understood the enormous sufferings they brought. My grandmother's books, my father's books were very sad but formative." While books helped form her attitudes, the very act of reading helped form her character. When Lionella answers a question, she does so thoughtfully: she analyzes her relationship with her brother; she has a theory about her mother's love of material things; she criticizes her parents' choices during the war. In short, she stands far enough back from her life to observe it clearly, as if it were a narrative and her family were characters in a book.

She is, in fact, a good reader of life. From seeing yourself in the world of a drama—from seeing yourself at Andrei's side—it is a mere skip of an intelligent mind to see a world of drama in your own life. Standing at her grandmother's deathbed, knowing that her presence, once so beloved by Mamma Ada, was now torturing her, Lionella must have suffered. But she must also have been aware of her suffering, aware of the scene as a scene. Readers, especially lifelong, sensitive readers, naturally begin to read their own lives. They become aware of various themes, they know the morals of their stories, they could discuss the historical perspective, political context, and psychological analysis of each of the major events and characters.

The moral of Lionella's story is survival. The war was not simply one event of her childhood, but the reigning theme of her life. Speaking of her mother's gloominess upon their return to Florence in late 1944, Lionella said, "Certainly she did not share my and my father's enthusiasm for being 'liberated' and for having *survived*, moments to which I still often turn, denying myself the right to complain about anything: I AM STILL ALIVE." Later she wrote of herself and her husband: "We consider ourselves to have survived the *shoah* for a will superior to our own; as far as I'm concerned, certainly not on account of the foresight of my parents—We feel very strongly our duty to give testimony on those years."

Lionella's parents responded to the second voice that, according to Tolstoy, speaks to the human heart in the advent of danger—the one that says, we can't foresee everything, let's just wait and see. And yet, they still survived. Primo Levi writes of the discomfort of surviving despite yourself.

> One always hesitates to judge foolhardy actions, whether one's own or those of others, after they have proved to be successful: perhaps therefore they were not foolhardy enough? Or perhaps it is true that there exists a God who protects children, fools, and drunks?[39]

Certainly, for Lionella, it was God's will that she and her family should survive despite their tardy escape from Florence. A protective God did exist, and gave her the responsibility, as a survivor, to carry on her Judaism, pass on her knowledge, keep the faith. That she was determined to do after the war. She was also determined not to be foolhardy again. To trust in God, yes, but to trust in herself as well.

Lionella describes her Judaism as a "natural thing, born with me." But she also recalls in detail the elements in her life—that is, after her birth—that *made* her Jewish, that cultivated her Jewishness. Her spiritual life began with Mamma Ada and her father.

> My grandmother was profoundly Jewish, she gave me a great feeling for it, not coercively, but with her example, with her talk, her teaching, her memories. She was very, very good. Papa took us to Temple all the time, he kept us down with him [in the men's section] . . . he taught us to follow the prayers and the songs, it was very

beautiful . . . So I grew up very easily in the faith. What had a very strong impression on me was this atmosphere of prayer that there was in the house, Papa wrapped his *tefillin*, he put on his *tallit*—it was necessary not to disturb him while he was saying the prayer—and then he went to Grandmother's room . . . I could do everything with my grandmother, she adored me, but if she was saying the morning prayer, I had to stay there and watch her, good and quiet. Then I learned Hebrew along with Italian; Papa taught us to read Hebrew on Saturdays, so I maybe even knew how to read Hebrew before Italian.

Rosh Hashanah (Jewish New Year) eve services in Florence were scheduled for 6:30 P.M. Six policemen patrolled outside. In the little guardhouse a member of the community checked my sister's and my purses—a notebook, some money, pens, and a postcard—and we filed inside, clinging to one another. We looked, trying not to look as if we were looking, for the entrance to the women's gallery. A man was standing there ushering hushed women up the stairs. The quiet gradually loosened as we climbed up and left behind the world of the men and the Temple elders, and we began to realize we weren't the only Americans there. In fact, we listened hard to the whispers and could discern no Italian at all. Had we, intending to blend in to an authentic Italian service, been tricked into attending a service for American Jewish college students abroad? Where were the Florentines?

Our mistake (in terms of blending) had been to arrive on time. Punctuality, like smiling directly at strangers in the street, is a distinctly American habit. Here at the synagogue it seemed to be particularly out of fashion. The Florentines arrived within the next forty-five minutes to an hour, in everything from jeans to pearls, chatting, cheek-kissing, marshaling their children. Down below, though the rabbi had begun the service at 6:30, the six or seven Very Important Jews meant to share the *bema* with him arrived gradually, one by one, shook hands, greeted each other, said the prayer before putting on the *tallit*, and then joined in the service. Throughout, they blew their noses, hitched up their pants, and talked.

Up above, the chatting was ceaseless, and so was the movement from gallery to gallery: we were in the center, but there was one on each side that at various points in the evening would become more or less desirable depending on who had arrived and whether the children were acting up. In the hubbub, the individual words of the service were indistinguishable, a distant hum.

Whatever it was that made these people Jewish, it wasn't in the synagogue. If it were, they would have taken their High Holiday seriously, shown up on time, dressed up, and shut up. If they came in late, they would have come in the back on tiptoe, as we did in our Reform synagogue as children, cringing as heads turned our way. They would have glanced at the rabbi for a nod of forgiveness and reassurance. These Jews barely seemed to notice the rabbi, nor he them. With or without him, they seemed to imply, this thing, this Jewishness would go on; it wasn't something you tried to make a part of your life, it was your life. To these congregants, other Jews were family, not acquaintances; synagogue is their house, not someone else's. There's no need to be polite and respectful in your own house.

Lionella was not at services that night; she was at her farm in the country, living a Jewish life so deeply a part of her that much of it was as natural and casual as brushing her teeth. The ease of her faith came from her early immersion in Jewish culture and ritual, thanks to her grandmother and father. The strength of it, its determination, came from Nathan Cassuto.

Cassuto was a doctor and a rabbi, born and raised in Florence. In early 1943, he was working in Milan as a vice-rabbi, when his home community called him back. The post of head rabbi had been empty since 1939; synagogues weren't exactly brimming with wealth, since congregants were for the most part unemployed. But the community realized it needed a leader, so it called on Cassuto. He was thirty-three years old.

Lionella was twelve. The Neppi Modonas had returned from Galluzzo and were living in Florence, in Via dei Banchi. Lionella could not go to public school, so she went to classes provided by the community, and studied for her *bat mitzvah*. February 6, 1943, was when she would become a Jewish adult, an official member of the community. As it turned out, that's when Cassuto became official too.

Even though he had not yet been officially installed, when I approached the *tevah* on my father's arm to the singing of the *baruch ha-bah*, Rav. Uzzielli accompanied me to the future Rabbi because he wanted him, as *chakkam ha-shalem*, to give me the benediction. Rav. Cassuto had a little *tallit* on his shoulders and to cover my head, as one does, with the corners that have the *tzitzit* he had to pull me close: the pressure of the buttons of his vest on my front is still connected to that moment in which I felt myself deeply moved to receive the "first" *beracha* from the new Rabbi. In the afternoon Rabbi Cassuto found the time to come to my house, where I had gathered my classmates to eat the famous cakes made of yellow flour and grapes that were then the ultimate in gluttony; the unexpected and very welcome visit of Rabbi Nathan and his gentle wife Anna gave a particular character to my party; from that day, I considered Rav. Cassuto to be "my Rabbi."

When I saw him in Temple seated on his bench with his two oldest children at his side, I was unhappy to be up above now in the women's gallery and no longer next to my father, whence I could have demonstrated how good I was at following the reading of the Torah! In the following weeks, the Rabbi started lessons at school on Jewish thought and ethics and they became my most eagerly awaited hours. It's surprising, reflecting on it now with the perspective of an adult, how he succeeded in speaking of extremely elevated concepts with such a simplicity of language: in the few months of school that followed he succeeded in consolidating my Judaism and in preparing me to confront with courage the storm that was nearing . . .

. . . His words became a constant instruction to hope but not to wait supinely for salvation. We had to count on all our physical and moral energy to keep us alive during the hardships we would encounter, trusting that thus we would find the help of the Lord as well . . .

To fulfill the *mitzvah* of the *Sukkah*, a little hut was erected, half-hidden by the hedge that surrounded the Temple custodian's house in Via Farini. Here, after the tragic deportation of the Jews from the ghetto of Rome, Rabbi Nathan Cassuto took leave of his *kehilah*; there would be no more public *tefillot*, each one of us would take our own path, sustained by the certainty that we would find one another again. In each of us remained the strength and the courage to live as a Jew.

My brother and I were the only children present.

I repeated and repeated Rav. Cassuto's words to myself and they truly helped me in the most terrible moments of the following tragic days. I looked to a future, I trusted in a return to normal life, and so I found the courage to go back home with Papa to get my student papers, my notebooks, and my most important textbooks. I carried them with me to various hiding places and in the study I imposed on myself I found a way of getting from today to tomorrow without seeing my time pass emptily: everything would end and I would not have lost a school year.

The reports of the deportations reached us one after the other, like a torturous trickle of water: Rav. Cassuto captured by treachery in Via dei Pucci, while he was leaving one of so many meetings to help the poor, Anna Cassuto taken by treachery, with an atrocious deceit, in the center of town two days later. But still we weren't totally aware that deportation almost always meant death as well.

In January my father buried my grandmother in a Jewish ceremony in the cemetery. At Purim, while the sirens sounded and the bombs from the airplanes could be heard exploding nearby, and my mother sighed at having to remain cooped up in the back of a shop, our temporary hiding place, to show myself that one must continue to hope, I finished off our miserable provisions by frying some strange pancakes in a saucepan from one egg. At Pesach in the little town in the mountains where we had fled, we succeeded in mixing and cooking matzoh.

I would have liked to tell all this to my TEACHER.[40]

Lionella took her title for this recollection from Proverbs 22:6: "Train up a child in the way he should go, and when he is old, he will not depart from it." In Cassuto, Florentine Jews got their leader, and Lionella got a mentor and a hero. It was he who voiced and confirmed in her both a sublime spirituality and a fierce instinct for survival. The lesson she learned from Cassuto was driven deep into her heart by his death. She repeated it to me in the cool of her apartment. *Si deve defendersi*, he had said: one must defend oneself.

The defiant pancakes, the makeshift matzohs, the determination to continue her studies—these were her early battles for the sake of her Judaism. They continued after the war, when she returned to public school and thus to a world full of gentiles. She went on studying Torah, accompanying her father to the synagogue, throwing her energy into following ancient rituals. But personal religiousness would not be enough. To Lionella, being a Jew requires one to pass Judaism along. "Having survived the *shoah*," she said, "I had the task of transmitting to my children (and I didn't conceive of marriage without this end) the values of Judaism, and therefore it was my duty to create a Jewish family." She could see that she enjoyed the ritual of Judaism and her brother didn't; she could see that so much of what she valued about Judaism did not get passed to him. But she could also see that he was still Jewish. She wrote:

> Being Jewish does not in itself imply being "observers of 613 commandments"—this can be an aspiration. "Religiousness" is not everything in Judaism. An adherence to Judaism cannot be based only on this. The children of religious people can be non-religious—but the children of a Jewish couple are certainly Jewish.

Religiousness is not all one needs to be Jewish because, since it has to do with intellect and temperament, you cannot necessarily pass it on to your children. But if you're born of Jewish parents, then some part of you, no matter what, is a Jew.

Lionella intended to marry a Jew—intended without question— "after having seen," as she wrote, "many families 'disappear' from the Jewish world in 1938, baptizing themselves because there was a Catholic mother or even only a grandmother." But she was not simply going to assume that she would end up with a Jew, she was going to ensure that she would. She wasn't simply going to hope that God would protect her from foolhardiness. Proverbs 22, verse 3 says, "A prudent man sees danger and hides himself; but the simple go on and suffer for it."

So she studiously avoided romance with non-Jews. She knows what it's like, she wrote once, "to impose on oneself, perhaps even unconsciously, a form of distance from so many friends for fear of falling in love." It hurt, it was hard, but it was, she felt, her responsibility.

Of course I distanced myself "consciously" from many college friends when I saw that their friendship was becoming too dangerous—this in order not to suffer or make others suffer. And this also outside the world of study because in Italy one always lives with non-Jewish acquaintances, being in such a small community.

Lionella married a man with whom she felt no culture gap, no political gap, no philosophical gap. In 1957, she married Giuseppe Viterbo, about whom she would later write, "What I say for myself goes for Giuseppe too—we are very united in our judgments." She met him "in our common work for Israel, for the community, for the Jewish culture." His father was the publisher of *Israel*, the Zionist paper from Rome (the one Fascist Jews bombed around the advent of the racial laws to show their allegiance to Mussolini).

Together they raised serious, studious, Jewish children. In their minds always was the specter of the war, the sense of themselves as survivors. "You can well understand," writes Lionella, "that the war is not 'a piece' of my childhood. Even now I live it inside and all this has certainly influenced the upbringing I gave my children. Like me, they have never been allowed to lead a superficial life: nightclubs, dances, beach parties, etc." Their life instead was filled with the rhythms of Jewish rituals Lionella remembered from her childhood—rituals maintained despite both the hardship of war and the ease of modern life. Like the boiling of the pots for Passover.

All these dishes of lean and fat, the cleaning for Pesach, Papa in the kitchen, he threw boiling water on everything to make the kitchen ready for Passover, which he cleaned personally, you understand. Mama said "We can use our dishwashers, there's no need to boil it. What are you doing? I would do it this way by now." No, for me great copper pots to boil in, I taught my husband, and I do the boiling, because I feel it's like being a child, drying with my father who does the boiling. And he did it because his grandfather did it.

In short, this transmission didn't die. It's very nice. I try to teach my children, I don't know if I succeeded in transmitting it, I don't know. My daughter is coming for Pesach, she's already reserved her return trip on the night before Pesach. She'll arrive when everything's done, but still. Simply the fact that she's coming here with her husband and her daughter to have *seder*, already means a lot, no?

She was determined not to be foolhardy—not to let her children's Jewishness (or lack thereof) happen by chance. But she's too sharp not to realize that some things, like religious feeling, are beyond her control. So when her daughter comes home for Pesach, she feels relieved, reassured. "It was my duty to create a Jewish family," wrote Lionella. "Thank God I have succeeded." She doesn't thank God for his work in making her children Jewish; she thanks Him for her own success. Her son, Emanuele, works in the administration of the Jewish community. He has an office in the school attached to the synagogue of Florence. His wife, Lia, works in the Jewish nursing home across the street.

Lionella's daughter, Ada, lives in Israel and married an Israeli. They had a baby girl named Tal. "To have a 'sabra' granddaughter," says Lionella, "was a great recompense for us." A *sabra* is a native Israeli.

Israel, for Lionella, is the key to Jewish survival and self-preservation. When the war ended, she looked to Palestine as the answer. "I wanted to go to Eretz Israele with a group of other kids from Florence and while Papa was favorable, Mamma was opposed—I could have been there still . . ." Though it never became her personal answer (or it did only indirectly, through her daughter), Israel remained for Lionella, as it was for many Jews, a philosophical and political answer to the Holocaust. Jewish scholar Irving Greenberg explains it this way:

> The answer to absurd death is unreasoning life; it is *chesed*—lovingkindness that seeks to create an object of its love, that sees that life and love can overcome the present reality, which points to and proves a new creation and final redemption . . . After the war, one of the highest birth-rates in the world prevailed in the displaced-persons camps, where survivors lived in their erstwhile concentration camps.
>
> The reborn State of Israel is this fundamental act of life and meaning of the Jewish people after Auschwitz.[41]

Once, I wrote to Lionella that I felt pained when Israel was unjust to its neighbors, because as a Jew I am connected to Israel, and I expect more from myself than I do from others. I would rather suffer, I said, than make someone else suffer. And I want Israel—and America—to act the same way. She replied,

> Dear little cousin, you weren't here when we yearned to have a nation of our own. Perhaps therefore, having seen it born and grow like a child of ours, we are much readier to justify certain of its attitudes. He who has suffered greatly does not always still have the possibility of enduring the outrages of others. I don't see that Israel was ever unjust to its neighbors.

Lionella, too, uses the image of childbirth when she speaks of Israel; as if the two sides of the commandment to survive—raising a Jewish family and supporting a Jewish nation—were essentially the same thing. But building a new nation isn't just like having a baby. To have a baby, two people engage in "an act of life and meaning"; it is a personal act, in which the only people who can get hurt are the three involved. Building a nation can hurt other people. You're not starting from scratch with two people and a house that needs filling; you're starting with land that's already lived on, with houses that must be emptied.

I would rather suffer than make others suffer. But that is, some would say, a pre-Holocaust view. After Auschwitz, says rabbi and philosopher Emil Fackenheim, Jews must "suspend the time-honored Jewish exaltation of martyrdom."[42]

> Jewish survival, were it even for no more than survival's sake, is a holy duty as well . . . The commanding Voice of Auschwitz singles Jews out; Jewish survival is a commandment which brooks no compromise. It was this Voice which was heard by the Jews of Israel in May and June 1967 when they refused to lie down and be slaughtered.[43]

Some would say that the Six Day War—indeed, much of Israel's military history—was more aggressive, and more complicated, than a simple refusal to lie down and be slaughtered. Some would argue that the position of a Jewish state should always be defensive and never offensive. Jews, after all, should know what it means to be attacked, what it means to die without cause. Jews, of all people, should value life. To them Fackenheim replies:

> I distinguish with utmost sharpness between a) the view that because of Auschwitz the justification of Jewish existence depends on Jews behaving like superhuman saints toward all other peoples ever after and b) the view that because of Auschwitz Jews are obligated to 1) Jewish survival as an end which, less than ever, needs any justification [and to] 2) work for oppressed and suffering humanity everywhere. I accept the second view and . . . the inevitably painful conflicts that go with it. The first view is totally unacceptable.[44]

The painful conflicts come, of course, when Jews oppress and cause suffering *in order to survive.* Marc Ellis argues that "the desire to remain a victim is evidence of disease; yet to become a conqueror after having been a victim is a recipe for moral suicide."[45] Is there a place between conqueror and victim? Between oppressor and oppressed? Two voices clamor for attention: the first, the commanding voice of Auschwitz, cries simply, "Survive!"; the second, the commanding voice of God, calls out as it does in the book of Exodus, "You shall not oppress a stranger, for you know the feelings of a stranger, having yourselves been strangers in the land of Egypt" (Exod. 23:9).

Maybe the only way to survive is to try not to hear the conflict, the clamor; to say, "I don't see that Israel was ever unjust to its neighbors." To listen—as did those parents who may not have been protecting their lives very well but were trying as hard as they could to protect their sanity—to the second voice in Tolstoy's formulation: In the advent of danger, even emotional danger, one must "shut one's eyes to the disagreeable . . . and think instead of what is pleasant."

When I first met Lionella, or at least when I first remember meeting her, she and her husband had just returned from their daughter Ada's wedding in Israel. It was 1991, during the Gulf War. Like any proud parent, she took out the wedding pictures after dinner, ordinary pictures of a small wedding: bride, groom, in-laws, and a few friends lined up in various permutations. Except that they were all carrying these funny little boxes, about the size of lunch boxes children carry to school. What are those? I asked Lionella, and she grinned. She is proud of the wedding, but she is proud of this too: they are gas masks.

There was no attack, thank God. But they had their masks just in case.

Blood Matters

D A S C U D I E R I was Rachel's choice. By virtue of its location on the Piazza del Duomo, it was an astronomically expensive café, and therefore a fitting place for her to do homage to my grandmother Amalie, on a brief visit to Florence, or perhaps for Amalie to do homage to her. Amalie was the guest, but Rachel was, after all, the Florentine, and at eighty-six, four years worthier of respect.

Since all conversation between the two ladies had to be interpreted, it ended fairly quickly. Not that we weren't willing to interpret, but so many things that one would say in an ordinary polite exchange seem too frivolous to ask someone to translate. The act of translation gives words a weight that meaningless niceties can't bear; it's simply too odd to say, "Tell her, 'the weather has been a bit warm.'" So instead, two conversations were going on, one around each lady, one in English and the other in Italian.

I was listening to the Italian one. Rachel was agreeing with my father on the subject of taxi drivers. They both loved them. "Once," said Rachel, "I was coming home late and there were all these blacks in the piazza, and the taxi driver was very kind. He got out and walked to the door with me and waited for me to go in." I raised my eyebrows to my father: did he understand what she had said, or should I translate?

"I got it," he said, and smiled. "All of it."

He meant that the comment about blacks had not escaped him. The smile was one of recognition and tolerance. He had some experience with prejudiced elderly relatives. I had always thought that his liberal leanings were slanted even more because he was Jewish, because he was beaten up for being Jewish in his all-white, almost all-Christian Montgomery public schools. But of course, those relatives were Jewish too, and their Judaism didn't seem to make them more sympathetic.

Rachel is no more racist than most Italians (or most people, for that matter), who are generally unsophisticated when it comes to questions of race and vulnerable to anti-immigrant propaganda. But she certainly is no less racist, though the connection between her and the recent Ethiopian immigrants is historically much stronger than the connection between my father's relatives and southern blacks.

When Fascism was persecuting Jews, it was also persecuting Africans, even above and beyond colonizing their land. Italian men and women were forbidden to marry members of either the Semitic or the Hammitic races—the Hammitic race includes Ethiopians, whose country Italy had invaded three years earlier. Historian Denis Mack Smith writes that "Marriage or concubinage with 'natives' in Africa was punishable by five years in prison."[46] And indeed, presumably because racism was more acceptable to the world than anti-Semitism, "The representatives of Fascist diplomacy abroad received from Rome continuing instructions to minimize the significance of the racial laws. They were to insist above all on the fact that their principal objective wasn't the Jews, but the colonial populations: with the racial legislation, it was desired above all to avoid the spreading of the phenomenon of the half-bred, fairly diffused in the conquered lands of Ethiopia."[47]

So the laws defending the integrity of the Italian race defended it against Africans as well as Jews, though really only in the sexual realm. No laws were necessary to keep Africans from teaching in the public schools or owning too much property or working their way up the military ladder. Those things were simply out of the question. And if Jews did not recognize that injustices were being perpetrated against others as well as themselves, it was really no wonder; they simply shared enough of European racism to keep them from seeing as unjust the prevention of marriages between Africans and Italians. As for the Italian invasion, one was told, at least, that some Ethiopian aggression had provoked it. And of course, those Africans lived so far away; one could not tell how they were treated, nor did one have much occasion to consider it.

Today there are North African immigrants in the streets of Florence. They hawk wares from big nylon bags spread out on plastic in the streets: little electric camouflaged soldiers that shimmy forward with a machine gun in an endless buzz, clunky beaded jewelry, belts, and posters of toddlers kissing. All the merchandise exactly the same. They sell near the official markets, the ones with stalls and operating hours, but not in them. The women wear scarves wrapped tightly around their heads and many layers of skirts; they have round faces and narrow lips. I never saw them selling, only talking with one another in the square near Rachel's house. Nearby, some sat in a little unintimidating bar with friendly proprietors, a favorite of mine. As we were passing one day, I said to Rachel, "I like that bar," and she said, "It's nice," and then shrugged. "Too many blacks."

When the women aren't talking in the square or sitting in that little bar with its blue neon sign, they work as domestics. Rachel was complaining as she put on her thick fur coat, hat, scarf, and gloves, that Lionella wanted her to get a live-in maid so she wouldn't be alone at night. "Who am I supposed to get?" she asked me, yanking her sleeve up her arm. "A black? A Filipino?"

"Why not?"

"Why? Because . . . I don't know. I don't like them." And she told me the story of an old lady whose Filipino maid slept through a robbery perpetrated by her Filipino friends.

Out the door, we headed down the stairs, getting our balance on each step before continuing to the next. We were going for a walk. "Where to?" I asked. "Let's go over to Piazza Santa Maria Novella to see how many blacks there are," she chuckled.

She would not say that they did not have their rights. One day as she dressed, in her white slip, stockings, and slippers, she mulled over the amount of money she was paying out for maid service. To one lady alone she paid 300,000 lire for six weeks when she didn't even work—Rachel was out in the country and didn't want her to look for another job in the meantime. "You can't find maids anymore, you can't find them," she said. "Blacks, Ethiopians, yes, but I don't like them."

"Why?"

"I don't know," pouting. "And you have to pay the same for them as for whites."

"That seems fair."

"Very fair," she said, nodding. At first I thought this assent contradicted her complaint, but then I realized the connection: if you have to pay the same for both, what's the point in hiring blacks.

The Fascist racial laws defined Jews as a race; this assertion, along with the assertion that Catholic Italians were Aryan, was perhaps the most outrageous aspect of the laws, especially given the fact that, only three years earlier, the *Enciclopedia Treccani* stated categorically, under its entry for "race," "Neither a Jewish race nor a Jewish nation, but a Jewish people exists. An Aryan race, the gravest error of all, does not exist."[48] The strangeness of this new racial definition might have blinded Jews to other victims of the laws. Those other victims belonged indeed to other races and therefore their exclusion (or persecution) made more sense.

Being defined as a race was an indignity Italian Jews had not previously suffered. Racial definitions admit no culture, no intellect, no belief system, no connection between one human being and another beyond the animal connection of blood. According to Article 8 of the Provisions for the Defense of the Italian Race, published in November 1938, "He is of the Jewish race whose parents are both of the Jewish race, even if he belongs to a religion different from that of the Jewish religion."[49] Or, if one parent is Jewish and the other is a foreigner, or if the mother is Jewish and the father is unknown, or if one parent is Jewish and the subject belongs to the Jewish religion, or the Jewish community, or has shown some manifestation of Judaism. Presumably, if both parents are Christians and you convert to Judaism, you're safe. It's a question of blood, of race with—yes, of course—a religion attached. The Fascist racial logic was simply too confused not to throw in a little religion. But essentially it was blood that mattered.

About once a week, Rachel would tell me, "That lady is coming to see me this evening." "That lady" was Anna, a retired teacher, recently bereaved by the death of her sister. She moved her swollen feet and legs slowly, bemoaned and gloried in her ailments. When she rang the bell at street level, Rachel would send me to buzz her in and then open the door for her, and then I stood in the hallway waiting, awkward, listening to her shuffling steps. "Can I help you, ma'am?" I asked, relieved as she turned the last corner into view. She grimaced. "If you can give me another pair of legs."

She spoke so slowly she should have been easy to understand, but her jaw moved more from side to side than up and down, and her words came out chewed and garbled. At length and unswervingly (try as Rachel might to get hold of the conversation) she described her sister's death; finally, she said, she called a priest. "I'm a Catholic, you see," she said to me, "and for Catholics the tradition is to have a priest deliver the last rites." Amazing, I thought, for a Catholic in a Catholic country not to assume I understood.

Later I discovered that this was part of her teacherly tendency to explain everything, carefully and at length, as if to a roomful of children. But she was also a member of the Amicizia Ebraico-Cristiana and prided herself on religious sensitivity. She told of inviting a Moslem parent to speak to her class, and of taking the class on field trips to the synagogue. She said she wanted her students to seek to understand one another.

Rachel responded that she has many Catholic friends, but when they start to talk about "Christian goodness," she always stops them. "I say, listen, I'm your friend, but don't talk to me about Christian goodness. They killed six million Jews." Anna corrected her as if she were a child. The ones who did the killing weren't really Christians, she said; they may have been baptized but they weren't Christians at heart. Real Christians were killed in concentration camps along with the Jews.

"Those Germans were all Christians," said Rachel.

"In name, yes, but—"

"And the Italians who did the spying were all Catholics."

"But deep down they were atheists."

Rachel grumbled. She was sitting on one edge of the sofa, her legs, crossed at her slender ankles, perpendicular to Anna's swollen feet, which were bare to relieve the pain. Anna was sitting in a deep, comfortable armchair, the ruling chair of the parlor. I was sitting across from Rachel. The little coffee table was too far away for any of us to reach gracefully for a cookie. I lurched forward, half-rising, and passed them to Anna. She accepted one, and gave up on the argument. "In any case," she said, and returned to the subject of her sister's burial.

Christian goodness is a redundancy to Anna. For her, a Christian is someone who, regardless of birth or ceremony, follows the teachings of Christ. By definition a Christian would not kill anyone or turn anyone over to be killed, and so no Christian has ever murdered or spied. Christians cannot be blamed for the Holocaust any more than they can be blamed for the Crusades or the Inquisition. If they were involved, they weren't Christians, period. Perhaps they called themselves Christians, but that is merely unfortunate. No wonder she explained last rites to me—in her world view there must be far more Jews than Christians. Real Christians, Christian Christians, were few and far between.

To Rachel, everyone's Jewish who's born Jewish, and then they may be defined as more or less observant unless they convert. Then they might still be considered Jewish (and in fact, according to Jewish law, they are). Jews don't have the luxury of vast numerical superiority; they can't pick and choose which of them is worthy of the name "Jew."

And often when they are abused, they're defined by other people as a race rather than as a religion. Jews as a group have been blamed for conspiracy, thievery, the death of Christ—not religious Jews or active Jews, or the Jewish system of belief, just Jews. From the point of view of the persecutors, it's the blood that matters. If the SS knocked on your door on a tip from your unchristian neighbor, you couldn't say, "Well, actually, I've taken the Lord's name in vain, coveted my neighbor's wife, and had a ham sandwich for lunch, so you'll just have to keep looking."

Oddly this racial persecution has led Jews to take a racial view of themselves, to define themselves not by beliefs or culture but by birth, by blood. Many Italian writers on the racial laws and the Holocaust say that before 1938 they did not particularly think of themselves as Jews: they were not religious, they did not keep kosher, they did not attend synagogue. After 1945 many more of them actively considered themselves to be Jewish—"It . . . took the racial campaign to reawaken us and remind us that we were Jewish"[50]—not because they had necessarily begun to believe in God or obey Jewish law, but because the racial definitions *of their oppressors* lumped them in with other Jews and forced them to suffer the same fate as other Jews. Vulnerable to discrimination, deportation, and death as Jews, they were Jews. Thus they emerged from the Holocaust with a sense of connection that, indeed, had nothing to do with religion at all. An inescapable, unalterable connection to certain other people.

Jews who never attended synagogue, who've never spoken a word of Hebrew, who never contemplate God, are still called Jews and call themselves Jews. Jewish theologian Marc Ellis complains of a "double standard" in which "Ariel Sharon symbolizes a fascist militarism and is identified as Jewish; but is Harry Truman, who ordered the atomic bombing on Hiroshima and Nagasaki, identified as Christian or, for that matter, is Richard Nixon or Ronald Reagan? More often, 'American President' is the prefix, and, when 'Christian' is affixed, a denial of their authentic Christianity occurs."[51] Perhaps it is unfair. And yet the two systems of identification *are* different, and it's not simply the Gentile world that constructs it as different. Ellis himself refers often to "religious" and "secular" Jews—"secular" Jews being, of course, Jews who are Jewish without necessarily following the tenets of the religion. Can one speak of "secular" Christians? *Is* a Christian a Christian the way a Jew is a Jew, that is, no matter what he or she believes and does?

My friends can say, "Well, my parents are Episcopalian, but I haven't decided," or "My family's Baptist but I don't really go in for organized religion." But I, no matter what the state of my faith or education, I always say, "I'm Jewish." The worst sin in a member of an oppressed group (or a group that is vulnerable to oppression) is denial of membership. Thus blacks who talk like white people or pale-skinned blacks who try to "pass" might be criticized by the black community, while Jews despise no one so much as the "self-hating" Jew. Rachel and Lionella speak of the Jews who were "Aryanized" to avoid the consequences of the racial laws with a mixture of pity, contempt, and revulsion.

So there is a history that produces a moral obligation for me to say, "I'm Jewish." And yet, when I say it, it's a reflex, not a conscious decision. I feel Jewish; it's not a choice I have made. Yet I do not believe that if I had been adopted at birth, baptized, and raised in a Christian family, I would still feel that way once the "truth" of my birth were discovered—though by Jewish law I would still be Jewish. I think I feel Jewish because I was raised that way, with Shabbat dinners and at least a loose appreciation of the holidays, with a Sunday school smattering of Hebrew and a joyful *bat mitzvah*. I was raised, moreover, in an overwhelmingly Christian community that required me (in a friendly way) to define and explain myself over and over again. My mother dutifully brought in the Chanukah candles to all of my elementary school classes; my teachers willingly released me from religious class (which took place in a trailer just off school property, neatly sidestepping the U.S. Constitution). I was different; I was Jewish. And I liked that. And surely, as my friends went through soul-searching and confusion about the question of whether they did or did not want to follow their parents' religion, I was spared the worst. I could not not be Jewish simply by attrition. I would have to convert (and even that wouldn't suffice to redefine myself officially), which means that simply rejecting religion per se wouldn't work. I was spared the fear of not belonging or the worry of not believing; I could not help belonging and it did not matter if I didn't believe. So in a way, being a member of a "people" instead of a religion relieves one of having to make some difficult decisions.

But shouldn't it be these very decisions that define a human being—rather than her birth? "People" Judaism, a-Jew-is-a-Jew-is-a-Jew Judaism, tempts one toward a blood-based view of the world, a view of the world that sees birth first before beliefs, ideas, and even actions; a view of the world that can reflect the visions of some of the Jews' most terrifying oppressors. Article 1 of the racial laws declares, "The marriage of an Italian citizen of the Aryan race with a person belonging to another race is prohibited."[52] Before the Holocaust, before Jews were defined as a race and separated from their Christian neighbors, there were many intermarriages. Paola Pandolfi says that before the racial laws in Italy, "precisely because of the high grade of assimilation reached by the Italian Jews, the number of mixed marriages exceeded, though just by a little, that of marriages among co-religionists."[53] Now civil marriages between Jews and non-Jews were considered null and void by the state. Perhaps some Jews would say that this is one good thing that came out of the racial laws. Bemporad seems to; he says, "If the brusque rebuke of the racial campaign had not been made, now there might be few whole Jews in Italy."[54]

But shouldn't we examine carefully any view that corresponds with Fascist law, with a law that persecuted thousands of people? And if we oppose mixed marriages now in response to the Holocaust, have we given Nazis and Fascists some victory over us, some control over our lives? Or are we just responding to a lesson we learned the hard way—that we must defend ourselves against all outsiders?

My sister Amy was married in a Jewish wedding, to the son of a Lutheran minister. It took her and my mother months to find a rabbi to perform the service.
Chris isn't planning to convert, but Amy is planning on having a Jewish home.
She first asked a rabbi and friend of the family who told us once that our blood
was too precious to squander on the Gentile world. That was a formality; we
hadn't expected her to budge even for Amy. But then came a long series of phone
calls and rejections and leads and failures. My mother (famed for her unraisable
blood pressure) became incensed. It was stupid, she said; this is the way to drive
people away, not keep people in the faith.

The biblical interdiction against intermarriage is quite clear. "He dislodges
many nations before you—the Hittites, Girgashites, Amorites, Canaanites, Per-
izzites, Hivites, and Jebusites, seven nations much larger than you . . . You shall
not intermarry with them; do not give your daughters to their sons or take their
daughters for your sons" (Deut. 7: 1, 3). But equally clear is the reason for the interdiction: "For they will turn your children away from Me to worship other
gods." The mixture of blood isn't the issue here; the problem is clearly religious,
an attempt to protect the integrity of an incipient faith.

Relaxed deep into a plush grey couch, in the waiting room of Rachel's ophthal-
mologist, I mentioned Sady's boyfriend, Paul, to Lionella. "He's not Jewish, I
suppose," said Lionella. I hesitated as if I were trying to remember—trying instead to think of the least incriminating answer. I said I thought he was an agnostic. Lionella smiled and leaned forward to share a secret with me, eyes bright.
"You were the best child," she said. My boyfriend is neither a Paul nor a Chris,
but an Adam—Adam Daniel Greenberg, no less. Between us we know less about
Judaism than Amy. We have never been to synagogue together. But any rabbi
would be pleased to marry us. It's the blood that matters.

When he wrote home from the isle of Rhodes to say he wanted to marry Rachel,
Aldo heard a lot of criticism. His best friend, Alberto Olivetti, wrote to ask Aldo
why he would go off and marry an "Oriental" when there were so many nice Florentine women around. His mother was concerned. Rachel said they thought she
would be a dirty savage. "But we're actually cleaner than the Italians."

She left Rhodes as Aldo's fiancée in 1929. The buildings were small on her island, the streets unpaved. Her school was across the street and her whole family
lived within a square mile. She had no degree and her Italian was unpolished at
best. Now she was headed to a big city to show her fiancé's upper-middle-class
academic family and friends that she deserved him. But when Alberto Olivetti

invited them over for a party to get to know Rachel, she refused. She was a tiny woman: fine ankles, fine hair, fine wrists. "Let him come here first," she said to Aldo. "After what he wrote to you, he can come here first."

Rachel does not like the idea of intermarriage, but she is not an idea-driven person. She judges people according to how she feels about them, not whether or not they've followed certain principles. When this leads her to contradictions, she does not notice.

Leo's wife was not Jewish and Rachel still loved her; she left Leo and Rachel loves her still, though she knows perhaps she oughtn't. She disapproves of rabbis who give converts and half-Jews a hard time. An outsider should be allowed to try to be an insider, should be given a chance to prove herself, just as Rachel was given a chance as an "Oriental" to prove herself civilized. But it is I who deduce the principle, not she. She simply tells stories. One rabbi she disparaged wanted a young lady, the daughter of a Jewish mother and a Gentile father, to commit right away to the synagogue by participating in a ritual bathing, without allowing her to work toward it slowly. "And her mother was Jewish, and they say that if the mother is Jewish, so are the children," said Rachel, shaking her head. But she will argue oppositely for another case dear to her heart: Lia, the wife of Rachel's grandson Emanuele. Lia's mother is Catholic and her father is Jewish, but her mother never converted, because, according to Rachel, the father didn't like people who changed their religion. So although Lia was raised Jewish, the rabbi gave her a hard time—to Rachel's disgust.

So she does not necessarily subscribe to the legal definitions of Judaism, but she does concern herself with who is Jewish and who is not. On our walk over from her apartment in Via dei Banchi to Da Scudieri, she pointed out various buildings and businesses owned by this Jew or another, some relatives and some not. There was a vague sense of some heyday past, when it seemed as if everything important in Florence was owned by Jews. That must have been before the war.

Even when we watched TV, she would point out which journalist was Jewish, which Catholic authority figure had been good to the Jews. She was proud of the ones who were Jewish, regardless of what they said or how well they did their job; their simple presence was some sort of proof to her, a source of pride.

It was a score-keeping kind of Jewishness that didn't have anything to do with God or much to do with religion, and that made me uncomfortable. Once again it made reference not to thought or belief but only to simple, bald belonging, birth. But I felt acutely that I had nothing to counter it with—I didn't keep score, didn't triumph in the knowledge of who belonged and who didn't, but I didn't do anything else either: I didn't keep kosher, didn't observe the sabbath, didn't belong to a synagogue, didn't believe in God or try to.

And I didn't want her to know any of this either. I didn't agree with her belief system, but I wanted to fit into it easily, wanted her to approve of me even as I disapproved of her. When my sister brought back little sandwiches from the café's pastry counter, I headed her off: they were filled with ham. I was embarrassed about stories that revealed we had traveled on the sabbath. I didn't like to be caught breaking the rules, though they were never rules I had accepted. Belonging may mean that you are accepted no matter what, but it does not mean you are invulnerable to criticism—on the contrary. And I've never been able to stand being judged lacking, even if I don't agree with the criteria.

I couldn't help feeling, too, that I was doing my research on false pretenses. I was welcomed and confided in partly because I was family but largely because I was Jewish. A young Jewish woman researching the Holocaust. That would have gained me entrance into many houses in Florence, relatives or not. I knew that Rachel thought I would be a simple, sympathetic conduit for her stories, and my being Jewish was a large part of that assumption. Some part of me felt that, since I couldn't be uncritical, since my point of view was so vastly different from theirs, I would be betraying my relatives' story rather than rescuing it.

So as I returned home with Rachel from Da Scudieri, listening to her stories of Jewish store-owners, Jewish success, and Jewish suffering, I paid attention, nodded respectfully, asked the right questions. I was interested, too, even if it was interest more in her single-mindedness than in her subject matter. But all of a sudden she stopped me and we turned into a fabric store, Casa dei Tessuti. She knew the owners and wanted to say hello.

They were two brothers, both extremely gentlemanly and attentive, white haired and balding, immaculately dressed. One of them started to explain to me how the textile industry began in Florence. Machiavelli came up, whom this gentleman called "a political genius." There were artistic geniuses and political geniuses as well, he said.

"Not now," said Rachel. "No, now, everything is corruption and stupidity."

"No, in fact, there are some now, there are," he said. "Rabin and Arafat." They had just agreed to a peace plan.

Rachel disagreed. "Rabin, no."

"Yes, Rabin too has understood." What Rabin understood, he said, was that people can't live with hate and terrorism. The world was made in love. He quoted the last line of the *Divine Comedy*: "the love that moves the sun and the other stars" (*l'amor che move il sole e l'altre stelle*). That's why we're here, he said. And he pointed to me. "You are here because of the love your parents had for each other. Her too. Me too."

Who was this man who believed something so beautiful, so simple, who spoke in gentle loving tones like a sage? Was he Jewish? Rachel had not said. Fiercely I hoped that he was.

Seeing the Darkness

We don't love men so much for the good they have done us
as for the good we have done them.

Tolstoy, *War and Peace*

RACHEL IS TOO PRACTICAL, too material, to cry about abstractions. And the death of six million Jews or eight thousand Italian Jews or even two hundred forty-eight Florentine Jews, for all its significance, is an abstraction. She cries instead about the death of her husband and the death of her son—her own losses. I spent many hours with her and discussed many things, and she never took out her embroidered white handkerchief on anyone else's account.

After all the time we spent talking, I had become accustomed to thinking of the Holocaust not in terms of its larger human meaning, but as a series of small personal stories. This was not what I had expected when I went to Italy; I had expected to confront good and evil in my conversations with Rachel and even on the streets of Florence where good and evil had fought. I took my camera to each of the places mentioned in the journals—the piazza where Aldo was stopped by the SS, the building in Borgognissanti where the owner threatened to turn them in—photographing each one for the sake of journalistic completeness, but looking for each one because of some other need. I think I had the vague notion that when I reached each house, each square that I had heard so much about, I would recognize it, it would produce emotion in me, a sense of the time, memories almost. As if I were not I, but Rachel herself, not visiting, but revisiting. I thought I could feel the emotional power of the war that she didn't seem to.

Well, of course, it hadn't happened that way. They were just buildings, and what's more, buildings that had been hard to identify. They were not marked by the past, just as Rachel wasn't marked by the past. And just as her stories moved without hesitation out of the war period, these buildings—buildings where Jews had hidden for their lives, where some people had sheltered them and others had threatened—blended maddeningly with the buildings next door.

I had about half an hour before I was supposed to meet Rachel and I decided to take my camera over to Via Serragli; it was close and I was in a hurry. I was looking for the Salumeria Celli, a little grocery store, which I had passed many times on my way to an English-language cinema farther down the street. Emo Celli had helped Rachel and her family eat during the war, and I wanted to find someone who remembered. Mostly, though, I was proceeding out of a sense of duty—I wanted to check Via Serragli off my list. My expectations were already low; they dropped further when I approached the store. Orange construction plastic and a red truck parked smack in front of the narrow façade would make a good picture impossible. Worse, I realized suddenly that I would have to talk, to ask questions, and I had been asking questions only of family. I had not planned what to say. I took a few pictures, stalling, and then made myself walk inside.

It looked like any other Italian grocery. The shelves were full, there was a refrigerated case to the right full of cheeses, the space was narrow. An elderly woman and two elderly men were talking to one another around the counter. They looked up and I had to speak.

"Excuse me," I addressed them all together. "I've been staying with an old cousin in Florence and she told me this store helped her during the war. She's Jewish. Her name is Rachel Neppi Modona." Or something like that. At some point I used the phrases "I wanted to know" and "do you remember."

They repronounced the name, with the accent on the wrong syllable, and said yes, they remembered. The professor, the son, the daughter—Via dei Banchi, right? "I delivered their groceries," said the thinner, colder man. His name was Walter. Piero, the fleshier and younger-looking one, said it was his father and uncle who helped. He and Walter had been eighteen and twenty. "They were hard years . . . After the liberation when we returned . . ." He was unable to continue; there were tears in his eyes and he turned his face.

I told them who was alive and who was dead and that Rachel was still very "strong"—it was the only word I could think of. Piero said that he had often read Aldo and Leo's names in the paper and had thought about them, but that he had

Piero and Walter Celli in their store (1993).

avoided going to lectures where he knew they would be for fear of remembering those times. And yet he wanted to remember, to know more. That desire never left him.

Italians are much less socially mobile, even today, than we Americans are, which means, paradoxically, that it is much harder to pigeonhole them. A man might work for his family store whether or not he is capable of advancement or of leading a thinking life, and thus to hear him speak of attending lectures should not be surprising. To find a security guard who is better read than a philosophy professor is a much simpler thing in Italy than in America. My sister and I made friends with one Florentine waiter whom we only half-jokingly dubbed "The Smartest Boy in Italy."

I turned my attention entirely to Piero, who seemed more interested than his brother. Did they know, at the time, what their father was doing? Yes, he said, they were part of the National Liberation Committee. His uncle, in fact, had been killed by the Germans. He was imprisoned by the Fascists, released when Mussolini fell (in July 1943), jailed again after the declaration of the armistice on September 8, escaped, and then was killed in the mountains. He started to say that his sister had hidden some people, when he got choked up again and went into the back room to blow his nose. I could just see his white handkerchief through the doorway.

He came forward a step. We were Communists, he said, and we still are, in here—he tapped his head. Piero's eyes shone with tears and nostalgia: the store was once, he explained, a hub of anti-Fascist activity. He said that during the war, "We cared about one another, without making distinctions . . . We were all against the Germans, Fascism . . . Only afterward did egoism, individualism, and self-interest arrive."

They had hoped in Russia, yes they had hoped. But man was basically bad. Beasts are better, because they don't have brains to say this is yours and this is mine.

He also said that many other people helped the Jews too. But they would say, yes you can buy this (and he picked up a package of risotto mix) for 100,000 lire. He said his father wouldn't do that.

He spoke of the war as if it really mattered, as if it were the shattering, soul-testing time that I had imagined it to be, as if people then did good and evil, instead of just living their lives and making small daily choices.

He said that I looked like Rachel, that he could see her standing in front of him. He kissed me goodbye. I promised to come back and see him and I did call once, but I didn't try very hard. His tears had cast a spell on me I didn't want to break. I was afraid that he might tarnish his beautiful words with dogma or bitterness or even small talk. And of course he might have. He was moved by an idea, an abstraction that had been a part of his life, and that is really all I wanted from him. That's what I had been waiting for, without knowing it.

What made the Cellis see the war years differently? Why were they the ones offering help, organizing resistance, seeing anti-Fascism not as the answer to personal oppression, but as a universal goal? Why did Emo Celli take Rachel aside and offer to make her a fake ration card? What makes someone do something decent while everyone else does not—that is, what makes someone a hero?

I'm beginning to think of it in terms of proofreading. Humans have a tremendous capacity not to see error. A whole field of cognitive psychology deals with why and how our brains transpose letters back when they're in the wrong order, read only one "and" when there are two in a row, turn "dack" into "dock" when the word "boat" is nearby. Our brains are so sophisticated that when they come across a mitsake in a sentence, they don't stop short, puzzled. They don't say, hmm, what does "mitsake" mean, perhaps a German-Japanese hybrid? Let me get my Webster's. They figure it out in a flash, without alerting the conscious mind, and then they go on. The same mechanism that lets a writer type "their" when she means "there" is there in the reader's brain as well. It's a marvelous mechanism, really: it allows us to read, among other things, letters from six-year-olds, truck-stop menus, and the daily paper. To go on with our lives in an imperfect world.

Well, I'm learning to be a proofreader. A proofreader's brain has to snag error, not smooth it over. Proofreaders have to learn not to assume that the next word is correct. Oddly, it requires a lot of concentration to read stupidly, uncomprehendingly—to read like the trained monkey my friend claimed I might as well be, when I described to him a proofreading test. I said a monkey would probably do much better than I.

That ability to smooth over error, to make the wrong word fit is a particularly human trait. We are creatures of habit; we need our expectations to be filled. We need things to be normal. Our brains adjust to new information so fast, we don't see a friend's new haircut; we search frantically for clues when our spouse says, "Notice anything different?" and gestures toward the kitchen. We don't see anything because the new microwave has already been assimilated into our image of this room.

A related mechanism must be at work in our moral lives. Our brains adjust to seeing homeless people on the street, to voting for politicians we don't trust, to passing people broken down on the highway. We are so ready to assimilate new information, good and bad, to make it normal, that we have to train ourselves not to assume that the *world* is correct. A couple of months ago, on my way to a shift in a soup kitchen, I was driving through a residential neighborhood when I saw a woman walking up ahead. A man in a car pulled up to her, she yelled something in the window and walked on. He pulled up to her again. This time she turned around and started walking the other way; he reversed to pull up beside her again. By this time I had passed them, but I turned around, pulled up across the street from them, rolled down my window, and yelled to the woman, "Are you O.K.?" She looked up, smiled and nodded, and I drove on.

I must drive past people in some sort of trouble every week; ordinarily, I do nothing. Is it a coincidence that I stop to help when I'm on my way to a shift at a soup kitchen? I don't think so. I think my mind was already focused not just on the fact that people need help, but on the idea that I was capable of providing it. I was poised to read my environment differently and was therefore ready to confront a situation I didn't anticipate—just as if I were sitting at my desk, red pen in my hand, and someone handed me a personal letter instead of a manuscript. That letter would be error-free when I got through with it.

If you are a Communist in a Fascist country, you have your red pen poised perpetually over the text of your life. Emo Celli was ready to understand Rachel's predicament when he noticed she wasn't buying anything that was rationed—he was ready to notice what she bought in the first place. And he was ready to help.

The years 1938 to 1945 were not "the period of the racial laws" or "the Holocaust" while they were being lived. Children were growing up, holidays came and went, money was made and spent. People got on with their lives. They were sometimes selfish and petty and spiteful, and most of them were not aware that their selfishness, pettiness, and spite could have unusually dire consequences. They had their own worries. No one conveniently darkened the heavens and lit up the darkness with the words, "This is a soul-testing time; your every decision is vital. It will all be over in seven years." If someone had, how many more people would have shown courage and love? The heroes were the ones who could see the errors in the text, who could see the darkness despite the fact that the sun was, inexplicably, shining.

Back at Via dei Banchi, I told Rachel about my visit and gave her a note Piero had written, bearing formal greetings. Rachel was pleased to hear that they'd remembered, she was grateful for their help, but she was not moved by the *idea* of their helping. That it was rare or dangerous or constituted a stand against oppression that very few were willing to take, that it took not only courage but vision for them to see all men as equals—these things did not enter her judgment. They had been good, had acted well, had treated her kindly. And that was all.

The Cellis reminded me of something I had seen at the beginning of my visit to Italy. It was a plaque in Bologna honoring the victims of the Nazis and the Fascists. Almost every good-sized city in Italy has one, but usually on its synagogue. This one was on the town hall. What it said was different, too, probably because the city is different. Bologna has a Communist government and a Communist history; its politics are almost as famous as its food. The plaque read:

> To the children to the women to the men of every race and nation
> whom ferocious Nazism savagely killed in death camps
> the community and the province of Bologna
> dedicate this memento of sorrow and recognition
> so that the cause for which they died
> may be present and admonitory
> in the supreme battles of human liberty
> for the independence of peoples
> for the coming of a more just society
> in the peaceful union of all humankind.

The inscription, unlike all the others I read in Italy in honor of death camp victims, does not mention Jews. It clearly states that where these people came from, who they were, does not matter. What matters is that we remember that it happened, and let that spur us on to battle for justice everywhere. I thought, as I read it, that the plaque probably angered some people when it went up. Under-standably. Couldn't it be a kind of forgetting or equalizing to throw all the vic-tims of the Holocaust in together? Should the plight of the Jews be singled out, be remembered as special? In the words on this plaque, the sense of hope and pos-sibility overwhelms the sense of despair. Is that appropriate?

Certainly there are those who feel the Holocaust belongs to Jews, who bristle at the mention of the war dead or of gypsies, cripples, and homosexuals—it wasn't *their* Holocaust. People who feel that way probably wouldn't like the idea of the Holocaust being used as a reminder—being used at all—for anything not confined to Judaism.

Rachel got angry once when we were watching the news and there were re-ports of people dying in Bosnia. She said, "They compare it to the Holocaust, but those whom the Germans preyed on, after two weeks they looked like this"— she held up her index finger. Then she gestured back to the television. "These people are fine." It angered her to think that the Holocaust was being compared to anything; in her mind it was an insult.

There is nothing heroic about being a victim, unless you can be considered a martyr. Jews killed during the Spanish Inquisition, when the choice was convert or die, were martyrs. Martyrs die for their beliefs. But Jews during the Holocaust were killed for their "race," for their birth, not for their religious faith. And to be a victim who wasn't killed at all, who lost property, some friends, and a few years of productivity while the "true" victims were being burned or shot or gassed or starved to death by a terrible international obsession—that kind of victimhood lacks even the grandeur of tragedy.

> There is an unmistakable rank order among the Jews who lived through the wartime Nazi years. In this hierarchy, the decisive criteria are exposure to risk and depth of suffering. Members of communities that were left intact and people who continued to live in their own homes are hardly considered survivors at all. At the other end of the scale, individuals who emerged from the woods or the camps are the survivors par excellence.[55]

Camp survivors, as "possessors of a special kind of knowledge," have a kind of heroic quality—they are like prophets who survived a trip through hell and re-turned to speak about it. But most Jews who made it through the war did not survive concentration camps. And many victimized by the Holocaust suffered obliquely, losing distant relatives, trust in the good faith of Western culture, a sense of security. They are not heroes and they are not prophets. What are they?

Some seek comfort in being "special" victims. They emphasize the uniqueness of the Holocaust, the unique character of anti-Semitism, unlike any other sort of hatred. They consider themselves a chosen people, not biblically, not religiously, not morally, but because they feel they have been singled out for persecution for two thousand years. That persecution becomes a source of pride and comfort, a way to feel important and a way to explain the past.

Being a victim is rarely instructive. It does not teach you to empathize with others, it does not teach you to identify other victims, it does not teach you to be a better person. Being a victim does not even teach you not to victimize other people. It might even make it harder for you to be see their pain.

The girl who is shunned in the cafeteria does not compare herself to all the other children who are persecuted by the popular crowd. She thinks of herself as specially persecuted, either deservedly so (because she is too fat or clumsy or un-cool) or not (because she's just a little too smart or rich or poor or dresses differently). Very few girls who are shunned think of themselves as anything but spe-cial—specially deserving or undeserving of their punishment. To look across the room and identify herself with another outcast would be to relinquish this feeling of specialness, which may be the only thing sustaining her as she suffers. And so, through her suffering, she becomes not more understanding of a mistreated class-mate, not more willing to help, but less.

This was hard for me to learn because, though I am Jewish, and though the Neppi Modonas are family, it's the Cellis' idea of the Holocaust that I share. For me the Holocaust is about racism and Fascism, injustice and compassion. For me it's about ideas, ideas that can be applied to everyone, not just to Jews. When I felt uncomfortable with Rachel and Lionella, I often thought it was because I didn't feel like a real Jew, that I was too assimilated. Maybe it was assimilation, but the problem isn't just that I have lost Jewish culture; it's also that I have lost Holocaust culture. I have lost the perspective of the victim; I simply don't feel like a survivor. You don't have to have lived through it, of course, to feel that way: my father was born in 1945 and the Holocaust is still personal for him. But when I think about the Holocaust, when I think "What would I have done?" I'm not asking myself, would I have left the country in time, would I have gone into hid-ing, would I have believed the stories coming out of Poland. I'm asking, would I have kept talking to Jewish friends, would I have hidden Jews, would I have protested on someone else's behalf. Two generations later, I have assimilated the perspective of a bystander.

It's a lot to ask of someone that they see the darkness when the sun is shining; Emo Celli was an unusual man. To Jews in Italy in the fall of 1938, seeing the darkness was easy: it surrounded them. They were losing their jobs, their rights, their honor, and the people they thought were their friends. It's easy to see your own suffering. The hard part is to see past it—to see, during the Holocaust, that other people are hurting too, to see afterward new injustices on the horizon. Celli risked prison, execution, exile for what he did. He was a hero. But he never had to risk a sense of himself, and that's what you have to do to look across the room, past your own loneliness, and identify with another child in pain. I once thought all survivors should be able to do it—I had the fantasy, the bystander's fantasy, that being persecuted *should* make you more compassionate, more understanding. Now I realize how much that would be asking. The hardest way to understand someone's pain is through your own. Maybe it's the best way, maybe it yields the greatest understanding, but before you can do it, you have to give up thinking your suffering is special, you have to give up seeing your suffering as personal, you have to give up seeing it as yours. And if suffering is all that seven years of your life have given you, it can be a hard thing to give up.

1. Renzo De Felice, *Storia degli ebrei italiani sotto il fascismo* (Turin: Giulio Einaudi, 1993), p. 376.
2. Letter from Leone to Aldo, January 12, 1917, from Silvia Baldi, "Biografia del Prof. Aldo Neppi Modona dal 1895 al 1921," dissertation, University of Florence, p. 21.
3. Letter from Ada to Aldo, November 1, 1918, Baldi, p. 39.
4. Vittorio Segre, *Storia di un ebreo fortunato* (Milan: Tascabili Bompiani, 1990), pp. 13–14.
5. Susan Zuccotti, *The Italians and the Holocaust* (New York: Basic Books, 1987), p. 27.
6. H. S. Hughes, *Prisoners of Hope: The Silver Age of the Italian Jews 1924–1974* (Cambridge, Mass.: Harvard University Press, 1983), p. 68.
7. Ibid., p. 20.
8. Memo Bemporad, *La macine: Storia di una famiglia israelita negli ultimi 60 anni di vita italiana* (Rome: Carrucci Editore, 1984), p. 38.
9. Bemporad, pp. 37–38.
10. Fausto Coen, *Italiani ed ebrei: Come eravamo. Le leggi razziali del 1938* (Genoa: Casa Editrice Marietti, 1988), p. 18.
11. *Il Popolo d'Italia,* September 3, 1938.
12. De Felice, p. 573.
13. *Il Popolo d'Italia,* November 6, 1938.
14. Coen, p. 19.
15. Segre, p. 86.
16. Ibid., p. 87.
17. Ibid., p. 89.
18. Hannah Arendt, *Eichmann in Jerusalem: A Report on the Banality of Evil* (New York: Viking Press, 1963), p. 160.
19. Bemporad, p. 9.
20. Ibid., p. 54.
21. Ibid., p. 51.
22. Arendt, p. 111.
23. Ibid., p. 117.
24. Primo Levi, *The Periodic Table,* trans. Raymond Rosenthal (New York: Schocken Books, 1984), p. 40.
25. *Il Popolo d'Italia,* August 31, 1938.
26. Bemporad, p. 47.
27. According to Silvia Baldi's dissertation on Aldo's World War I years (p. 37), Aldo had studied for his exams while at the front. He read Cicero and Virgil, and studied modern history and the English language as an infantry officer.
28. Bemporad, p. 185.
29. Luigi Preti, *Un ebreo nel fascismo* (Milan: Rusconi Editore, 1974), p. 160.
30. Moravia, from *Il Ponte,* July 1953, p. 1350. Quoted in Coen, p. 38.
31. Natalia Ginzburg, *All Our Yesterdays,* trans. Angus Davidson (Manchester, England: Carcanet Press Limited, 1985) p. 136.

32. Arendt, p. 80.

33. Gaia Servadio, *Un'infanzia diversa* (Milan: Rizzoli, 1988), pp. 33–34.

34. Elie Wiesel, *A Jew Today* (New York: Random House, 1978), p. 11.

35. Giorgio Bassani, *The Garden of the Finzi-Contini,* trans. William Weaver (New York: Harcourt Brace Jovanovich, 1977) p. 5. Copyright 1962 by Giulio Einaudi editore.

36. Ibid., p. 6.

37. Levi, p. 110.

38. Leo Tostoy, *War and Peace,* trans. Rosemary Edmonds (London: Penguin Books, Ltd., 1982) p. 887.

39. Levi, p. 145.

40. Lionella Viterbo, in *Memoria della persecuzione degli ebrei con particolare riguardo alla Toscana* (A.N.F.I.M., editors: Florence, 1989), pp. 29–31.

41. Irving Greenberg, "Cloud of Smoke, Pillar of Fire: Judaism, Christianity, and Modernity after the Holocaust," paper delivered at International Symposium on the Holocaust, Cathedral of St. John the Divine, 1974. Published in *Auschwitz: Beginning of a New Era? Reflections on the Holocaust,* ed. Eva Fleischner (New York: The Cathedral Church of St. John the Divine, 1977), p. 43.

42. Emil Fackenheim, *God's Presence in History: Jewish Affirmations and Philosophical Reflections* (New York: New York University Press, 1970), p. 87.

43. Ibid., p. 86.

44. Ibid., p. 103, n. 51.

45. Marc Ellis, *Toward a Jewish Theology of Liberation* (Maryknoll, N.Y.: Orbis Books, 1987), p. 26.

46. Denis Mack Smith, *Italy: A Modern History* (Ann Arbor: University of Michigan Press, 1959), p. 463.

47. Coen, p. 115.

48. Ibid., p. 39.

49. De Felice, p. 577.

50. Bemporad, p. 49.

51. Ellis, p. 114.

52. De Felice, p. 576.

53. Paola Pandolfi, *Ebrei a Firenze nel 1943: Persecuzione e Deportazione.* From *Argomenti Storici,* vol. 5 (Florence: Università di Firenze, 1980), p. 22.

54. Bemporad, p. 50.

55. Raul Hilberg, *Perpetrators Victims Bystanders: The Jewish Catastrophe 1933–1945* (New York: HarperCollins Publishers, 1992), p. 187.

ARVIT: evening worship service.

BARUCH HA-BAH: literally, "blessed are those who come" in the name of the Lord, the traditional blessing of welcome.

BEMA: the raised platform—the pulpit—in the synagogue.

BERACHA: blessing.

CHAKKAM HA-SHALEM: fully ordained, head rabbi.

HAGOMEL: from "birkat hagomel," a prayer of thanksgiving said in the case of recovery from great illness or rescue from grave danger.

HAMIM: Sephardic Jewish dish, a stew with meat and bulghur.

HA-TIKVAH: literally, "the hope." Refers to a song about "the hope of two millennia, to be a free people in our land, the land of Zion and Jerusalem." It is now Israel's national anthem.

HAZZANIM: official in the Jewish community, responsible for certain synagogue duties.

KADDISH: a prayer in praise of God, recited in daily synagogue services and by mourners after the death of a close relative.

KEHILAH: the community.

MENORAH: a nine-branch candelabrum used in the celebration of Chanukah.

MEZZUZAH: literally, "doorpost." A small hollow plaque affixed to the door of a house to symbolize that it is a Jewish home consecrated to God. Inside the plaque is a parchment scroll inscribed with the Shema, one of the central prayers of Judaism.

MITZVAH/MITZVOT: commandment/s. A *bar (bat) mitzvah* is a "son (daughter) of the commandment."

PESACH: literally, "passover." Springtime holiday, lasting eight days, celebrating the exodus from Egypt.

SEDER: the ritual feast held to celebrate Passover or Pesach.

SEFER: a shortened form of "bet sefer" or "school" (literally "house of the book"). It is often used to mean "synagogue," as is the Italian word for school, "scola" or "scuola."

SHEMA: a central Jewish prayer: "Hear, O Israel, the Lord is our God, the Lord is One" (Deut. 6:4).

SHOAH: literally, "calamity." The Holocaust.

SUKKAH: a temporary hut erected for the harvest festival of Sukkot. During the weeklong holiday, families might take their meals in the Sukkah, decorated with fruits of the harvest; its impermanence is meant to remind Jews of their dependence on God's bounty.

TALLIT: fringed prayer shawl worn at prayer and on certain solemn occasions.

TALLIT KATAN: small tallit worn under the clothing.

TEFILLIN: two small leather boxes, each containing strips of parchment inscribed with quotations from the Hebrew Scriptures. One is strapped to the forehead and the other to the left arm by observant Jewish men during morning worship.

TEFILLOT: prayers.

TEVAH: literally, "ark." Used to designate the cabinet in which the torah scrolls are kept. The focal point of a synagogue.

TISHAH B'AV: literally the ninth day of the month of Av. A day of national mourning over the destruction of the First Temple in 586 B.C.E., the Second Temple, 70 C.E., and other catastrophes in Jewish history. It is customary to fast, beginning at sundown the night before and ending at sundown on Tishah B'Av.

TZADDIK: a righteous individual.

TZITZIT: the fringes on the four corners of the tallit, intended as reminders of God's commandments.

UNIVERSITY PRESS OF NEW ENGLAND publishes books under its own imprint and is the publisher for Brandeis University Press, Dartmouth College, Middlebury College Press, University of New Hampshire, Tufts University, Wesleyan University Press, and Salzburg Seminar.

LIBRARY OF CONGRESS CATALOGING-IN-PUBLICATION DATA

Cohen, Kate.
    The Neppi Modona diaries : reading Jewish survival through my
Italian family / Kate Cohen.
        p.   cm.
    ISBN 0–87451–783–4 (alk. paper)
    1. Neppi Modona family—Diaries.   2. Jews—Italy—Biography.
3. Holocaust, Jewish (1939–1945)—Italy—Personal narratives.
I. Title.
DS135.I9N463 1996
940.53′18′0922—dc20   96–24968